STAGFLATION

A. STEPHEN VON GLAHN

STAGFLATION: A Radical Theory of Unemployment and Inflation

HOWARD J. SHERMAN
University of California, Riverside

Harper & Row, Publishers
New York, Hagerstown, San Francisco, London

Sponsoring Editor: John Greenman
Project Editor: Karla B. Philip
Designer: Michel Craig
Production Supervisor: Kewal Sharma
Compositor: Bi-Comp, Inc.
Printer and Binder: The Murray Printing Company
Art Studio: Danmark & Michaels Inc.

STAGFLATION: A Radical Theory of Unemployment and Inflation

Library of Congress Cataloging in Publication Data

Sherman, Howard J
    Stagflation: a radical theory of unemployment and inflation.

    Includes index.
    1. Unemployed—United States. 2. Inflation (Finance)—United States.
3. Monopolies—United States. 4. United States—Economic policy—1971–
5. Macroeconomics. I. Title.
HD5724.S493   330.9'73'0925   76-18752
ISBN 0-06-046106-3

DEDICATION

PAUL ROBESON
1898–1976

Paul Robeson was the leading black militant of the 1940s and 1950s. The son of a slave, he overcame every obstacle to win honors both in college and law school and was elected Phi Beta Kappa and captain of the debating team. Robeson first achieved fame from 1914 to 1919 as the top player at Rutgers University in football (all-American), baseball, basketball, and track. Walter Camp said that Robeson was "the greatest defensive end that ever trod the gridiron."

Robeson turned to singing and acting when discrimination turned his law practice sour. He had a magnificent voice, singing folk songs, popular songs, protest songs, and opera. Pete Seeger said "Robeson is one of the greatest voices, one of the greatest Americans I have ever met." The most moving artistic experience I have ever had was listening to Paul Robeson sing. His recordings are now available and they convey much of his exciting personality. Robeson, also a powerful actor, starred in many of Eugene O'Neill's plays in the 1930s. He played in eleven Hol-

26144

*lywood movies before he quit in disgust at the stereotyped roles
in which he was cast. He was renowned as Othello both in the
United States and London, and in 1943 Robeson's perfect por-
trayal of Othello ran in New York for 296 performances, an all-
time record for a Shakespearean play on Broadway.*

*In spite of his accomplishments, most Americans have never
heard of Paul Robeson. Why? At the height of his career in the
early 1950s, the House Un-American Activities Committee attacked him because he fought against the cold war. Robeson
refused to answer their inquisitional questions, he refused to
crawl, so he was blacklisted. During most of the 1950s Robeson
could not hire most halls, agents would not handle him, record
companies would not record him, radio and TV companies ignored him, and he was forbidden a passport. But Paul Robeson
never surrendered; he continued to fight for his people's rights
until the day he died. Robeson was best described by Oscar
Brown, Jr., a black singer and actor, who said: "He was a man of
great talent, courage, and integrity, probably the greatest man
America has produced."*

CONTENTS

PREFACE

Two of the most important problems facing the United States and all of the capitalist world today are unemployment and inflation. Together, they are called *stagflation*—stagnation plus inflation.

This text is written from a "radical" perspective. To be a radical economist means, roughly, to look critically at our present economic institutions, including big business and the politicians "owned" by big business. Radicalism means an attempt to look at every issue from the viewpoint of a mass of working people, especially oppressed minorities and women. Radicalism means the desire for a radically different and better society.

I have tried to utilize the latest economic knowledge and data in this book. I have also tried to avoid most of the jargon so dear to the hearts of most economists: It is my hope that this is as readable a book possible.

I wish to thank Faris Bingaradi and Abdol Soofi for excellent research assistance. I am also grateful to Shirlee Pigeon for a magnificent job of typing and editing. Most of all, I wish to thank Kathleen Pulling. Without the help of data from her very important unpublished dissertation, this book would not be of the quality it is. In addition, her specific criticisms were incisive and very helpful.

The book was also greatly improved by the advice and criticism of three graduate students, Brian Bock, Gary Evans, and Michael Sheehan. I am also profoundly grateful to Professor Robert Lekachman for a careful reading of the manuscript and constructive criticism.

Finally, I wish to sincerely thank Raford Boddy and James Crotty for the constructive criticisms they gave to several articles of my previous work. They forced me to reexamine both concepts and data, and in doing so, I found several errors and ambiguities which I have tried to correct in this book.

HOWARD J. SHERMAN

ACKNOWLEDGMENTS

For permission to use data from Thor Hultgren's *Cost, Prices, and Profits: Their Cyclical Relations*, I give thanks to the National Bureau of Economic Research. I am also grateful to the *Journal of Economic Issues* for permission to use, as a chapter in this book, my article entitled "Monopoly Power and Stagflation," given as a paper at the meetings of the Association for Evolutionary Economics in September 1976, and published in the *Journal of Economic Issues*, Proceedings Issue, June 1977. My thanks also go to E. K. Hunt for allowing me to use some data and some concepts from our joint book, *Economics: An Introduction to Traditional and Radical Views* (New York: Harper & Row, 1975).

STAGFLATION

1
THE HUMAN IMPACT OF STAGFLATION

What is stagflation? It is a new word to describe a new phenomenon:

STAGnation + *inFLATION* = stagflation

Inflation means rising average prices. Stagnation means a stagnant or declining economy, marked primarily by high levels of unemployment. Never before in U.S. history have Americans suffered from both unemployment and inflation at the same time. It was first noted on a small scale in the 1950s and 1960s, but became most dramatic in the depression of 1974 and 1975.

A depression is a large downturn in output and employment. A recession is a small downturn in output and employment. Since no one agrees on what is "small" or "large" in this context, the terms are best defined by means of an ancient, but accurate, old joke: A "recession" is when the other guy is out of work; a "depression" is when you are out of work. Some apologists for the present government prefer to call a depression by a more euphemistic term like "rolling readjustment." Whatever the term, it hides a lot of human misery.

HISTORY OF UNEMPLOYMENT
IN THE U.S. ECONOMY

Alternating periods of expansion and decline of output and employment—called business cycles—have occurred regularly in the United States for over 150 years. The very earliest cycles were clearly tied to events abroad. In its infancy, from 1776 to 1840, the American economy depended heavily on the export trade to Europe. The country prospered with every quickening in the flow of ships and goods from Atlantic ports. When this flow was interrupted, distress in the coastal towns persisted until some new stimulus brought a return of strong demand for American shipping. Most profits came from commerce, and large foreign commerce at that. It was in commerce and shipping that the most important capital investment was occurring. Therefore, between 1800 and 1815, a remarkably close correlation existed between the demand for American exports and the health of the American economy as a whole.[1] In 1836, when European economic activity declined and the American expansion faltered, Europeans sold many of their holdings and withdrew their funds, intensifying the major depression that followed.

After 1840, foreign influence persisted, but the course of the economy was increasingly shaped by the domestic environment. By midcentury, American business cycles were more clearly internally generated; a pattern of fluctuation characteristic of modern capitalist economies had set in. In the nineteenth century, depressions or recessions began in 1857, 1860, 1865, 1869, 1873, 1882, 1887, 1893, 1895 and 1899. The twentieth century witnessed depressions or recessions beginning in 1902, 1907, 1910, 1913, 1918, 1920, 1923, 1926, 1929, 1937, 1945, 1948, 1953, 1957, 1960, 1969, and 1973. There has been a somewhat regular pattern of expansion and contraction in business activity. The average business cycle of peacetime expansion and contraction lasts about 45 months. The economy always expands in wartime, so cycles with a war are much longer. In the majority of cycles, the expansion lasted much longer than the following contraction, but there have been several lengthy contractions.

During the period of American industrialization (1870s through 1920s) ". . . millions lived in abject poverty in densely packed slums. . . . They struggled merely to maintain their families above the level of brutal hunger and want for such little pay that their status was a tragic anomaly in light of the prosperity enjoyed by business and industry."[2] Prosperity was enjoyed by business and industry in most years. Output, productivity, and profits all climbed impressively. Yet the last decades of the nineteenth century saw frequent periods of distress and depression. From 1873 to 1879, thousands of small businesses failed, farms were lost to foreclosure, and the accumulated savings of thousands of families, caught by bank failure, disappeared. Estimates of unemployment during the long depression that began in 1873 range from 1 to 3 million. When recovery came in the 1880s, output expanded more rapidly than at any other time in U.S. history, and yet the decade was interrupted by three years of depression. Vigorous expansion did not return to the economy until late in the 1890s; the depression of the early 1890s is generally regarded as the most severe on record prior to the Great Depression. Over 4.5 million workers, or almost 20 percent of the labor force, were unemployed in 1894 and unemployment remained high until 1899.[3]

The inadequacies and deficiencies of the banking community and of the monetary system operated to aggravate the mild as well as the severe cyclic disturbances, not only in the nineteenth century, but also well into the twentieth century. As the economy matured, the frequency of banking crises accelerated. Precipitous monetary failures occurred in 1873, 1874, 1890, 1893, and again in 1907.

World War I brought economic expansion. It was followed, however, by the severe depression of 1920–1921. Production fell by 20 percent and employment dropped 11 percent within a year (Figure 1.1).

The rebound out of the 1921 trough was a strong one, and notwithstanding the downturns of 1923–1924 and 1926–1927, the 1920s were growth years. Major advances in productivity took place, employment was high, and prices were steady or gently falling. Major new industries led the expansion. Automobile production tripled during the decade, making up one-eighth of the value of manufacturing by 1929. The automobile's stimulus to the construction, steel, glass, rubber, oil, retail trade, and service industries led to widespread increases in production. These were boom years for new housing and business construction as well. Radio was a growth industry, while production of other consumer durables reached record levels.

In October 1929, the stock market collapsed. It would be difficult to support a view that the stock market break was the basic cause of the depression of the 1930s. Manufacturing had begun to falter at least three months earlier, and the construction industry had been depressed for almost two years. But the col-

FIGURE 1.1 INDEX OF INDUSTRIAL PRODUCTION, 1919–1939 (SEA-
SONALLY ADJUSTED; BASE: 1935–1939 = 100)

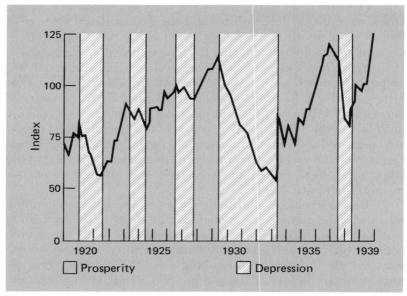

SOURCE: Federal Reserve Board, reprinted in U.S. Department of Commerce, Bureau of
the Census, *Historical Statistics of the United States, 1789–1945* (Washington, D.C.:
Government Printing Office, 1949), p. 330. Depression dates from the National Bureau
of Economic Research.

lapse of the stock market was spectacular. Buyers for securities
vanished as everyone rushed to sell. Debts that could not be paid
encompassed the lenders in the downward spiral of asset values.
Moreover, the loss of wealth was being matched by the loss of
income as prices, sales, and production continued to fall. There
were signs that the debacle had ended in early 1931, but instead
of beginning to recover, the downward momentum suddenly
quickened. By 1933, at least 25 percent of the labor force was
unemployed. The homeless, the hungry, and the desperate were
never fully counted. The economy improved slightly until 1938,
when it took another plunge downward. Full employment was
restored only by the all-out war spending of World War II.

Since World War II the American economy has been plagued
by instability, although depressions approaching the seriousness
of the Great Depression have been avoided. Several small recessions of the 1950s were followed by prolonged prosperity in the
1960s, but in 1969 another recession hit the economy. In 1974–

TABLE 1.1 TIMING OF BUSINESS CYCLES IN THE
UNITED STATES SINCE 1949

Standard Reference Dates

Monthly		Quarterly	
Trough	Peak	Trough	Peak
Oct. 1949	July 1953	4-1949	3-1953
Aug. 1954	July 1957	3-1954	3-1957
Apr. 1958	May 1960	2-1958	2-1960
Feb. 1961	Nov. 1969	1-1961	4-1969
Nov. 1970	Dec. 1973	4-1970	4-1973
May 1975	—	2-1975	—

SOURCES: U.S. Department of Commerce, *Business Conditions Digest* (monthly).
The 1973 peak and 1975 trough are the author's estimates. Method of dating
first proposed by Wesley Mitchell and Arthur Burns, *Measuring Business
Cycles* (New York: National Bureau of Economic Research, 1946). Further
developed by Geoffrey Moore and Julius Shiskin, *Indicators of Business
Expansions and Contractions* (New York: National Bureau of Economic Research, 1967).

1975 the economy suffered from the worst and longest depression
since the 1930s, with unemployment officially recorded over 9
percent.

Table 1.1 records the dates of business cycle peaks and
troughs since World War II. A *trough* is the low point of business
activity and employment. A *peak* is the highest point of business
activity and employment. A *business cycle* is defined as the expansion of business activity from initial trough to peak *plus* the
following contraction of business activity from peak to final
trough.

THE MISERY OF UNEMPLOYMENT

Even in minor depressions, millions of people are unemployed and suffer extreme deprivation; for example, cases of
malnutrition were found in 1975 among families of those long
unemployed. For the society as a whole, recessions and depressions mean periods of unused resources, lower output and
employment, and a much slower long-run rate of growth. Many
attempts have been made to calculate the amount of loss to society for unemployment. One careful estimate put the total loss for
the years 1953 to 1972 at 45 million man-years, valued at $1.8

trillion in 1970 dollars.[4] A *man-year* is the amount of work one person can produce in a year. If these calculations were extended back to cover all the depressions in U.S. economic history, the total loss would be astronomical.

Depressions and economic instability have other effects, however, that cannot be calculated in economic terms. There are sociological effects, as reflected in population growth, higher divorce rates, crime, physical and mental ill health, and even suicide rates.[5] If few resort to suicide, the total effect is nonetheless incalculably great on all who lose jobs, small businesses, or farms; who wander about on an enforced "vacation" with meager subsistence provided by private or public charities; who find all of their previous plans destroyed.

Even in the Great Depression, most unemployed workers tortured themselves with the idea that each of them, individually, was at fault:

> *The suddenly-idle hands blamed themselves, rather than society. True, there were hunger marches and protestations to City Hall and Washington; but the millions experienced a private kind of shame when the pink slip came. No matter that others suffered the same fate, the inner voice whispered, "I'm a failure."*[6]

Unemployment thus caused millions of individual tragedies as well as vast social wastefulness.

Conservatives do a lot of shouting about "law and order," yet they ignore the causes of crime—unemployment being one of the most prominent. Tom Wicker noted:

> *In 1974, as a declining economy progressively forced people out of work, the rate of crime rose by 17 percent nationally, compared to a rise of only 0.75 percent in 1973. The rate of violent crime doubled, the rate of property crime tripled, and . . . [a] link to rising unemployment was suggested.*[7]

What suggested the link between crime and unemployment to Wicker were three facts. Those cities that had the largest increases in unemployment also had the largest increases in crime. Those months that had the largest increases in unemployment also had the largest increases in crime. Finally, the type of crime that increased most was the type most likely to be committed by a poor, unemployed person, that is, street crimes of muggings and robberies for small sums of money. Nor is the relation between unemployment and crime purely economic; the unemployed are angry and frustrated and live in a society where affluence is flaunted at them every day.

When a newspaper casually mentions that 7 million Americans want to work but cannot find jobs, these are not just 7 million statistics but 7 million afflicted individuals. If a large firm closes down or moves to a new location, it leaves behind engineers and executives suddenly reduced from a useful job at $400 a week to enforced idleness on unemployment compensation, as well as a large number of unskilled workers with no future prospects. At times whole mining towns seem to lose animation, and hundreds of miners' wives line up at soup kitchens and welfare departments for food allotments. In the "prosperous" year of 1959, a 38-year-old unemployed auto worker represented millions of others when he said: "I've been looking for work all over but I can't get a job. I hate being on welfare. It's enough to make a man jump into the river."[8] When the majority of the people are working for good wages, very few really want to subsist as a useless stick of wood on a few dollars a week.

In the depressed years 1974 and 1975, there were hundreds of published reports of individual hardship cases. To cite two at random:

> In Athens, Ohio, Jonathan Patrick, an unemployed musician, tried to earn a living by selling flowers on the street, but he found that few people had the money to buy them. He said, "When people can't enjoy a flower, something is wrong, deep down. People say they don't have the money, or they pretend not to see, or they hurry by and look away."[9]

Skilled, well-paid workers are also caught by the depression.

> Robert Cleland, age 26, was a draftsman at Chrysler in Detroit. He has a wife, two children, a new house, a car, and many payments to make. In February 1975, he was unemployed and said: "Once upon a time, I believed in the American Dream. Everything I have, I earned by long hard work, and now it seems a total hassle to hang onto it. The good things of the dream are slipping away. You're damn right there's a depression."[10]

The depression of 1974–1975 put many white middle-class suburban families on food stamps for the first time. Many, many small businesses went bankrupt. Many small farmers were forced off the land.[11]

THE TRUE EXTENT OF UNEMPLOYMENT

Table 1.2 lists the official U.S. government estimates of maximum unemployment in various depressions.

The official data are horrifying enough, since every unemployed individual is a tragedy, but these data drastically understate the real amount of unemployment. Let us examine the unemployment data in detail for the trough of the 1974–1975 depression.

The officially recorded unemployment rate for the second quarter of 1975 was 8.8 percent. For the entire second quarter of 1975, there were 92,575,000 persons in the labor force including 84,384,000 employed and, officially, 8,191,000 unemployed (or 8.8 percent).[12] There were also 58,358,000 persons *not* in the labor force. Any reader of these statistics must be curious as to why over 58 million of the 151 million adult population are not in the labor force. According to the Labor Department survey most of that 58 million do not want a job now, however, some do want a job but are simply too discouraged to look for a job (at least, they had not looked in the last four weeks of the survey). It breaks down this way: 58,358,000 not in the labor force = 53,353,000 who do not want a job now + 5,156,000 who want a job, but are too discouraged to look. When asked why they do not want a job now, the 53 million said:

attending school	6,291,000
ill, disabled	4,780,000
keeping house	31,438,000
retired	7,607,000
other	3,237,000
Total	53,353,000

Some of these reasons, such as "keeping house," are clearly the result of social conditioning, but let us accept all of these people as voluntarily not working.

That leaves the suspicious category of over 5 million "discouraged" workers not counted in the labor force. This category is particularly suspicious because it always rises in recessions and depressions, so it automatically lowers the unemployment rate. For example, in the fourth quarter of 1973 at the peak of the expansion, there were 4,349,000 discouraged workers, but as the depression continued, the number of discouraged grew by 837,000. For this reason, strange things can happen in the official statistics. For example, from January to February 1975, the

TABLE 1.2 HISTORY OF UNEMPLOYMENT

Depression Years	Officially Reported Maximum Unemployment
1926–1927	4%
1929–1933	25
1937–1938	20
1945–1946	4
1948–1949	8
1953–1954	6
1957–1958	8
1960–1961	7
1969–1970	6
1974–1975	9%

SOURCE: U.S. Department of Labor, all except last reported in Geoffrey Moore, "Recession?" *Economic Outlook USA*, Vol. 1 (Summer 1974), p. 4. Annual rate in worst month of each depression.

number of people employed at jobs declined by one-half million, yet there was no change in the unemployment rate. The reason is that the official labor force shrank by the same amount. The New York Times explained this apparent lack of increase in the official unemployment rate by saying that:

> . . . There was a decline in the number of people at work in February, but the unemployment rate remained static because about 580,000 already jobless persons stopped looking for work last month, in many cases because they felt there were no jobs to be found. . . . the government did not count them statistically as unemployed.[13]

If unemployment can be solved no other way, it can always be solved by redefining the statistics.

The Labor Department also asked the over 5 million discouraged workers why they had given up looking for a job. Reasons for not looking were:

school attendance	1,394,000
ill health, disability	631,000
home responsibilities	1,135,000
think cannot get a job	1,153,000
other	873,000
Total	5,186,000

Remember that all of these 5-million-plus discouraged workers
want a job now! Clearly, the 1,153,000 who did not look (mostly
after many months of looking) because they "thought they cannot
get a job" should be counted as unemployed. If they are included
in the labor force as unemployed, then the quarterly rate rises
from the official 8.8 percent to 10 percent. This is a very minimal
adjustment.

The government, however, only recorded this answer of
complete discouragement if no other answer was given. Since all
these workers want a job now, "school attendance" meant answers like "I couldn't find a job so I went back to school." The
euphemism of "home responsibilities" meant "there aren't any
jobs for secretaries, so I'm keeping house now." Therefore, it
would seem more accurate to say that *all* these discouraged
workers were involuntarily unemployed. If they are all classified
as in the labor force and unemployed, then the unemployment
rate goes from the official 8.8 percent to 13.7 percent (or
13,777,000 people). This figure represents the maximum adjustment for discouraged workers, but still leaves out other causes for
the official understatement of unemployment.

The second largest cause for the official understatement is
the peculiar handling of part-time workers. In the second quarter
of 1975, the Labor Department found 79 million full-time and
13.5 million part-time employed, but the department states:
"persons on part-time schedules for economic reasons are included in the full-time employed."[14] What does the term *economic
reasons* mean? By economic reasons the department means that
people wanting full-time jobs could only get part-time jobs because the economy was in such a bad condition. So the department's statement really says: "persons on part-time schedules
who wanted, but were unable to get, full-time jobs are included
in the full-time employed." Peculiar indeed!

According to the Labor Department's own data, in the second quarter of 1975 an average of 3,878,000 persons could find
only part-time work "for economic reasons," though they desired
full-time work.[15] The average hours worked by these people were
only 21 a week, or about half the full-time work week. Therefore,
they should be counted as half-employed, an average of
1,939,000 additional unemployed. With this correction alone, the
unemployment rate rises from an official 8.8 percent to 10.9
percent.

From these two adjustments, then, we can examine a

TABLE 1.3 CORRECTED UNEMPLOYMENT RATE
(2nd Quarter of 1975, seasonally adjusted)

Minimum Correction	
1. Official unemployment	8,191,000 (or 8.8%)
2. Involuntary part-time unemployment	1,939,000
3. Minimum adjustment for discouraged	1,153,000
Minimum corrected unemployed	11,283,000
12.0% unemployed = 11,283,000/93,728,000 (in labor force)	

Maximum Correction	
1. Official unemployment	8,191,000
2. Involuntary part-time unemployment	1,939,000
3. Maximum adjustment for discouraged	5,186,000
Maximum corrected unemployed	15,315,000
15.7% unemployment = 15,315,000/97,761,000 (in labor force)	

SOURCE: U.S. Department of Labor, *Employment and Earnings* (July 1975).

minimum and maximum statement of unemployment for the second quarter of 1975.

Table 1.3 reveals that the official unemployment rate of 8.8 percent for the second quarter of 1975 should be raised to 12 percent on a very conservative adjustment, an increase of almost half. A more realistic adjustment reveals an unemployment rate of 15.7 percent, or almost double the official figure.

Unfortunately, even the maximum correction does not necessarily correct all the downward biases in the Labor Department unemployment data. The department treats as fully employed many *unpaid* family workers. In the peak expansion year of 1973, there were still 1.6 million unpaid family workers, including 700,000 in agriculture.[16] This phenomenon of work without pay in the family unit—because no other job is available—is called *disguised unemployment*. The person usually adds little or nothing to the family income (for example, on a very small farm), but shares in that small income. During a depression, disguised unemployment always increases as more people are forced to share the limited family resources, and final figures for 1975 will show a large increase in this category.

The averages at a given time also hide the extent of the spread of insecurity among workers. In the peak business year of

1973, the official unemployment rate was 4.9 percent, but some 14.2 percent of all workers were unemployed for some period during the year.[17] If the same ratio holds true in 1975, we may expect 25 to 30 percent of all workers to suffer a period of unemployment at some time during the year.

UNDEREMPLOYMENT

There is also what some economists call subemployment or underemployment. Because of general wide-spread unemployment, a skilled person may accept an unskilled job at low pay if that is all that is available. The threat of unemployment holds millions of workers to very low pay at jobs below their qualifications. Final data on 1972, a year of expansion and relatively low unemployment, reveal that there were six million full-time employed workers who earned less than the government's own official poverty standard.[18] In the depression years of 1974 and 1975 (with the added burden of inflation) the position of the working poor became considerably worse.

Underemployment means that millions of unskilled workers work full-time, but are paid below the poverty level. Underemployment means that millions of skilled workers must work in unskilled jobs far below their capacity. Finally, underemployment means that hundreds of thousands of college graduates work at jobs requiring almost no education. For example:

> In one case in 1975 Jim Stephens (a fictitious name, but a real case) earned his bachelor's degree in biology. He was unable to gain immediate acceptance to the limited number of spots in medical schools, so he tried to get work as a lab technician. Since it was the middle of the depression, he was unable to get even a lab technician job. Therefore, he became a cab driver.[19]

A survey of placement services found that among the college graduates of 1975, many architecture B.A.s became construction assistants, many English B.A.s have been reduced to clerical work, some people with education degrees have been forced to work in factories (because cities and states are too cheap to employ more teachers), and a few Ph.D.s have been discovered working as bartenders.[20] A year after the 1974 graduation 27 percent of the graduates "said they had more education than their jobs required and 24 percent said their work didn't make use of their skills."[21]

UNEMPLOYMENT OF
MINORITIES AND WOMEN

All women and both sexes in many minority groups—including blacks, Chicanos, Puerto Ricans, Jews, Italians, Irish, and many others—suffer discrimination in the United States. The discrimination is justified by various kinds of prejudices which falsely claim the groups are "inferior."[22] The discrimination includes discrimination in housing, education, loans, types of jobs, and employment. Here we consider only that facet of discrimination which results in higher unemployment rates. In the case of young people, some unemployment results from prejudice against youth, but some also results from lack of qualifications, to the extent that training and experience are qualifications. In the case of women and minorities, since anthropologists find that all groups are created with equal qualifications, *all* higher rates of unemployment must be due to discrimination, including some present employment discrimination and some previous discrimination in education, training, or previous jobs.

Even the official U.S. data show these extremely high unemployment figures. In June 1975 average unemployment for all workers was 9.1 percent.[23] Table 1.4 shows that women suffered more unemployment than men, blacks suffered more than whites (almost double), and youths suffered more than adults (far more than double). Thus white males 20 years and over were best off, while black women workers ages 16–19 suffered the most unemployment. A rate of 7.6 percent for all white males is bad enough, but an unemployment rate of 43 percent for all young black

TABLE 1.4 UNEMPLOYMENT BY RACE, SEX, AND AGE
(June 1975 rates, in percentages)

Category	All Workers 16 and Over	Young Workers, 16–19 Years
All	9.1%	23.6%
All whites	8.1	—
All blacks	15.4	—
All men	8.4	—
All women	10.2	—
White men	7.6	20.8
White women	9.4	21.4
Black men	15.4	42.8
Black women	15.5%	43.0%

SOURCE: U.S. Department of Labor, *Employment and Earnings* (July 1975).

FIGURE 1.2 UNEMPLOYMENT RATES BY COLOR (SEASONALLY ADJUSTED)

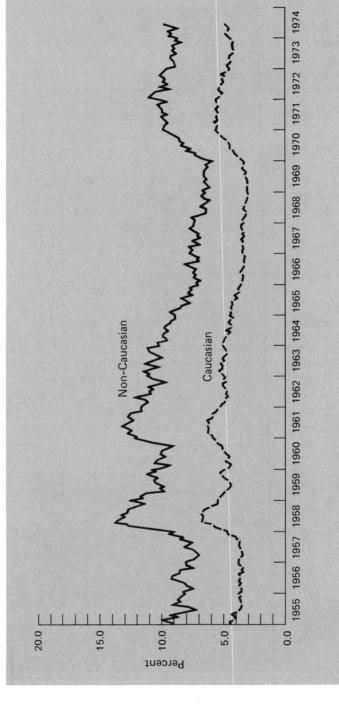

SOURCE: U.S. Department of Labor, *Employment and Earnings* (Washington, D.C.: GPO), monthly.

workers reveals a condition of unbelievable depression for this group. Figure 1.2 shows that blacks have had almost double the unemployment rate of whites for many years.

Yet these official data of unemployment do not tell the full story. The *underestimates* of unemployment are even greater for women, minorities, and youth than for white male adults. The two most important reasons are the same factors discussed above as major reasons for underestimating all unemployment. First, even more women than men and, proportionately, even more blacks than whites, fall into that strange category: "not in the labor force, but want a job now." In the second quarter of 1975, only 1,592,000 men, but some 3,583,000 women were counted as not in the labor force because they were discouraged from looking, even though they wanted a job now. At the same time, the discouraged workers included 3,699,000 whites and 1,196,000 blacks. As a proportion of the population or the labor force, this was much higher for blacks than whites. Even as a proportion of those counted as not in the labor force, the discouraged were 7.2 percent of the whites, but 16.6 percent of the blacks.

Second, both blacks and women (and youth) are proportionately much larger percentages than adult white males of those who are employed part-time, but desire full-time jobs and cannot find them. Corrected unemployment figures in Table 1.5, adjusting for only these two factors, give a more realistic picture of the burdens of unemployment by race, sex, and age of workers.

On any calculation, (1) a higher percentage of blacks than whites are unemployed, (2) a higher percentage of women than men are unemployed, and (3) a higher percentage of young than old workers are unemployed. Moreover, the differences become greater—both absolutely and relatively—when these corrections remove the various underestimations. For example, black women have only a slightly higher rate of unemployment than black men in the official data (15.5 to 15.4 percent), but the difference is much greater in the adjusted data (31.3 to 23.9 percent).

The group of black women, ages 16 to 19, reflects all three kinds of discrimination in an official unemployment rate of 43 percent. With a correction merely to include those part-time workers who want, but can't find, full-time work, the rate for this group for June 1975 rises to 49.2 percent unemployed. If data were available on how many are too discouraged to look for work from this group, but are not counted in the labor force, the minimum and maximum corrected rates of unemployment would be well over 50 percent.

TABLE 1.5 CORRECTED UNEMPLOYMENT BY RACE, SEX, AND AGE
(June 1975 rates, in percentages)

Category	Official Unemployment	Minimum Corrected Unemployment[1]	Maximum Corrected Unemployment[2]
White men	7.6	9.9	12.0
White women	9.4	13.3	18.8
Black men	15.4	20.1	23.9
Black women	15.5	22.9	31.3
All youth, 16–19	23.6	30.9	40.5
All workers	9.1	12.4	16.3

SOURCE: U.S. Department of Labor, *Employment and Earnings* (July 1975),
pp. 26 and 59. Not seasonally adjusted.

[1] *Minimum corrected unemployment* means that unemployment is adjusted to
include one-half of those part-time workers who desire full-time jobs, but
are unable to get them; and both unemployment and labor force are adjusted
to include those workers officially not in the labor force but who want
work now, but are discouraged from looking because they think they cannot
get a job. Discouraged are from quarterly survey.

[2] *Maximum corrected unemployment* means that unemployment is adjusted to
include one-half of those part-time workers who want full-time jobs but are
unable to get them; and both unemployment and labor force are adjusted to
include those workers officially not in the labor force but who want jobs
now, but are discouraged from looking for any reasons.

There are also other reasons to believe the official rates un-
derestimate unemployment of youth, minorities, and women. It
was shown earlier that large numbers of unpaid family workers
are counted as employed. Yet a disproportionate number of these
are young and/or female and/or blacks in the South.[24]

Furthermore, the category *white* includes Chicanos and
Puerto Ricans, whose unemployment rates are far higher than
average.[25] On the other side, the category *black* includes several
other small racial minorities, particularly Chinese and Japanese,
whose unemployment rates are much lower than blacks' rates.
Thus the unemployment gap between whites and blacks is
somewhat larger than it appears in the offical data.

Finally, subemployment or underemployment is far more
prevalent among young workers, women, and minorities than it is
among white male adults. For example, in 1970 the median wage
of full-time employed workers was $7,870 for white men, $5,314
for black men, $4,584 for white women, and only $3,487 for black
women.[26] As a result, in 1970 only 5 percent of U.S. families

headed by white males were below the official poverty line, but 33 percent of all black families were below the poverty line; 37 percent of all families headed by white women were below the poverty line, and 62 percent of all families headed by black women were below the poverty line. The official poverty line was $4,275 per family. Since the average wage of full-time employed black women was only $3,487, it is easy to see how most families headed by black women were in poverty even though most of these women worked full-time. Of course, in the depression of 1974–1975 when unemployment was especially bad among blacks and women, their poverty situation worsened.

In addition to underemployment causing their low wages, underemployment is also reflected in the poor jobs given some highly qualified groups. For example, in 1972 women with college degrees had only a slightly higher median wage than men with eighth-grade education. Among women with 4 years of college, 17 percent take jobs as unskilled or semiskilled workers. Even among women with 5 years or more of college, 6 percent take unskilled or semiskilled jobs.[27]

Why is unemployment so high among women and minorities. The reason lies both in prejudice and in the fact that this unemployment pattern is also profitable to employers. If an employer has ten black and ten white workers, and must fire half for a couple of months, which will he fire? If "he is rational and seeks to minimize his labor turnover costs, he will lay off his ten black workers on the assumption that they will be unlikely to get permanent or better jobs elsewhere because of the discriminatory practices of other employers."[28] Thus the capitalist fires black workers (and women) in each recession and hires them back in times of expansion. He also gains by not paying the fringe benefits due workers who stay on the job for a longer time.

SEASONAL UNEMPLOYMENT

In addition to general or cyclical unemployment, workers are also unemployed in a seasonal pattern. For example, agricultural workers are very fully employed at harvest time, but are often unemployed many months in the year.

To eliminate the seasonal pattern from consideration and analysis, the Labor Department publishes seasonally adjusted unemployment rates. Although the techniques now used are quite complex, the basic idea of the adjustment is quite simple: raise the unemployment rate in months that normally have high

TABLE 1.6 UNEMPLOYMENT RATES,
SEASONALLY ADJUSTED AND NOT
SEASONALLY ADJUSTED, 1975

Month	Not Seasonally Adjusted	Seasonally Adjusted
January	9.0%	8.2%
February	9.1	8.2
March	9.1	8.7
April	8.6	8.9
May	8.3	9.2
June	9.1%	8.6%

SOURCE: U.S. Department of Labor, *Employment and Earnings* (July 1975), p. 19.

seasonal employment and lower it in months with normal by low seasonal employment. Accordingly, the Labor Department reported in the first 6 months of 1975 the data in Table 1.6.

The seasonally adjusted results, which are the ones given publicity, were more pleasant for the Ford administration since they put the unemployment rate over 9 percent only in one month, whereas the unadjusted rates were 9 percent or more in four months. One should always take the seasonal adjustment with a grain of salt because it may, in a sense, understate or overstate the impact of a depression depending on the time of the year. Nevertheless, all data used in this book from here on is seasonally adjusted.

The whole concept of seasonal unemployment is dubious if it means that this sort of unemployment is an act of nature and nothing can be done about it. It is true that nothing can be done about it in a pure unplanned capitalist economy. But in a planned economy, like Cuba, which under capitalism had large numbers of unemployed sugar workers in the winter, these workers can easily be given other work, such as constructing rural housing, roads or dams.

FRICTIONAL UNEMPLOYMENT

Frictional unemployment is supposed to mean those workers who are temporarily unemployed only because they are moving from one job to another, usually in the wake of technological progress. For example, workers building stage coaches may be unemployed for a short time until they move into the automotive industry. This concept has a small grain of truth, but has been used in deceptive ways.

It is said that frictional unemployment is natural because it results from technological progress, so nothing can be done about it. Yet in a planned economy all such workers could be retrained by the government. The main problem, however, is that conservatives overestimate frictional unemployment in order to deny that there is much (or any) general unemployment caused by capitalist business cycles.

In World War II, when there was unlimited government demand, unemployment fell to one percent. Since frictional unemployment results from technological progress, and since such progress was very rapid in World War II, frictional unemployment should never be higher than the 1 percent recorded in World War II. Yet in the Truman period Democratic economists started saying frictional unemployment was 1.5 to 2 percent. In the Eisenhower administration Republican economists said frictional unemployment was 2.5 to 3 percent. In the Kennedy-Johnson administrations Democratic economists spoke of 3.5 to 4 percent frictional unemployment. Nixon's economists talked about 4.5 to 5 percent and Ford's economists talk about 6 to 8 percent frictional unemployment.

THE PROBLEM OF INFLATION

Inflation is defined as a rise in the average price level of all goods. A rise in one price offset by a fall in another is not inflation; this is constantly occurring as a result of shifting demand, such as a shift from butter to margarine. Furthermore, we must distinguish the effects of a slow and gradual inflation from those of a very rapid, or galloping, inflation. If inflation results in the rise of prices by a few percent per year, then it is only a social irritant. It does work a great injustice on those who possess savings, who have made loans, who must live on a fixed income, or whose wages lag behind prices, because these groups find the purchasing power of their incomes steadily declining. In particular, the aged face an economic disaster when they retire. This decline of real wages and real savings exacerbates many economic and political conflicts. For a country as a whole, gradual inflation of domestic prices may reduce the volume of goods sold abroad; and for goods that still face competition, entire overseas markets may be lost.

The situation is much more serious, however, when the rate of price inflation reaches several hundred percent per year, as happened in Germany in the early 1920s. Rampant inflation brings such a rapid decline in the value of money that ultimately there can be complete dislocation and collapse of the economy, with correspondingly violent political reactions. At such times money and the market system fail completely. Productive effort is paralyzed, and exchange retrogresses to barter. In recent years there have been several underdeveloped countries, such as Brazil and South Vietnam, in which galloping inflation threatened to disrupt all normal economic processes.

Even in the United States, the magnitude of inflation is indicated by the fact that the consumer price level quadrupled between 1900 and 1958, and doubled between 1938 and 1958.[29] During the 6 years from 1945 to 1950, wholesale prices rose 52.6 percent and consumer prices 33.7 percent. Nevertheless, inflation in the United States was in the very gradual category of 1 or 2 percent a year in most years from 1951 to 1965. After the escalation of the war in Vietnam in 1965, however, inflation became progressively worse. It was one of the major economic issues in the 1968 and 1972 presidential elections. By 1974 the Gallup poll reported that 62 percent of Americans felt it was the worst single national problem.

In U.S. history mild inflations have occurred in almost every business cycle expansion. Major inflations also occurred in every war, including the Revolutionary War, the War of 1812, the Civil War, World Wars I and II, the Korean War, and the Vietnam War. On the other hand, deflations, or declining prices, occurred in almost every depression or recession up through the recession of 1948. Although it seems hard to believe, there have been long periods of declining prices in U.S. history.

Until 1950 there was never any inflation during a recession or depression. In the recessions of 1954 and 1958, however, there were price rises in several industries in the midst of unemployment, though the overall price level didn't change much. In the recessions of 1969–1970 and 1974–1975 there were *both* high unemployment and inflation. Inflation in 1974 and 1975 reached rates of 12 percent to 14 percent in several months in spite of unemployment rates of 8 and 9 percent and over. This is a new phenomenon in U.S. history.

THE HUMAN IMPACT OF INFLATION
Inflation hurts everyone whose income does not rise faster than the rate of inflation. When it comes in a time of high unemployment, it means a crushing burden on those whose money

income is actually falling. Economists use the term *real* income to refer to an income after adjustment for price changes. If your income in money terms rises by 10 percent, but the consumer price level rises by 15 percent, then your real income has declined. Obviously, those on fixed money incomes will suffer the greatest declines in real income. So the elderly and retired are hurt the worst. Any unemployed worker has a miserable fixed income on the government dole.

The combined impact of depression in keeping wages . down—and of inflation in raising prices—has brought lower real wages to most American workers in the decade from 1965 to 1975. Thus the weekly take-home pay, after federal taxes, of a nonfarm worker with three dependents rose rapidly from 1965 to 1968 in money terms, but the worker's *real* pay (in dollars of constant 1967 purchasing power) rose only from $91.32 in 1965 to $99.44 in 1968.[30] Because of recession (and inflation) in 1969 and 1970, money wages continued to rise, but real wages *fell* to $89.95, or below the 1965 level. In 1971 and 1972 industrial expansion brought a considerable rise of money wages, and even real wages rose to $96.40 in 1972 in spite of price rises. This is usual because when output and productivity are expanding the workers usually get some part of the much larger pie.

In the final phase of expansion, however, for the first time in peacetime "prosperity," real wages fell while output was still rising. Money wages rose in 1973 but not by as much as prices, so the real wage was down to $93.83 by December of 1973. This was the result of President Nixon's stiff controls on workers' wages, while keeping only slight controls on business prices.

In 1974 with recession added to inflation, money wages rose very, very slowly, while prices continued upward. So by June 1974, real wages fell to $91.48. By April 1975, with a long period of stagnant money wages and rising prices, real wages fell further to $87.46, far below the 1970 and 1965 levels. Besides showing how labor has suffered from inflation, these data cast doubt on the theory that inflation has been caused by high wages.

As a result of both unemployment and declining real wages, in the year 1974 some 24.3 million Americans (or 12 percent of the population) were living below the official poverty level of $5,038.[31] This included 7.3 million families with total incomes below $5,000. For *all* blacks the median income was only $7,810 for a family of four. For all full-time working women, the median wage or salary was only $6,770. The total number living in poverty actually increased by 5.6 percent in 1974—and probably more in 1975.

Of course, U.S. inflation is not as bad as German inflation was right after World War I. The price level often doubled in a day or even an hour. By 1923, one U.S. dollar was worth 4.2 billion German marks. According to the novelist Thomas Mann:

> Peasants filled their houses with sewing machines, pianos, and Persian rugs, and refused to part with their eggs and milk except in exchange for articles of permanent value. . . .
>
> You took your money as fast as your legs would carry you to some innocent grocer. . . . If you were lucky, he had the mark quotation for 9 A.M., but not for noon. . . . You might drop in at the tobacconist's for a cigar. Alarmed at the price, you'd rush to a competitor, find that his price was still higher, and race back to the first shop, which may have doubled or tripled its price in the meantime. . . . On Friday evenings, you could see workers coming out of the factories with baskets, sacks, and suitcases full of money. . . . It became necessary to pay wages daily. . . .[32]

That inflationary experience was the breeding ground of Hitler's fascism.

The current U.S. inflation (and depression) is bad enough for many individuals. For example, many retired workers find their retirement income is below poverty levels, so they must sell many of their small stock of possessions just to stay alive.[33] Many people still working have to give up all quality foods and change to cheaper kinds of food.[34] It must be stressed that inflation usually hurts the poor worse than the rich. Inflation redistributes income to the rich by raising the value of the property they hold, including property in land, buildings, and corporate stock.

BLAMING THE VICTIM

Conservative economists have always tended to blame the unemployed for unemployment. Some conservative politicians still claim that anyone who *really* wants a job can get one. In the next chapter we shall see that, using the strange proposition called Say's Law, conservative economists for many decades proved to their satisfaction that a general depression is impossible, so involuntary unemployment on a large scale is impossible. They admitted only *frictional* unemployment—that is, a temporary depression in a few industries until workers can move to other industries that are booming.

On the basis of these arguments, conservative economists concluded that all unemployed (beyond the frictional unemployed) must be lazy loafers unwilling to work at the prevailing wage. The unemployed must, according to these economists, voluntarily leave their jobs to look for easier or better-paying jobs elsewhere. Imagine arguing this notion during the 1930s when official unemployment was over 25 percent. Do all workers periodically get fits of laziness or greed? Are millions only pretending to be unhappy when out of a job and living on a thin handout from the government?

As we shall see in the next chapter, this argument always leads conservative economists to the conclusion that all workers would be fully employed if only they would accept lower wages. These views have been revived in more sophisticated technical form by modern conservatives. For example, Armen Alchian argues that when demand declines, workers are faced with a choice.[35] They can agree to continue working at a lower wage or voluntarily quit their present jobs and go hunting around for a better one. Since many workers are ignorant of the true facts of the job market, they spend many months hopping around looking for nonexistent jobs at their old wages. Meanwhile, these millions of ill-informed workers may be considered voluntarily unemployed or frictionally unemployed or "employed" in acquiring information.

One of the problems with this argument is that its description is contrary to fact. Bosses (such as General Motors) seldom call their workers together for a cozy chat to say "you accept a lower wage or be fired"; they usually just fire thousands of workers without warning. (Moreover, we shall see in the next chapter that accepting lower wages would *not* lower the unemployment rate.) Alchian has tried to answer this criticism. He claims that capitalists have learned from experience that, when given the choice of lower wages or quitting, most workers will quit. Instead of going to the bother of offering this choice, employers just anticipate the workers' choice and fire them "to the mutual satisfaction of both employee and employer."[36] Since in reality most unemployed would accept lower wages, and since there is no evidence that employers think in this contorted fashion, it is hard to see why so many economists have treated his theory so seriously.

Alchian's argument about voluntary, frictional unemployment while looking for better jobs has been particularly applied to women workers and young workers. Three authors of a recent textbook say:

> *The size of frictional unemployment is rising. Voluntary quits and job hopping represent a large and growing phenomenon in the*

*United States labor market. Unusually large numbers of younger
(and inexperienced) workers and middle-aged women have been
entering the labor force recently. These workers are typically more
selective about the types of jobs they will accept.*

*Unemployment during job search to improve wages or working
conditions is considered to be voluntary and not a proper concern
of government policy.*[37]

So women and young workers "voluntarily quit" and "job
hop" and they "are typically more selective about the type of jobs
they will accept." The mildest comment one can make about this
argument is that it is both illogical and a travesty of the facts.
Logically, one would expect that women and young workers
would be far more anxious to hold on to any job, no matter how
bad and lowly paid, than an older male because they know that
they will face discrimination in getting a better job. They are
certainly not more selective because they cannot afford to be. The
fact is—according to numerous Labor Department surveys—that
women voluntarily quit any given job much *less* than men at that
job.[38] The argument, therefore, seems compounded less of evidence and more of prejudiced notions about women and unemployed young workers (of whom a high proportion are black,
though this is not always mentioned).

The conservative economists extend the argument to blame
the victims not only for unemployment, but also for inflation.
Alchian's view is that voluntary unemployment lowers the supply of willing workers, so raises wages and thus raises prices. In
Alchian's view, workers must suffer several months of futile job
hunting before they learn to accept lower real wages—and only
these lower real wages will stabilize the price level. In later
chapters, we shall see that conservatives now view some level of
unemployment as natural. The *natural* level of unemployment is
that level necessary to stop inflation; and they argue that any
steps to lower that natural level will only result in more inflation
(this argument will be discussed in later chapters).

NOTES

1. See W. B. Smith and A. H. Cole, *Fluctuations in American Business, 1790–1860* (Cambridge, Mass.: Harvard University Press, 1935).
2. Foster R. Dulles, quoted in Richard O. Boyer and Herbert
Morais, *Labor's Untold Story* (New York: Marzani & Munsell, 1955), p.
34.

3. See Stanley Lebergott, *Manpower in Economic Growth: The American Record Since 1800* (New York: McGraw-Hill, 1964).

4. Leon Keyserling, "What's Wrong with American Economics," *Challenge* vol. 16 (May/June 1973), pp. 18–25.

5. For the Great Depression of the 1930s, there is an immense literature on each area; for an overall study of the effects of earlier business cycles, see D. C. Thomas, *Social Aspects of the Business Cycle* (New York: Knopf, 1927).

6. Studs Terkel, *Hard Times: An Oral History of the Great Depression* (New York: Pantheon Books, 1970), p. 5.

7. Tom Wicker, "Unemployment and Crime," *New York Times* (April 25, 1975), p. 33.

8. Reported in an excellent survey by A. H. Raskin, "People Behind Statistics: A Study of the Unemployed," *New York Times* (March 16, 1959), p. 1.

9. This case is taken from among many in the excellent article by Associated Press writer Victoria Graham, printed in *Riverside Press-Enterprise* (Feb. 9, 1975), p. C1.

10. Ibid., p. C2.

11. Ibid., p. C2.

12. All data from U.S. Department of Labor, Bureau of Labor Statistics, *Employment and Earnings* (July 1975). Data for all persons 16 years and over, seasonally adjusted.

13. "The Labor Force Is Shrinking Drastically," *New York Times* (March 9, 1975).

14. U.S. Department of Labor, op. cit., p. 51.

15. This was the average for April, May, and June. See U.S. Department of Labor, *Employment and Earnings*, issues for May, June, and July 1975.

16. U.S. Department of Labor, *Manpower Report of the President* (April 1975), p. 274.

17. Ibid., p. 274.

18. See Thomas Vietorisz, R. Mier, and B. Harrison, "Full Employment at Living Wages," *The Annals* (March 1965). Also see the very clear analysis of unemployment and subemployment in Paul Sweezy and Harry Magdoff, "Capitalism and Unemployment," *Monthly Review*, vol. 27 (June 1975), pp. 1–130.

19. G. G. LaBelle, Associated Press release, *Riverside Press-Enterprise* (August 27, 1975), p. J1.

20. Ibid.

21. Ibid.

22. The best discussion of prejudice and discrimination against women in employment is in Barbara Deckard, *The Women's Movement* (New York: Harper & Row, 1975), Chapters 5 and 6. An excellent discussion of prejudice and discrimination against blacks in employment is in Ray Franklin and Solomon Resnick, *The Political Economy of Racism* (New York: Holt, Rinehart and Winston, 1973).

23. Data from U.S. Department of Labor, Bureau of Labor Statistics, *Employment and Earnings* (July 1975). *All workers* refers to everyone counted in the labor force age 16 and over. These data are not seasonally adjusted because they are not available in that form.

24. The data (from the Census Bureau) and a more complete argument are in the excellent book by Victor Perlo, *Economics of Racism, USA* (New York: International Publishers, 1975).

25. Ibid.

26. All data here from U.S. Department of Labor, discussed in E. K. Hunt and Howard Sherman, *Economics* (New York: Harper & Row, 1975), pp. 326–335.

27. See Deckard, op. cit., chapter 5.

28. Franklin and Resnick, op. cit., p. 20.

29. See Willard L. Thorp and Richard F. Quandt, *The New Inflation* (New York: McGraw-Hill, 1959), p. 1.

30. U.S. Department of Labor, Bureau of Labor Statistics, *Employment and Earnings* (August 1975 and earlier issues).

31. U.S. Census Bureau, *Money, Income, and Poverty Status of Families and Persons in the U.S., 1974* (Washington, D.C.: U.S. Government Printing Office, 1975).

32. Lecture by Mann in 1942, quoted by George F. Will in "The German Inflation of the 1920s," *Riverside Press-Enterprise* (February 7, 1975), p. D9.

33. Victoria Graham, "Great Recession," *Riverside Press-Enterprise* (February 9, 1975), p. C1.

34. Ibid.

35. Armen Alchian, "Information Costs, Pricing, and Resource Unemployment," *Western Economic Journal*, vol. 7 (June 1969), pp. 107–129.

36. William Hosek, *Macroeconomic Theory* (Homewood, Ill.: Irwin, 1975), p. 293. Hosek has a summary and discussion of Alchian.

37. William Mitchell, John Hand, and Ingo Walter, eds. *Readings in Macroeconomics* (New York: McGraw-Hill, 1975), p. 152.

38. The official data are fully presented and discussed in Barbara Deckard, op. cit., pp. 85–86.

2
CAPITALISM AND EFFECTIVE DEMAND

Why are millions and millions of people unemployed in the U.S. economy? It seems strange—like a scene from *Alice in Wonderland*—that millions of people lack jobs when there is so much to do. After all, by official government count, millions of people are in poverty; they lack the necessary food, clothing, and shelter for a decent life. Couldn't millions of unemployed be employed to produce these urgently needed amounts of food, clothing, and shelter? It seems barbaric and inexplicable to have even one person languishing in unemployment while there is so much to be done.

Unemployment results when capitalists decide not to invest in new factories and equipment, or to run their old factories and equipment at much lower rates of production, so that they need fewer workers. They do this because they don't expect to make a high enough profit from more production. If there were a high enough demand for their products, then capitalists would expect to make more profit, and would then hire more workers. But millions of people do want more food, clothing, and shelter—not to mention luxuries. Isn't this a *demand* for products? No, it is not an *effective demand* for products under capitalism. The only effective demand for products under capitalism is a demand backed by money. The poor may desire more food. That is not an effective demand unless they have the money to buy the food. Only if there is a demand in money terms is it effective in getting a capitalist to produce and to hire more workers.

THE CAPITALIST SYSTEM

What exactly is meant by capitalism? *Capitalism* may be defined as a system in which one class of individuals, the capitalists, own the means of production. These means of production are called *capital goods*, such as factories and equipment. The capitalists hire another class of individuals, called *workers*, who own nothing productive but their power to labor. The product of the worker's labor is owned by the capitalists. The capitalists sell the product in the market place for a certain amount of money. The capitalists will produce only so long as they expect to make a profit in the market above and beyond all their expenses.

It is this system that creates the possibility of an alternating cycle of boom and bust, with episodes of massive unemployment, sometimes accompanied by high rates of inflation. Previous economic systems, such as slavery or feudalism, did have unemployment or inflation at times, but they were rare and usually caused by a natural catastrophe, such as a flood or an epidemic. Only modern capitalism shows a systematic business cycle with periodic mass unemployment caused by a lack of effective demand. Only modern capitalism shows the unique phenomenon of high unemployment and high inflation at the same time, not as a function of natural catastrophe, but as a result of the normal functioning of the system. It is worth noting these differences from previous systems in some detail to understand the nature of the business cycle.

PRODUCTION FOR THE MARKET

In the capitalist economy, which was developed in England by the end of the eighteenth century, most production was directed solely toward its sale on the market. This was rarely true of earlier societies. In the most primitive societies, almost all productive activity is necessarily carried out by the collective unit of all the males and/or females of the tribe. Generally, almost all the produce is distributed according to some fixed scheme among the tribe's membership.

Even at a somewhat higher economic stage, production is

still for use, and not for sale. None of the Indian tribes of the Americas, not even the Aztecs, bought or sold land or produced crops to sell for a profit to others. In fact, "for the red man, soil existed only in order to meet the necessities of life, and production, not profit', was the basis of his economy. . . . Unemployment was certainly never a problem in the Indian communities of early America."[1] Because there was little division of labor within the tribe, there was little if any trade among its members. Furthermore, very little commerce was transacted between the most primitive tribes, and that "was virtually restricted to materials small in bulk and precious for their decorative or magical qualities."[2] We find that all over the world for thousands of years almost all economic systems, whether tribal or feudal, were based on relatively self-sufficient agricultural units.

In the Roman Empire, there was a great deal of trade, but most of it was in luxury goods.[3] This trade therefore did not affect the self-sufficiency of the basic agricultural unit, the slave-run plantation, although lack of surplus food could bring starvation to large numbers of city dwellers. As one author says, "Notwithstanding the phenomenal expansion of trade and industry, the vast masses inside the Empire still continued to win their livelihood from the soil. Agriculture remained throughout antiquity the most usual and the most typical economic activity, and land the most important form of wealth."[4]

The same was true of feudal England, where the primitive level of technology made impossible the supply of large urban populations and even greatly restricted trade between the villages. As a result, in the England of that day "towns developed slowly; each group of burgesses solved their local problems on their own initiative and in their own time. Even in 1377 not much more than eight percent of the population were townsmen, and only a minority of these had independent dealings with continental markets."[5]

Of course in the later medieval period there were areas of more highly developed industrial production, such as Flanders and northern Italy; and even relatively backward England carried on a systematic wool trade with Flanders. Yet these were exceptions to the general rule of the feudal-economy and may be considered early signs pointing to the end of that economy.

If there happened to be a surplus from the slave or feudal estate, it might be marketed in return for foreign luxury items to be used by the lord of the estate. Finding a market, however, was not a matter of life and death for the economic unit. If the surplus found no market, the manor was still supplied with its necessities for that year, and it could and would continue the process of production for the next year's needs. Only catastrophes such as droughts, plagues, or floods, or political troubles such as government interference, war, or revolution could disturb such economically self-sufficient societies. These phenomena could and did depress production at various randomly spaced intervals, as well as seasonally because of the special seasonal sensitivity of agriculture.

This type of economy could not, however, conceivably face the problem of lack of effective demand for all commodities because the economic unit directly consumed most of the products of its own land and could do without trade altogether. Thus in discussing the business cycle of depression and prosperity, Wesley Mitchell observes that "the total number of past business cycles may well be less than a thousand. For business cycles are phenomena peculiar to a certain form of economic organization which has been dominant even in Western Europe for less than two centuries, and for briefer periods in other regions."[6] The first truly general industrial depression of the modern type didn't appear until 1793 in England.

In the period of transition from feudalism to capitalism in the England of the sixteenth, seventeenth, and eighteenth centuries, the majority of the people still lived on the land and consumed their own products. As time went on, however, more and more products, both agricultural and industrial, were delivered to the market place. By the end of the eighteenth century, the private enterprise system of production for the market embraced most economic activity. By the nineteenth century, one business entrepreneur might own a factory producing millions of shoes, though his whole family could consume only a few pairs. The shoes had to be sold in order to buy other consumer goods for his family, pay wages to his employees, and replace and expand the plant and equipment of his business.

In the United States, the transformation to a market economy took place in the nineteenth century. In 1800, two-thirds of the U.S. population labored in agriculture, and most of the remainder were employed in commerce and shipping. Except for the foreign trade sector, markets were small and local. Many families and communities were almost self-sufficient. Native industry, which had a foothold in 1800, spurted during the War of 1812, when imports from England were cut off. By 1815, New England mills and factories were capable of supplying textiles and simple manufactures to the nation. Transportation networks were built to link communities and regions. This permitted farmers to specialize in commercial crops for cash income with which they purchased in the market the necessities of life. By 1840, a large national market for manufactures had been created. Families turned away from self-sufficiency and purchased cloth, flour, farm implements, and household items. Rapid industrialization followed.

The process of industrialization, starting first in England and spreading to the rest of western Europe and the United States, had changed the character of production and employment. In the modern market economy, every person's productive effort is related to sales in the market, and every person's income depends on the income of others. People working in an automobile factory, for example, depend for their continued employment on millions of other people buying cars each year. In turn, most of these car buyers depend on millions buying the products they produce. If consumers are unable to buy their cars, automobile workers immediately lose their jobs. The car manufacturer needs less steel, less rubber, less paint, and so on. Each of these industries, in turn, lays off workers. The process goes on and on because of the interconnectedness of the market economy. Each time more workers lose their jobs, their income ceases. They can no longer buy the hundreds of goods and services they normally purchase, and the crisis widens and becomes more severe.

The sale in the market of privately produced goods and services generates all income. Decisions to purchase are made by thousands of small- and large-income receivers, and the total of these purchasing decisions makes up the total, or aggregate, demand. In previous economic systems, the self-sufficient economic unit—the craftsman producing a trickle of handmade items for known customers—could not possibly be troubled by lack of demand for his product. In the industrialized private enterprise system, however, the businessman produces for the market and cannot continue production if there is no market demand for his products.

REGULAR USE OF MONEY

Another institutional condition that opens up the possibility of a lack of aggregate demand is the regular use of money in exchange. The monetary system takes the place of the barter system, which is the exchanging of commodity for commodity. It was seen that production for the market makes cyclical unemployment possible. Use of money in the market exchange will be shown to be a second necessary condition for the emergence of business cycles.

The use of money, even in ancient times, brought many new complications into the economic scene. In the Roman Empire, for example, vast amounts of money were needed by the government to support wars of expansion, large standing armies, police and bureaucracy, and an unfavorable balance of trade (due to import of luxuries from the East). The emperors were eventually forced to the expedient of debasing the coins by adding inferior metals. As there were more coins, but declining production of goods in the later days of the empire, the amount that could be bought with the coins declined rapidly; in other words, a catastrophic inflation occurred.

Despite these difficulties, the regular use of money did not lead to the modern type of depression because most of the Roman economy was still contained in self-sufficient agricultural units. The luxury trade did suffer from the extreme inflation, but only as one more affliction in addition to colonial wars and slave revolts, the extreme inefficiency of employing slave labor, and the Roman citizen's attitude that any participation in the work process was degrading (because only slaves should work).

With the breakup of the Roman Empire, trade suffered a considerable decline. In early feudalism, the pattern was over- whelmingly that of the isolated, self-sufficient manor. Barter therefore grew in importance, and the use of money declined. On each manor, in return for the lord's protection, the serf provided all the services and consumer goods needed and required by the lord, his family, and his retinue. However, when technology began to improve, industry and commerce slowly started to re- vive in western Europe. The widespread trade of the later medieval period eventually led to the replacement of barter by a money economy; at the same time, following the pattern dis- cussed in the previous section, production was increasingly de- signed for sale in the market rather than use at home.

The modern private enterprise economy demands continu- ous use of money as the go-between in market exchange by the entire population. In a barter economy it is possible for one com- modity to be brought to market in larger supply than there is demand for it; but it is impossible to have a lack of total or *aggre- gate demand.* For example, those who bring cows to market may find more shoes and fewer coats produced than they desire; that is, they would rather "spend" their cows for fewer shoes and more coats than are available. The excess supply of shoes is balanced by the excess demand for coats. The result is only a temporary, or frictional, unemployment of shoe producers, which could be cured by a shift to coat production.

In the modern economy, the seller obtains only money for his commodities, money that he may or may not use immediately or later to buy other commodities. Thus money functions as the means for the storage of value for future use. The wants of mankind may be infinite, but it is not always the case that all buyers have money to buy what they want. There is, therefore, no inherent necessity in a money economy that sellers should find buyers for all commodities brought to market.

The problem is not an aggregate lack of money in the economy. While those who wish to buy may have no money, those who have money may be taking it out of circulation and not using it in any way, or hoarding it. The chain of circulation may then be broken at any point at which the flow of money is stopped or withdrawn from the system. In that case the reduction of the flow of circulation, like the reduction of the volume of water flowing in a stream, causes a slowdown in the movement of products being circulated by this means. While it is basically true that products exchange for products even after the introduction of money, the mere necessity of the money bridge makes all the difference in the world. If the bridge is absent, finished commodities may pile up in warehouses, while potential customers are unable to buy them. Only money can make a possible consumer into an actual buyer in the capitalist system. The problem is not overproduction of the total commodities relative to what people want or desire. The problem is rather that there may be too many commodities on the market relative to the *effective demand,* which is limited by definition to desires that are backed by money in the marketplace.

PRODUCTION FOR PRIVATE PROFIT
We have examined two conditions—production for the market and regular use of money—that must be present if business cycles are to occur. These are cycles in which demand fluctuates below the full-employment level of supply. But at least one more institutional condition is necessary before we can contend that total demand may not equal supply in this economy. It is the existence of private ownership of production facilities and production for private profit. Even in an economy characterized by exchange in the market through the medium of money, supply

and demand can be kept in balance, or quickly brought back into balance, if both supply and demand are consciously planned by the same national agency.

A centrally planned socialist economy is one in which the government owns and plans the use of all means of production. Most business cycle economists admit that industrialized socialist economies do not experience the business cycle phenomena characteristic of industrialized private enterprise economies. This is the case because a socialist economy can make one unified plan for growth without concern for private profit. Thus all of the data on Soviet economic development indicate continuous full employment, except for retraining time or movement between jobs.

In a private enterprise economy, each individual enterprise makes its own plans on the basis of its own estimate of whether it will obtain a private profit by undertaking production. In the national plan of a socialist economy, the same agency decides both the aggregate supply and the aggregate demand. It sets the aggregate consumer demand by setting wages, and it controls the aggregate investment demand directly through the government budget.

Of course socialist planners may make mistakes in allocation of resources and new investment, especially because there are changes in technology and other new conditions each year. They may allocate resources to uses that are not as productive as others, or even order the production of one thing (e.g., automobiles) but not order enough production of other things going into it (e.g., rubber tires). In such cases there may be supply bottlenecks holding back production in some industries and temporary oversupply and unused capacity in others. Such mistakes may lower the rate of growth or even cause output to fall in one year (as happened in Czechoslovakia in 1963).

Moreover, much recent data on eastern Europe and the Soviet Union show a cyclical recurrence of slow-growth periods. Each time the economy starts growing rapidly, the bureaucrats get overoptimistic. They push production more rapidly than is physically possible, leading to supply bottlenecks. If they order too many new factories to be built at once, the result is half-built factories and little or no increase in current output. Nevertheless, there remain very important distinctions from a capitalist economy. There need be no secondary effects, no cumulative collapse of production, because socialist investment is not based on private profit (so the economy does remain at full employment).

In an economy based upon private ownership of individual competing units, the sum of decisions to produce may not equal the sum of decisions by other individuals and businesses to spend—that is, to consume and invest. If the sum of the outputs produced at present prices is greater than the sum of the effective demand, then there is not enough revenue to cover the costs of production and also yield a profit for the private entrepreneur. This criterion is decisive because if the private entrepreneur can make no profit, he will not continue production, his machinery will stand idle, and all his workers will be unemployed.

THE CONSERVATIVE VIEW OF J. B. SAY

Let us now see how these problems of capitalism are viewed by economists of various persuasions: conservative, liberal, and radical. The conservative view begins with the classical economists, J. B. Say and David Ricardo. The liberal view begins with J. M. Keynes. The radical view begins with Karl Marx. Of course, each view has less well-known forerunners as well as many followers who modify and expand it.

The conservative view, first presented by J. B. Say (1767–1832), is that unemployment and inflation are accidents caused by factors external to the economy. They are always minor and temporary; and the capitalist economy, if left to itself, will always automatically come back to full employment and stable prices in a short time. Say's law states that any increase in the supply of goods will, through various automatic processes, call forth an equal amount of demand. Say argued that every supply of goods to the market meant income for the producers of that supply, and this income would be spent as demand for other goods.

Aside from a few dissenters, whole generations of economists (from the 1800s to the 1930s) refused to accept the possibility that there could be involuntary unemployment or an excessive supply of goods. Furthermore, they never challenged the assumption that all commodities could always be sold at prices equal to their full, long-run costs (including an average profit margin). They admitted only the possibility of temporary, accidental maladjustments in one or a few industries. Such maladjustments were sure to be corrected as soon as competition could force capital to switch from one industry to another. In a typical statement Ricardo argued: "Too much of a particular commodity may be produced, of which there may be said to be such a glut in the market as not to repay the capital expended on it; but this cannot be the case with all commodities."[7]

The kernel of truth in Say's law is the platitude that every purchase constitutes a sale, and every sale means some money income to someone, which may again, and ordinarily will, be used for more purchases. Ricardo phrased the case for Say's law in this way: "No man produces but with a view to consume or sell, and he never sells but with an intention to purchase some other commodity which may be useful to him or which may contribute to future production. By purchasing them, he necessarily becomes either the consumer of his own goods, or the purchaser and consumer of the goods of some other person."[8] Ricardo viewed money as only a "veil" over the real process of exchange of commodity for commodity, so he did not believe that money would ever be withdrawn from circulation.

This argument *must* be wrong as applied to modern capitalist economies because observation reveals that such economies have never been without periodic depressions within the last century or more. Say's law is, indeed, true for certain earlier types of economies; these could not have less aggregate demand than supply because production was for the use of self-contained communities with little external trade and little use of money. Under capitalism, however, the economy has changed: (1) production is for private profit, (2) output must be sold in the market for a profit, and (3) money is used as a medium of exchange and may be hoarded rather than respent.

By ignoring these historical changes, the classical economists, such as Say or Ricardo, built an analytic model that fit a primitive economy or a Robinson Crusoe island, but is inadequate for modern capitalism. Leaving aside government and foreign trade for the moment, the essentials of J. B. Say's view of the economy can be portrayed in a very simple picture (Figure 2.1).

There is an important grain of truth in what J. B. Say claimed. It is true that output, which is supplied to the market and sold there, generates income. The capitalist pays out wages, rent, and interest. The residual from sales, whether positive or negative, may be called profits. These incomes all go to households (if we assume that corporations pay out all profits to stockholders). So it is normally true, as Figure 2.1 indicates, that:

$$\text{\$ supply of net output} = \text{\$ profit} + \text{\$ rent} + \text{\$ interest} + \text{\$ wages} = \text{\$ national income}$$

J. B. Say not only claimed that households received the flow

FIGURE 2.1   CONSERVATIVE (J. B. SAY) VIEW OF INCOME FLOW

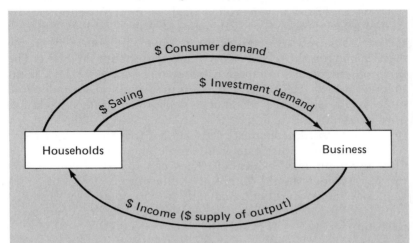

of money from sales of output, but also that households spent *all* of this money, thus completing the circle of circulation. As Figure 2.1 indicates, some of this income is spent for consumer goods, such as food, clothing, shelter and luxuries. The rest of the money is saved, since *saving* is defined as all of the national income that is not consumed. But, according to Say, saving causes no problem for monetary circulation and effective demand. It does not remove money from circulation because J. B. Say made the crucial assumption that:

$$\text{\$ saving} = \text{\$ investment}$$

Since investment means spending money on factories, equipment, or inventories of goods, such investment constitutes part of effective demand just as much as consumer demand does.

J. B. Say and the other classical economists claimed that all income not spent for consumption would always be invested because if more money is saved than invested, competition among lenders will cause the rate of interest to fall. A lower rate of interest stimulates investment which rises until it equals the supply of goods remaining beyond consumer demand. Secondly, if more investment does not correct the situation, the defenders of Say's law argued that competition will correct it. An excess supply means that capitalists cannot sell all their goods at present prices; therefore, competition for consumers will force prices downward. At the lower prices, all the output supplied can be sold because more output is demanded at lower prices. Third, if the excess supply of goods is not removed by competition, the classicals claim this causes very temporary unemployment. The unemployment causes competition among workers, which leads to lower wages. The lower wages stimulate capitalists to demand more labor (since it's cheaper now), which brings back full employment.

The classical economists thus argued that the capitalist system will automatically restore full employment with stable prices after any temporary dislocation. They concluded, of course, that the government should do nothing about unemployment, since unemployment would automatically be eliminated by capitalist activity. This position was accepted by all orthodox economists until the late 1930s. It is still the most conservative position.

THE LIBERAL VIEW OF J. M. KEYNES

J. M. Keynes (1883–1946) is perhaps the most important economist of the first half of the twentieth century. His background does not appear to be that of a radical or an earth shaker. Born into a respected English family and educated in the best British schools, Keynes worked for His Majesty's Civil Service and the Bank of England, edited the *Economic Journal,* and wrote careful treatises on Indian finances and formal logic as well as on the general problems of money. Keynes was always considered one of the Establishment in cultural, governmental, and financial circles, yet he rocked the Establishment both in England and the United States by demolishing the myth of Say's law and automatic full employment.

Say's law had been attacked before by such unorthodox economists as Malthus and Marx. Keynes, however, attacked it in detail, using the respectable academic tools of the classical and neoclassical economists. In his most famous book, written at the depths of the Great Depression, he destroyed Say's law and proved that the economy might function for a long time either at a point of heavy unemployment or at full employment and inflation.[9]

EQUILIBRIUM OF AGGREGATE SUPPLY AND DEMAND

Keynesian economists use the idea of an equilibrium of the forces of aggregate supply and demand as their most important

FIGURE 2.2   LIBERAL (KEYNES) VIEW OF INCOME FLOW

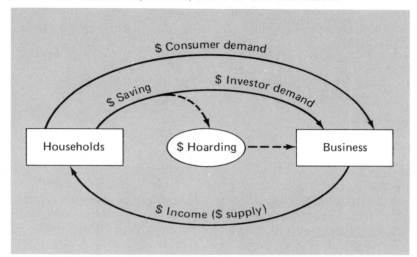

analytical tool for understanding the level of output and employment. *Aggregate supply* is defined as the total output that business produces and plans to sell. *Aggregate demand* is defined as the total dollar amount of final goods and services that consumers, businessmen, government, and foreigners *plan* to buy from the business sector.

Equilibrium exists when planned aggregate demand equals planned aggregate supply. Equilibrium means that buyers' and sellers' plans or intentions exactly agree at present prices. If, however, some goods—such as 1000 bushels of ripe tomatoes—go unsold, then the supply at present prices is greater than the planned demand.

The problem may be explained another way by saying: There is equilibrium only if consumption plus planned investment are equal to consumption plus saving. *Saving* is defined as the difference between income and planned consumption spending. Keynes argued that equilibrium is maintained only if saving out of income is just equal to planned investment spending.

The problem of economic equilibrium is illustrated in its simplest form in Figure 2.2. Business pays the national income to households. Then, if there is equilibrium, all of that income is spent by households to buy goods from business. This implies that all income that is not spent for consumption is saved in the form of investment spending. If some savings are not invested, but are diverted into hoards of money, then there will not be equilibrium of supply and demand. The picture in Figure 2.2 assumes that:

$investment demand + $ hoarding or $ dishoarding
= $ saving

DISEQUILIBRIUM, UNEMPLOYMENT AND INFLATION

Say assumed that all output supplied to the market meant income and that all income is invariably spent, either for consumption or investment. Keynes, on the contrary, points out that some income may not be spent for either consumption or investment in a given period. *Hoarding* means not spending income. If some income is not spent, then that income drops out of the circular flow of money into inactive hoards. For example, money deposited in banks, if the banks do not lend it to anybody, is not spent.

Keynes pointed out that if some of the money income—wages, profit, interest, and rent—from supplying goods to the market is not spent, then there may be disequilibrium. *Disequilibrium* here means simply that the total money demand for all goods is less than the value of all goods at present prices. When demand is less than supply, inventories accumulate and capitalists lose money, so they cut back on production and fire workers. The economy may reach equilibrium again only at a much lower level of supply, where vast numbers of workers are unemployed.

Keynes described this new situation—an unemployment level of equilibrium—as one in which some savings are not invested but are hoarded, thus reducing demand. He pointed out that Say was wrong to think lower rates of interest would automatically stimulate investment. Investors invest only for profit. Suppose, however, the outlook is for very little profit or even losses in the future? No capitalist will be willing to borrow money even at very low interest rates because of the risk involved, so saving may remain permanently higher than investment.

Moreover, Keynes argued that Say was wrong to think lower prices would automatically increase demand. He pointed out that lower prices will decrease wage and profit incomes, but the lower incomes mean less spending and even less demand.

Further, Keynes argued that Say was also wrong to think lower wages would mean more demand for labor. Wages are the largest single component of consumer demand. If wages are lowered, demand for goods falls. Yet a falling demand for goods means capitalists' demand for labor may fall even further.

The opposite situation may result in inflation. By definition, inflation means rising average prices, whereas deflation means falling prices. Suppose that planned demand is greater than supply. At present prices, excess demand drives prices and outputs upward. At first, the only effect might be prosperity or rising output and employment. But when the barrier of full employment is reached, output can rise no higher, so a still higher demand can result only in higher prices or inflation. In the case of inflation, according to Keynes, spending may be greater than national income because additional money moves out of hoards into investment. This movement of money out of hoards is called *dishoarding*. Spending can also exceed income if the spenders are borrowing from banks and the banking system as a whole is creating new money.

KEYNES AND CONSUMER BEHAVIOR

Having decided that inflation and depression are determined by the movements of aggregate demand relative to supply, Keynes' main enterprise is the explanation of these movements. He gives particular attention to deducing the psychological bases for the decision of households to save or consume at different economic levels.

Keynes begins by classifying the elements of aggregate demand for output into two categories: consumer spending and net investment spending. He first considers the behavior of consumer spending, which he believes is determined for the most part by the level of national income. His reasoning as to consumer behavior is based on certain broad psychological presumptions: (1) at a very low income level, the average individual still needs some minimum consumption and therefore will spend all his income on consumption and may even dip into savings or go into debt to spend more than his whole current income on consumption; (2) as his income rises, he needs a smaller percentage of it to cover his minimum needs, so at some break-even point he reaches an equality of income received and consumption spend-

FIGURE 2.3 CONSUMPTION AND INCOME

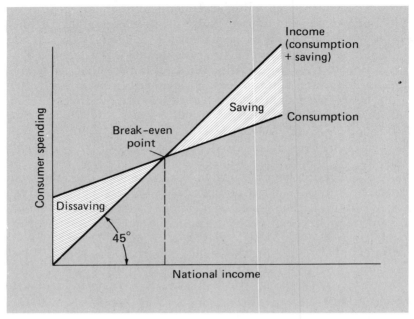

ing; (3) as income rises to a very high level, consumption needs and desires may be filled through the use of a smaller portion of income, so an increasing percentage may be saved.

This usual behavior of consumers is illustrated in Figure 2.3. The line labeled *Income (consumption + saving)* shows the total income at each point; it is equal by definition to the income spent for consumption plus the income saved. If income exactly equaled consumption at every income level, that line (at 45°) would also show consumer spending. In reality they are different. The line labeled *Consumption* shows how much consumer spending there actually is at each level of income. The space between these two lines obviously reflects the amount by which consumption differs from income. At low levels of income, consumer spending is greater than their income, so there is *dissaving* (using up of reserves or going into debt) by consumers. At high levels of income, consumer spending is much less than their income, so there is saving.

This Keynesian schedule of aggregate consumer spending at different income levels is called the *consumption function*. It tells us that in the short run consumption is not some constant

FIGURE 2.4 KEYNESIAN VIEW OF SUPPLY AND DEMAND

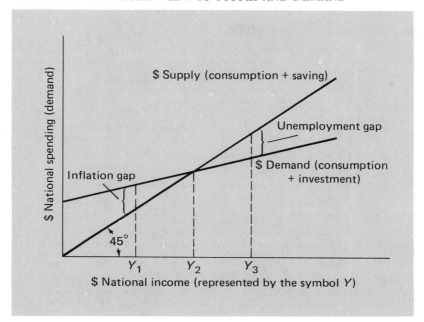

proportion of income. Rather, as income rises, the proportion of income spent on consumption declines.

KEYNES AND AGGREGATE DEMAND

Consumption spending is the largest component of aggregate demand. In a simple economy, with no government and foreign transactions, consumption and investment together constitute aggregate demand. Consumption spending is generally considered the most stable component of aggregate demand. If consumption really behaves in a stable fashion, then, given any level of investment, our knowledge of consumer behavior enables us to derive the level of aggregate demand at each level of income.

Take any arbitrary level of investment. Assume that this level of investment is constant (i.e., does not change when income changes). In Figure 2.4, this investment is combined with consumer demand, according to Keynes' view of consumer behavior. The aggregate demand, or spending, line is derived by adding the constant amount of investment to the consumption schedule at every level of income. The dollar amount of income is by definition equal to the dollar value of output. This is why the supply of output is shown as rising at a 45° angle, always remaining equal to income received.

Figure 2.4 illustrates the economic results at three levels of income or output. If there is a relatively small labor force available, full employment can produce only income 1 (Y_1), a relatively low level of output. If there is a larger labor force, then full employment can produce income 2 (Y_2). With a still larger labor force, full employment can produce income (Y_3), a relatively high level of output.

It is clear that there is only one level of income at which aggregate demand (consumption plus investment) is equal to aggregate supply (consumption plus saving): income 2. This is called the *equilibrium level of income and output*. If full employment happens to produce this level, there is no problem.

Assume, on the contrary, that there is a large labor force, which at full employment produces income 3. At this level it is obvious that the total of planned spending (aggregate demand) is less than the level of output (aggregate supply). The difference, labeled *Unemployment gap*, represents goods and services produced that neither businesses nor consumers want to buy. These goods and services become unwanted inventories. In the next production period businessmen will cut back on production to avoid the continued buildup of unwanted inventories. This decrease in production (and in the number of workers employed) must continue until output at income 2 is reached. At this point output is just equal to what will be voluntarily purchased. The expectations of both businessmen and consumers are consistent at income 2. There are no longer forces at work that will lead to changes in output and income. This is why income 2 is called the equilibrium level of income. But we have assumed that all the workers fully employed could produce output at income 3, so at income 2 there is unemployment. It is an equilibrium *below* full employment. Only if all the unemployed workers died of a plague or were killed in a war would this be an equilibrium with full employment.

Now consider the opposite case. Assume there is a much smaller labor force that can produce only output at income 1. Then aggregate demand will be higher than aggregate supply (see Figure 2.4). Businessmen will be able to sell more than they have produced. This can be accomplished only with an unplanned and unwanted reduction of inventories. If inventories are reduced to zero and no more can be produced (because full employment has already been attained), then how will the businessman react to the excess of demand over the supply of goods? Obviously, because he can produce no more goods, he will raise prices. This is the inflation situation.

If, in this case, full employment of workers can produce only output and national income at income 1, the aggregate supply available at that level is less than the aggregate demand. In other words, in that instance saving (plus consumption) is less than investment (plus consumption). This implies that there is an excess of investment funds, which comes from dishoarding of previous savings or from an increased money supply. Then there may be attempts to increase output beyond the full-employment level. Because output cannot rise beyond the full-employment level, prices must then begin to rise. Therefore the result of the gap between the demand for output and the smaller supply of it is price inflation. The inflationary tendency will continue until the money value of national output and national income approaches the income 2 equilibrium level (although *physical* output cannot go above the given full-employment level of income 1.)

The Keynesian analysis, in its simplest form, demonstrates how the nation's income is determined by the equilibrium between aggregate demand and aggregate supply. It shows that this level of income may be well below the level that could be generated by producing with the labor force fully employed, so the equilibrium level of a capitalist economy may be such as to cause large-scale unemployment. On the other side, the Keynesian analysis shows that the level of income and spending may be above the production possible with the labor force fully employed, in which case the equilibrium level of a capitalist economy may be such as to cause considerable price inflation. Notice that this simplest Keynesian analysis does not explain how there could be both inflation and unemployment at the same time; it seems to exclude that possibility.

Keynes' solutions to unemployment and inflation are those of the liberal reformer. He proves that unregulated capitalism may produce long periods of unemployment or inflation. Nevertheless, he believes that capitalism can be saved by government intervention. If there is unemployment, aggregate demand can be raised by more government spending or lower taxes. If there is inflation, aggregate demand can be lowered by less government spending or by higher taxes.

THE RADICAL VIEW OF KARL MARX

Long before Keynes was born, Karl Marx (1818–1883) made the same critical attack on Say's law; he also proved that capitalism is subject to periodic attacks of mass unemployment. Unlike Keynes, however, he argued that the capitalist diseases of unemployment and inflation cannot be cured by reforms but only by replacing capitalism completely with the new economic system of socialism. These policy differences are discussed in later chapters.

Marx's distinctive contribution to income determination analysis is to point out the very different demand behavior resulting from workers' wage income and from capitalists' property income. This distinction is shown in Figure 2.5.

Marx divides income into two flows:

$$\$ \text{ wage income} + \$ \text{ property income} = \$ \text{ national income}$$

Wage income here includes all income earned from labor, such as piecework wages, hourly wages, and salaries. Property income includes all unearned income deriving from ownership of property, such as profits from ownership of capital, rent from ownership of land, and interest from ownership of money. Later chapters will discuss Marx's position that all property income is derived directly or indirectly from the labor done by workers.

The important point here is that workers' wages and capitalists' property income reveal very different spending patterns. On the one hand, most workers' income is in the lower income categories. Thus most of workers' income is spent for consumption, while very little, if any, is saved. For simplicity, Marx considers that the low wages of debt-ridden poor workers are balanced by the higher wages of better paid workers. Therefore, Marx assumes that aggregate wages just equal the consumer spending of workers:

$$\$ \text{ wage income} = \$ \text{ workers' consumption}$$

The data in later chapters will indeed indicate that the *average* worker—the average of poorly paid and better paid, in good times and bad times—saves almost nothing.

Capitalists, on the other hand, receive very high incomes from profits, rent, and interest. Therefore, as will be shown in later chapters, capitalists do save large parts of their income. As a result, the pattern of spending from capitalist income shows two

FIGURE 2.5   RADICAL (MARX) VIEW OF INCOME FLOW

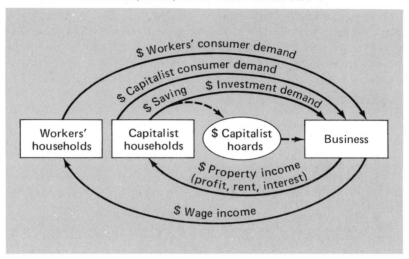

flows. Capitalists not only spend on consumer goods, including luxuries, but also save some of their income:

$ capitalist consumption + $ capitalist saving
   = $ property income

What happens to capitalists' savings? In what forms do they save? A large part of it will be invested for profit. The capitalist buys stocks and bonds in corporations, and the corporations invest the money in factories, equipment, and inventories of goods on hand. Some of the money is invested indirectly through deposits in banks and insurance companies, who lend it to corporations, who use it to buy capital goods. It often happens, however, that there are no more profitable ways to invest the remaining amounts of capitalist saving. In that case, some of capitalist savings are not profitably invested, but are held idle in banks or other hoards. As a general proposition:

$ capitalist investment + $ capitalist hoarding
   = $ capitalist saving

Of course, in a year with very high profit expectations, capitalists may invest beyond their current income by lowering their saving hoards or dishoarding.

Marx thus agrees with Keynes that saving may be greater

than planned investment (causing unemployment) or saving may be less than planned investment (causing inflation). Marx, however, stresses that these problems arise because of (1) the distribution of income under capitalism and (2) the behavior of capitalists seeking profits.

NOTES

1. John A. Crow, *The Epic of Latin America* (Garden City, N.Y.: Doubleday, 1948), p. 54.

2. Grahame Clark, *From Savagery to Civilization* (London: Cobbett Press, 1946), p. 96.

3. See, for example, the brief account in F. W. Walbank, *The Decline of the Roman Empire in the West* (London: Cobbett Press, 1956), pp. 11–13.

4. Ibid., p. 18.

5. Marion Gibbs, *Feudal Order* (London: Cobbett Press, 1949), pp. 7–8.

6. W. C. Mitchell, *Business Annals* (New York: National Bureau of Economic Research, 1926), p. 47.

7. David Ricardo, *The Principles of Political Economy and Taxation* (London: Gonner, Bell, & Sons, 1891), p. 276.

8. Ibid., p. 273.

9. John Maynard Keynes, *The General Theory of Employment, Interest and Money* (New York: Harcourt Brace Jovanovich, 1936).

3
INEQUALITY AND
CONSUMER DEMAND

The largest single element of spending for U.S. products comes from the consumer demand for goods and services. What determines consumer demand? Obviously, the total amount of income available is an important factor. Rich and poor, however, have very different spending patterns. Therefore, another factor determining consumer demand is the degree of inequality in the distribution of income between rich and poor.

INEQUALITY IN INCOME DISTRIBUTION
The official data on income distribution shown in Table 3.1 illustrate the wide range in the United States from very poor to very rich.

The poorest 10 percent of U.S. families each made less than $2700 a year, and all together received only 2 percent of all U.S. income. In addition, 40 percent of the families in the second poorest 10 percent of Americans also fell below the official poverty line, which was only $3940 in 1970. Yet this official definition appears to be set much too low by contemporary U.S. standards. It is based on what the government admits is "an economy diet . . . meant for emergency or temporary use when funds are

TABLE 3.1   INEQUALITY OF U.S. INCOME DISTRIBUTION, 1970

Income Group of Family	Income Range	Percent of Total Income Received by Group
Lowest tenth	$ 0– 2,700	2%
Second tenth	2,700– 4,000	3
Third tenth	4,000– 5,500	5
Fourth tenth	5,500– 7,000	6
Fifth tenth	7,000– 8,600	7
Sixth tenth	8,600–10,045	9
Seventh tenth	10,045–12,010	11
Eighth tenth	12,010–15,000	13
Ninth tenth	15,000–20,000	17
Highest tenth	$20,000 and over	27%

SOURCE: U.S. Department of Commerce, *Statistical Abstract of the United States, 1972* (Washington, D.C.: Government Printing Office, 1972), p. 324. Income is before taxes, but there is very little change in equality after taxes.

low—in other words a diet which over long periods of time does not meet minimum nutritional requirements."[1] By the official definition, a family that just achieved the official poverty income would still not eat enough nutritional foods, and would live in substandard housing.

At the other end of the income spectrum, the richest 10 percent of the families each made over $20,000, and all together received 27 percent of all U.S. income. These figures give some idea of the inequality in the United States. They indicate that the average family in the richest 10 percent received more than 13 times the income of the average family in the poorest 10 percent.

Moreover, income is still more concentrated in the very highest brackets. The richest 5 percent of families had over 14 percent of all family income. The richest 5 percent of unrelated individuals had 21 percent of all individual income. Only the top 2 percent of all taxpayers make over $30,000. Only the top one-tenth of 1 percent of all taxpayers make over $250,000 a year. About 2000 taxpayers make over $1 million a year.

Because income is highly concentrated, saving is also. A small number of individuals and firms do most of the saving and investing of capital. In 1965 personal savings of individuals amounted to only $25 billion, whereas saving by businesses and corporations was $83 billion. Even within the category of per-

TABLE 3.2 HISTORY OF INEQUALITY OF
U.S. INCOME, 1910–1970
(Percentages of U.S. personal income, before taxes,
perceived by richest 20 percent and poorest 20 percent of U.S. families)

Year	Richest 20 Percent	Poorest 20 Percent
1910	46%	8%
1918	47	7
1929	51	5
1937	49	4
1947	48	4
1957	45	4
1965	44	4
1970	44%	5%

SOURCES: U.S. Department of Commerce, Bureau of the
Census, *Statistical Abstract of the United States, 1972*
(Washington, D.C.: Government Printing Office, 1972),
p. 324; also James Weaver, *Modern Political Economy*
(Boston: Allyn & Bacon, 1973), p. 142.

sonal savings, households in the lower two-thirds of the income
range did no saving at all. On the contrary, most of this two-thirds
consumed more than their total income; that is, they went into
debt. More than half of all the personal savings available for
investment was supplied by those in the upper 5 percent income
bracket.

In the course of the twentieth century, has there been any
reduction of inequality in the distribution of U.S. income? The
answer is shown in Table 3.2.

The first thing we notice is how very little change there has
been over this 60-year period. The most noticeable change is a
fall in the share of the poorest 20 percent of Americans from 7 or 8
percent down to 4 or 5 percent, a fall by almost half. On the other
hand, the share of the richest 20 percent of Americans has fluctuated in a narrow range, rising from 46 to 51 percent in 1929,
then falling to 44 percent in 1970. Therefore, we conclude that in
spite of all the liberal rhetoric and all the government promises to
reduce inequality, there has been no improvement since 1910.

LABOR INCOME AND PROPERTY INCOME
Income is not randomly distributed among all individuals.
On the contrary, distribution is closely related to type of income.

Does most of a person's income come from labor (wages) or does it come from property (rent, interest, or profits)? If this fact is known, a good guess can be made about his or her income bracket.

Almost all the bottom 80 percent of families in 1970 were working-class families, and most of their income came from wages and salaries earned by their labor. At the other extreme, most of the income of the top 2 percent came from ownership of property in the form of rent, interest, or profit—in short, the income of the capitalist class. Moreover, the very, very rich elite (less than one-tenth of 1 percent of all taxpayers) collect 23 percent of all dividends and 37 percent of all capital gains. Fully 90 percent of the income in that top tax bracket is from property, and only 10 percent is from wages and salaries.[2]

Privately held wealth, the total someone owns at a given time, is even more concentrated than current income. In 1953, three American academic economists estimated that only 0.2 percent of spending units (i.e., 1 in 500 individuals or families reporting to the Internal Revenue Service) owned 65 to 71 percent of all publicly held stock.[3] In 1956, according to another conservatively calculated estimate, one-fourth of all U.S. privately held wealth was owned by one-half of 1 percent of all Americans. Moreover, just 1.6 percent of the people held 82 percent of all corporate stock.[4]

Notice the cumulative and self-reinforcing nature of the concentration of wealth and income. High concentration of stock ownership leads to a high concentration of income from profits. This income is so concentrated that its recipients are in the highest income brackets. But it is only these highest income brackets that are able to save significant amounts. Therefore they are the ones who make large investments, thus increasing their stock ownership. In other words, large ownership of stock leads to high income in the form of profits, but high income leads to more stock ownership.

The process of wealth and income concentration is self-reinforcing in other ways. For example, one vital prerequisite of upward mobility is education. But many careful studies have revealed that in a large percentage of cases "the father's income rather than the boy's brains determines who shall be college trained."[5] If you are poor, it is hard to support yourself through college even if you are of above-average intelligence. If you are rich but not bright enough to get into top universities, you can always find some private university willing to accept you for enough money.

Even with an education, though, the poor man can attempt to work his way up in business only from the point at which he is hired. The rich heir to a business may have little education and less intelligence but may still step into his father's shoes if he controls enough stock in the corporation. "It is very difficult to climb to the top. . . . It is easier and much safer to be born there."[6] In fact, many of the wealthy today merely inherited a great deal of stock. From 1900 to 1950 some 70 percent of the fathers of the very rich were big businessmen.[7] It is true that most of the very rich have "worked" as big businessmen; nevertheless, completely at-leisure coupon clippers increased from 14 percent of the very rich in 1900 to 26 percent by 1950.[8] The overall conclusion is that Horatio Alger's stories of poor boys rising into great wealth are myths. There is a certain amount of mobility from poor to middle-income status, but very little upward mobility from middle income into the richest elite groups.[9]

Not only have class divisions become more rigid, but very few people remain in the self-employed, independent middle class; most people are simply employees of businessmen. In 1780 the wage and salary earners were only 20 percent of the population, while 80 percent were self-employed, mostly farmers.[10] By 1900, after industrialization, the situation was drastically changed: Wage and salary workers rose to 68 percent, while self-employed farmers, professionals, and businessmen fell to 31 percent; another 1 percent were managers and officials. The process continued so that, by 1970, 84 percent of all Americans were wage and salary workers. Only 9 percent in 1970 were self-employed. When we subtract from that 9 percent the very small farmers, small businessmen, and independent professionals who exploit no one but themselves, this leaves only about 2 percent capitalists living mainly on profit, rent, or interest. In addition, there are 7 percent who are listed as managers or officials; they are salaried workers in theory, but receive some profits and side with the capitalists in all disputes with the workers.

For simplicity, we shall ignore the small intermediate groups in this chapter, speaking only of *workers* who get *wages* and *capitalists* who get *profits*; small farmers and small businessmen are considered in a later chapter. It must always be remembered that most poor and low-income people are wage workers (including women, youth, minorities, and unemployed workers).

Capitalists receive the profits taken from workers, yet most capitalists fall in the very highest income bracket.

CONSUMER PSYCHOLOGY
AND SOCIAL STRUCTURE

Keynesian economists use certain shorthand terms to describe the relationship between consumption and income. The *average propensity to consume* is the portion of income spent for consumption, or the ratio of consumption to income at any particular level of income. Similarly, the *average propensity to save* is the ratio of saving to income at this particular level of income. (Remember that saving is defined as all income not consumed.)

Keynesian economists also speak of the *marginal propensity to consume*, which can be thought of as the portion that will be spent out of any additional increment to income. It is defined as the ratio of the change in consumption to the change in income. Similarly, the *marginal propensity to save* is the ratio of the change in saving to the change in income.

The use of the word *propensity* to describe consumer behavior seems to imply that consumers follow some purely innate psychological laws. On the contrary, according to radical economists, consumer behavior is determined not by any natural drives but by social conditioning. We are not born with a desire for television sets. Nor is there any innate compulsion to consume exactly 90 percent of our income and save 10 percent. Our desires for television sets, as well as our decisions on the ratio of consumption and saving to income, are determined by society's attitudes, ideologies, and institutions. Certainly family background has a significant influence on consumption habits, as do secular and religious educational systems. And last but not least, the vast volume of advertising in the U.S. economy affects the pattern and even the aggregate amount of consumption.

Thus consumer psychology is largely socially determined. Even more important than consumer psychology or desires, however, are the objective social facts of how income is distributed. Even if they have the very same psychological attitudes, an unemployed worker with a tiny income will not be able to save anything (and may dissave, or go into debt), whereas a businessman with a million-dollar income may consume only 10 percent of his income (and still have a very high consumption standard). Thus the data show that groups with very low incomes spend all (or more than all) their incomes on consumption.

Groups with very high incomes spend only a small percentage (but more dollars) on consumption; the rest they save in various forms.

Obviously, a change in the distribution of income will affect the proportion of income spent on consumption. Hence if society taxes the rich and gives to the poor, the proportion of income spent on consumption (the propensity to consume) will usually rise. But if society taxes the poor and gives to the rich, the proportion of income spent on consumption will usually fall.

Propensity to consume for the whole nation therefore depends mainly on just two factors (although it is influenced by many others): (1) consumer psychology as determined by social conditioning and (2) how society distributes income. In this context the term *propensity to consume* is perhaps misleading. A more neutral term, perhaps *consumption ratio*, might more easily include behavior based on both psychological desires and income distribution. Because most economic literature does use *propensity to consume*, it is used here; but the reader must remember that it refers, not to innate drives, but to socially conditioned psychology and the objective facts of income distribution.

Using the usual terminology, we can say that an income shift from the rich to the poor will tend to raise the national propensity to consume because the poor have to consume all their income. An income shift from the poor to the rich will tend to lower the national propensity to consume because the rich consume a much lower proportion of their income.

Further, most of the income of the rich comes from ownership of property (profits, rent, interest, and dividends). But most of those whose income comes almost solely from wages and salaries fall into the lower income groups. Thus we expect to find workers forced to spend almost all of their low incomes; while capitalists are able to save a good-sized proportion of their high incomes. This theoretical expectation is confirmed by some data given by the conservative Milton Friedman; his data show the reality of this difference in class behavior. In the period 1948–1950, Friedman found that business owners saved 23 percent of their income, farmers saved only 12 percent, and nonfarm wage workers saved a mere 4 percent.[11] Friedman's data thus reveal that the average worker spends 96 percent of his or her income for consumption. Although a few better paid workers save some money (especially in expansions), large numbers of poorly paid

workers go into debt (especially in depressions). Other studies
have found capitalists saving as high as 30 to 40 percent of their
incomes, so the difference is truly striking.

Thus the effects of shifts between property income and wage
income are similar to those of shifts between rich and poor. If less
goes to capitalist property owners and more to wage workers, the
result is a higher propensity to consume because wage workers
consume almost all their income. If less goes to wage workers
and more to property owners, the result is a *lower* propensity to
consume because property owners consume a small percentage
and save a very large percentage of their income.

CONSUMER BEHAVIOR
OVER THE BUSINESS CYCLE

The changes in consumption and saving at different levels of
income, as postulated in consumption theory, may be illustrated
by actual data. In 1929, at the peak of prosperity, the level of
consumer expenditure reached its highest point of the decade, as
did national income. Personal saving was also at a record level of
$4.168 billion.[12] By 1933, in the depth of the depression, aggre-
gate income had fallen by half. Consumption had also fallen, but
not as swiftly, because people were spending on consumption
more than their aggregate income by dipping into their savings
accumulated in previous years and by going into debt. As a result, personal saving was actually negative in 1933, at −$648
million (dissaving).

From these data, the conclusion is: total consumer spending
rises when national income rises, and falls when national income
falls. Consumption, however, rises more slowly than income and
also falls more slowly than income. In an expansion a sizable
portion of high incomes is usually saved; whereas in a depression, when income suddenly falls, all or more than all income is
often spent on consumption. In other words, when national income rises in prosperity, the average propensity to consume (the
ratio of consumption to income) generally falls; but when national income declines in a depression, the average propensity to
consume generally rises.

There is, in fact, a great deal of evidence from other cycles
which indicates "that as income falls in the business cycle, consumption will fall proportionately *less* than income; and again
when income rises cyclically, consumption will rise proportionately less than income."[13] For reasons that are not important
here, the average propensity to consume in the long run has re-

TABLE 3.3 CYCLICAL PATTERNS OF NATIONAL INCOME
AND CONSUMPTION
(United States, quarterly data, 4th quarter 1970 to 2nd quarter 1975)

		Expansion					Contractions		
		Trough			Peak		Trough		
Stages	1	2	3	4	5	6	7	8	9
National income	89	98	97	104	106	103	102	98	97
Aggregate consumption	91	98	96	104	104	103	104	100	102
Ratio of consumption to income	101	100	99	99	97	99	101	102	105

SOURCE: U.S. Department of Commerce, *Survey of Current Business* (July 1972, July 1973, July 1974, August 1975). Dates of peaks and troughs of cycle from Table 1.1.

NOTE: Average value from 4th quarter 1970 through 2nd quarter 1975 set equal to 100. Average value of national income was $660 billion. Average value of aggregate consumption was $528 billion. Average value of the ratio of consumption to income, i.e., average propensity to consume was 0.81.

mained remarkably constant (average consumer spending varied only between 84 and 89 percent of net national product in estimates for whole decades between 1869 and 1928).[14] The important fact, however, is that the average propensity to consume, or the proportion of consumer demand to income, has declined in every expansion and risen in every depression.

These cyclical patterns can be seen most clearly if each cycle is divided into nine stages. Stage 1 is the initial trough at the bottom of the last depression; stages 2, 3, and 4 divide up the expansion; stage 5 is at the cycle peak; stages 6, 7, and 8 divide up the contraction; and stage 9 is the final trough in the new depression. The cycle average for each series is set at 100, so the figure for each stage is a percentage of that cycle's average. The patterns in the 1970–1975 cycle for national income, national or aggregate consumption, and the ratio of consumption to income are shown in Table 3.3 and Figure 3.1.

National income rises from the initial trough at stage 1 (in the fourth quarter of 1970) to the cycle peak at stage 5 (in the fourth quarter of 1973) by 17 points. The term *points* is used throughout this book to refer to the amount of rise or decline in one of these cycle patterns, in which the average over the whole cycle is al-

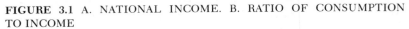

FIGURE 3.1 A. NATIONAL INCOME. B. RATIO OF CONSUMPTION
TO INCOME

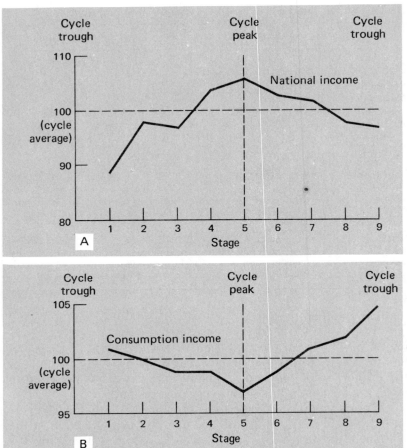

SOURCE: U.S. Department of Commerce, *Survey of Current Business* (July 1972, July
1973, July 1974, August 1975). Dates of cycle peaks and troughs from Table 1.1.

NOTE: Average value of variable from 4th quarter 1970 through 2nd quarter 1975 set
equal to 100. The data is quarterly from 4th quarter 1970 to 2nd quarter 1975 for the
United States.

ways set at 100 points. The term *percentage points* is not used
because that is a slightly different measure (here, the base is
always the average over the whole cycle).

While national income rose 17 points in the expansion, consumption rose only 13 points in the expansion. Similarly, in the
contraction from the peak at stage 5 (in the fourth quarter of 1973)

down to the final trough at stage 9 (in the second quarter of 1975) national income fell 9 points, while consumption only fell by 2 points. These data illustrate the fact that consumption rises and falls more slowly than income. The result of these different movements of income and consumption is that the ratio of consumption to income, the average propensity to consume, is highest at the trough of the contraction. As shown in Figure 3.1B, the ratio of consumption to income then falls to its lowest point at the cycle peak, rising to another high point at the end of the following contraction.

In the four previous cycles, from 1949 through 1970, the result is the same. Since the index for each cycle is based on setting its own average equal to 100, the patterns can be averaged without distortion. For those four cycles, in the average expansion national income rose 25 points, while consumption rose only 18 points. For those four cycles, in the average cyclical contraction national income fell by 3 points, while consumption actually rose by 0.6 points.[15] In these very mild contractions, income fell little and consumption stayed almost constant. (All these data are in terms of real purchasing power; everything rose more in money terms).

In the more violent contractions of the 1920s and 1930s, the behavior is clearly the same as the 1970–1975 cycle. In the average of four expansions, from 1921 through 1938, national income rose by 23 points, while consumption rose only 15 points. In the average of the four contractions in that same period, national income declined by 18 points, while consumption declined only 10 points.[16]

Why does the average propensity to consume tend to fall in each business expansion? Many Keynesians argue that, as income rises, the average psychological propensity of consumers is fixed at the norm set by their previous spending level. There is a long lag before they consider a higher level to be normal and necessary. In the meantime the percentage saved must increase.

Many other economists, particularly radicals, have considered more specifically the differing consumer behaviors of affluent capitalists and lower income workers. As capitalist income rises in an expansion, capitalists do consume a smaller and smaller proportion of it. Partly, this is because they still consider their earlier consumption level normal and satisfactory. Partly, it is because the profit outlook has become more optimistic, so they wish to save a larger part of their income in order to invest it in profitable enterprises.

Workers, on the other hand, continue to spend almost their whole income on consumption. Since their standard of living was below normal at the bottom of the depression, they use most of their increased income to pay off debts and buy necessities. At any rate, their propensity to consume remains over 95 percent even at the peak of the cycle.

Since the capitalists have a much lower propensity to consume than the workers, the distribution of income between worker and capitalist is very important in determining the national average propensity to consume. Even if there were no changes in psychological propensities to consume in either class, a shift in income distribution could explain a change in the average propensity to consume. The declining average propensity in an expansion may be explained by a shift of income from workers (with high propensities to consume) to capitalists (with low—and falling—propensities to consume). The rising propensity to consume in a depression could be explained by an income shift back from capitalists to workers.

CYCLICAL SHIFTS IN
INCOME DISTRIBUTION

Wages do rise and fall proportionately less than aggregate income, while profits fluctuate more than the total national income. "Thus in a time of great activity, wages and salaries constitute a smaller fraction of increased national income than in a time of depression."[17] The aggregate data demonstrate that the ratio of wages to national income falls in economic expansion but rises in depression. During the four business cycles from 1921 through 1938, wages (or aggregate employee's compensation) rose on the average in expansion periods by only 20 points. At the same time, the nonwage part of national income (profits, rent, and interest) rose by 23 points. In these same four cycles, wage income fell on the average in contractions by only 13 points, whereas nonwage or property income fell by 26 points.[18] Furthermore, the single most important part of property income is corporate profits. In the years 1921 through 1938 the average net profit of all corporations rose in expansions by an astounding 169 points and declined in contractions by an equally startling 175 points.[19]

A very similar pattern occurred in the 1970–1975 cycle. Wages (employee compensation in terms of real purchasing power) rose 14 points in the expansion, and fell 6 points in the contraction.[20] It is worth noting how close this was to the rise and

FIGURE 3.2   RATIO OF PROFITS TO WAGES, 1970–1975 (100 = AVERAGE
OVER WHOLE PERIOD, 4TH QUARTER 1970 TO 2ND QUARTER 1975)

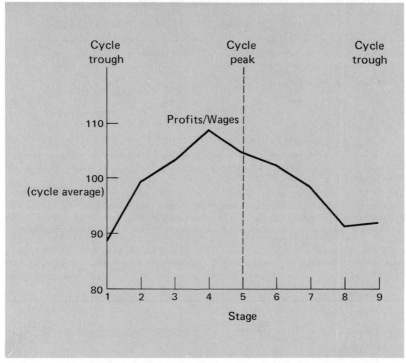

SOURCE: U.S. Department of Commerce, *Business Conditions Digest* (Oct. 1974); also
U.S. Department of Commerce, *Survey of Current Business* (January 1973, July 1974,
August 1975). Data from Table 1.1.

NOTE: Ratio of corporate profit and inventory valuation adjustment (before taxes) to
compensation of employees (before taxes).

fall of consumption, which rose 14 and fell 4 points. On the other
hand, profits (corporate profit and inventory valuation adjustment
in terms of real purchasing power) rose 32 points in its expansion
and fell 22 points in its contraction. While wages peaked in stage
5, profits peaked in stage 4.

As a result of the more rapid rise and fall of profits, the ratio of
profits to wages changes systematically over the business cycle.
In the 1970–1975 cycle, the ratio of profits to wages rose 21 points
to its peak in stage 4 and fell 18 points to its trough in stage 8
(Figure 3.2 and Table 3.4). Thus there was an income shift toward high-income capitalist profits in the expansion and back
toward lower-income workers' wages in the contraction. This was
a major reason for the declining propensity to consume in the

TABLE 3.4 RATIO OF PROFIT TO WAGES
(United States, quarterly data, 4th quarter 1970 to 2nd quarter 1975)

	Expansion					Expansion		
	Cycle trough			Cycle peak		Cycle trough		
Stages	1	2	3	4	5	6	7	8	9
Wages	91	94	99	104	106	104	102	101	99
Profits	78	97	99	110	108	104	99	87	88
Ratio of profits to wages	87	98	102	108	104	101	97	90	90

SOURCE: U.S. Department of Commerce, *Survey of Current Business* (January 1973, July 1974, August 1975). Cycle troughs and peak from Table 1.1.

NOTE: The average value from 4th quarter 1970 through 2nd quarter 1975 is set equal to 100. The average value of wages (all employee compensation in real terms) was $485 billion. The average value of corporate profits (with inventory valuation adjustment, all in real terms) was $62 billion. The average value of the ratio of profit to wages was 0.19. The value of this ratio is consistently understated in the official data for a number of reasons (including some overstatement of "wages" and drastic understatement of profits). All property income is 25% of national income in the same official data, also badly understated.

expansion and the rising propensity to consume in the contraction.

To avoid confusion, it must be stressed that real wages, profits, consumption and income all rose in the expansion and all fell in the contraction. But the *ratio* of consumption to income and the *ratio* of wages to profits both declined in the expansion and both rose in the contraction. In the expansion workers have more real income, but a smaller proportion of all income—and vice versa in contraction. Thus, in the 1970–1975 cycle, the ratio of wages to national income declined 3 points to its low point at the cycle peak and rose by 3 points to its peak during the cyclical contraction. On the contrary, the ratio of corporate profits to national income rose 18 points in the business cycle expansion and fell 16 points in the business cycle contraction.

In the four business cycles from 1949 to 1970, the patterns of profit and wage behavior were similar, except that the downturns in profit and profit ratios occurred much earlier in the expansion. This led some observers to make it an absolute rule that profits and profit ratios decline in early expansion, although this was true only for these particular expansions. In these four expansions, total corporate profits in real terms reached a peak each time in stage 3.[21] In all four expansions total real wages rose to its peak in stage 5. As a consequence, in these four cycles the ratio of profit to wages rose to its peak in stages 2, 2, 3, and 3 respectively; while it fell to its trough in stages 6, 8, 9, and 9 respectively (see Appendix at the end of chapter).

Why do wages rise so slowly in expansions, particularly in the early half of expansion? In the recovery phase of the cycle, there are still large numbers of unemployed willing to take new jobs at low pay. The bargaining power of unions in the early phases of business expansion is also relatively weak, partly because of the existence of the reserve of unemployed workers, but also because of the general attitudes toward wage changes. The public is sympathetic to workers resisting wage cuts, but less sympathetic to fights for wage increases. Even workers are more easily aroused by anger and militancy to resistance to wage cuts than they are enthusiastic to strike for wage increases. In early expansion, however, the big profit increases come primarily from increased productivity. Expansion, particularly the initial recovery, is a period of investment in new machinery, which increases productivity of workers and lessens the need to hire more workers. Finally, increased demand for goods causes prices to rise during expansion. It takes workers a while, however, to realize that these price increases are holding down their real wages (this is called the money illusion).

Why do wages usually keep rising to the peak of expansion? By the peak of expansion, there is much less unemployment. This gives unions greater bargaining power. Worker militancy also increases as workers become fully aware that productivity increases are raising profits, while price increases are slowing the increase of real wages. For these reasons, real wages as well as money wages usually continue to rise to the peak of expansion.

Why do real wages fall relatively slowly in contraction? During the recession, workers strongly resist wage cuts, while productivity and prices usually rise much more slowly than in expansion (because of declining demand). Thus the recession usually witnesses a shift to a lower ratio of profit to wage as profits fall faster than wages. In the next chapter we will examine why profits usually rise so rapidly in early expansion, level off (or even decline) in late expansion, decline rapidly in early contraction, and usually bottom out (or even rise) in late contraction.

CYCLICAL INTERACTION OF INCOME
DISTRIBUTION AND CONSUMPTION

Earlier sections have implied how cyclical changes in income distribution affect the cyclical behavior of consumer demand, but it is useful to make this explicit as a summary of this chapter. Early in cyclical expansions, the ratio of profits to wages rises drastically. This income shift lowers the ratio of consumer demand to income and output. In the later stages of expansions, the ratio of profit to wages levels off or declines a little, though it is still above the cycle average until the business peak is reached. This slight easing of inequality is not enough to get consumer demand to rise rapidly (and is too late to stop the process of contraction), but it does keep consumption steady or slowly rising.

In the early part of most contractions wages fall, but profits fall even more rapidly. The improved equality of income distribution raises the ratio of consumption to income. Therefore, consumption does not fall as rapidly as income, so consumer demand sets some floor to the contraction. At the bottom, profits level off or even start to rise before wages. This would again lower the propensity to consume, but increasing total demand and profit expectations have already set the processes of recovery under way.

NOTES

1. Donald Light, "Income Dsitribution," *Occasional Papers of the Union for Radical Political Economics*, December 1969, p. 2.

2. U.S. Internal Revenue Service, *Statistics of Income: Individual Income Tax Returns* (Washington, D.C.: Government Printing Office, 1970).

3. Keith Butters, Lawrence Thompson, and Lynn Bollinger, *Effect of Taxation on Investments by Individuals* (Cambridge, Mass.: Riverside Press, 1953), p. 400.

4. Robert Lampman, *The Share of Top Wealth-Holders in National Wealth* (Princeton, N.J.: Princeton University Press, 1962), p. 24.

5. C. Wright Mills, *White Collar* (New York: Oxford University Press, 1956), p. 257. For precise data, see Chapter 19.

6. C. Wright Mills, *The Power Elite* (New York: Oxford University Press, 1959), p. 115.

7. Ibid., p. 105.

8. Ibid., p. 108.

9. Ibid., p. 109–111.

10. All the estimates here are from Michael Reich, "The Evolution of the U.S. Labor Force," in R. Edwards et al., *The Capitalist System* (Englewood Cliffs, N.J.: Prentice-Hall, 1972).

11. Milton Friedman, *A Theory of the Consumption Function* (Princeton, N.J.: Princeton University Press, 1957), pp. 69–79.

12. All data here are from U.S. Department of Commerce, Bureau of the Census, *Statistical Abstract of the United States, 1964* (Washington, D.C.: Government Printing Office, 1964).

13. Alvin Hansen, *A Guide to Keynes* (New York: McGraw-Hill, 1953), p. 76.

14. Simon Kuznets, *National Product Since 1869* (New York: National Bureau of Economic Research, 1946), p. 119.

15. Data from U.S. Department of Commerce, *Business Conditions Digest* (October 1974), and U.S. Department of Commerce, *National Income and Product Accounts of the United States, 1920–1965: Statistical Tables* (Washington, D.C.: Government Printing Office, 1966).

16. Wesley C. Mitchell, *What Happens During Business Cycles?* (New York: National Bureau of Economic Research, 1951), p. 155.

17. John Maurice Clark, *Strategic Factors in Business Cycles* (New York: National Bureau of Economic Research, 1951), p. 155.

18. Data derived from Wesley C. Mitchell, op. cit., p. 79.

19. Ibid., pp. 154–155, 324.

20. All data in this and the following two paragraphs are calculated from U.S. Department of Commerce, *Survey of Current Business* (Washington, D.C.: Government Printing Office, August 1971, August 1972, August 1973, August 1974, and August 1975).

21. All data in this paragraph were calculated from U.S. Department of Commerce, *Business Conditions Digest* (Washington, D.C.: Government Printing Office, October 1974).

APPENDIX
Ratio of Profits to Wages

Since there has been much interest in the ratio of profits to wages, but much disagreement over the facts, it is worth presenting the cyclical pattern of this ratio in some detail.

TABLE 3.5 HISTORY OF RATIO OF PROFITS TO WAGES

| | Level of Profit/Wage Ratio at Each Cycle Stage | | | | | | | | |
| | Expansion | | | Peak | | Contraction | | |
Stage Cycle	1	2	3	4	5	6	7	8	9
1949–1954	96	114	108	95	90	75	81	82	87
1954–1958	98	110	105	99	94	89	82	77	80
1958–1961	96	98	108	104	101	96	93	90	88
1961–1970	91	103	112	96	75	70	70	70	65
1970–1975	87	98	102	108	104	101	97	90	90

SOURCES: U.S. Department of Commerce, *Business Conditions Digest* (October 1974). U.S. Department of Commerce, *Survey of Current Business* (August 1975).

NOTE: Quarterly data. "Wages" include all compensation of employees. "Profits" include all corporate profit and inventory valuation adjustment. Ratio for each quarter is profits divided by wages. Average value of ratio over each entire cycle is set equal to 100. Actual averages in the five cycles were 0.21, 0.19, 0.17, 0.17, and 0.19, respectively, all badly understated in the official data as shown earlier.

4
INVESTMENT AND PROFITS

Attempts to explain investment behavior constitute the heart of many business cycle theories. Economists have long realized that, from the standpoint of understanding business cycles, investment spending is the most crucial and violently fluctuating component of aggregate demand. Yet it is also the most difficult to explain and accurately predict.

GROSS AND NET INVESTMENT

Gross investment is defined as the total value of all capital goods produced in a year. *Net investment* is simply the change in the stock of capital within a given period. The stock of capital grows as new capital goods are produced and purchased. On the other hand, the stock of capital is steadily diminished through use, wear and tear, and obsolescence. To determine net investment, the amount by which the old capital stock has diminished in the period is subtracted from the amount of gross investment.

For example, in the crucial year 1929, $8.7 billion was invested in new construction and $5.8 billion in new producers' durable equipment, and there was a $1.7 billion increase in business inventories, or a total of $16.2 billion gross investment.[1]

Because allowances for depreciation (or decline of the old capital stock) amounted to $8.6 billion in that year, it can be assumed that $8.6 billion of the gross investment was for replacement. By definition the net investment must have been at the level of $7.6 billion.

Although it was assumed that the amount of replacement investment can be measured by the estimated depreciation, the decision to replace depreciated capital goods is not automatic. In 1933 gross investment was only $1.4 billion, but depreciation was still $7.2 billion. Therefore net investment was actually at the negative level of −$5.8 billion. The capital stock, and hence the economy's productive capacity, was rapidly diminishing. (Notice that gross investment could never be negative, for at worst no new capital goods would be produced. In that event, net investment would be negative and equal to depreciation).

In an investigation of aggregate demand, it is gross investment that is important. Any investment spending is a part of the demand for currently produced capital goods. If growth of productive capacity is being considered, however, then net investment indicates by how much the capital stock has increased and thereby permits an estimation of the increase in the economy's capacity to produce.

INVESTMENT FLUCTUATES VIOLENTLY

In the last chapter, it was shown that consumption fluctuates much less than national income. This is because in an expansion, when income is increasing and shifting from wages to capitalist profits, capitalists do not increase their consumption proportionately. Capitalists already have more than adequate consumption and they are tempted in the boom to invest more of their income. In expectation of high profits and expanding demand, investment rises rapidly.

Conversely, in a depression, demand is falling and the profit outlook is miserable, so capitalists rapidly reduce their investment. Capitalists then spend for consumption a higher proportion of their declining income. Moreover, income shifts back toward workers who spend an even higher proportion of their own declining income for consumption.

It is, therefore, no surprise that investment fluctuates far more violently than consumption. During the 1970–1975 cycle consumption rose 14 points in the expansion and fell 4 points in the depression. Gross investment, on the other hand, rose by 36

FIGURE 4.1 INVESTMENT AND CONSUMPTION, 1970–1975

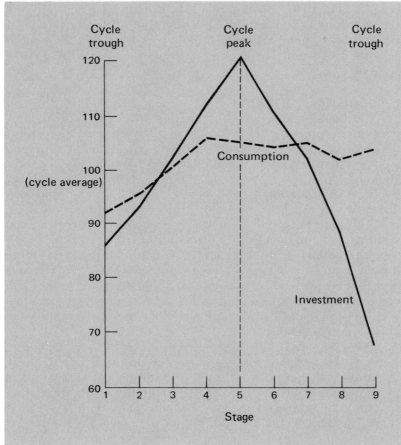

SOURCE: U.S. Department of Commerce, *Survey of Current Business* (Washington, D.C.. GPO, August of 1971, 1972, 1973, 1974, and 1975). Data from Table 1.1.

NOTE: The average value for each variable over the whole period, 4th quarter 1970 to 2nd quarter 1975, is set at 100. Average value of gross private domestic investment was $121 billion. All data are in real terms, quarterly, for the United States.

points to the cycle peak and fell by an enormous 55 points to the cycle trough.[2] Incidentally, net investment fluctuated, as usual, even more violently. Figure 4.1 compares the cyclical behavior of consumption and gross investment in this cycle.

The same relationship has held true in most previous cycles. Thus, in the four cycles from 1921 to 1938, consumption rose an average of only 15 points and fell an average of only 10 points. In the same four cycles, gross investment rose an average of 55

points and fell an average of 49 points.[3] In the four mild cycles
from 1949 to 1970, consumption rose in the expansions an average of 18 points and actually rose slightly in the contractions an
average of 0.6 points. In the same four mild cycles, investment
expanded an average of 30 points and contracted an average of 13
points.[4]

DECISION TO INVEST

The businessman who contemplates the purchase of new
plant or equipment will not decide to make the purchase unless
the profit he expects to receive from this investment is greater
than, or at least equal to, the purchase price of the capital goods.
Obviously profits are exceedingly important in determining
the level of investment—and hence output, income, and employment—in the U.S. economy. Indeed the prime motivation
for investment in a private enterprise economy is the expectation
of future profit on the new investment. But because future profits
cannot be known with certainty, it is mainly on the basis of the
present level of profits and changes in profits that businessmen
form their expectations. Accordingly, high or rising profits will
lead to optimistic expectations and new investment, whereas low
or falling profits will lead to pessimistic expectations and a decline in new investment.

The other and quite distinct reason for the importance of
profits is the fact that more profits provide the funds for more
investment. If there are no profits, the firm may lack funds to
invest even if it wishes to do so. Although the capital funds can
sometimes be borrowed, more profits make it easier for the firm or
its stockholders to obtain credit. Moreover, most firms are quicker
to invest from internal sources, and in practice most expansion is
financed with retained profits.

A great many empirical studies have found a close relationship between investment decisions and total profits or profit
rates.[5] One study of data from 1947 to 1960 in fifteen industries
found a significant correlation between total profits and investment decisions (evidenced by new capital appropriations) in
every one of the industries.[6]

Various other studies have found a positive correlation of
investment with profits after taxes as well as profits before taxes,
total profits, the rate of profit (on sales or on investment), the level
of profits, the change in profits, present profits, and previous profits lagged by one quarter or two.[7] One reason that all these variables have been correlated with investment in various studies is

that they are all correlated with each other; in other words, most of the different measures of profits move in the same direction in each period. Nor can we say that only one of these measures is appropriate to all problems; different ones are needed to answer different questions. For example, a long-run investment decision between different industries is probably most influenced by the rate of profit on investment in each industry. On the other hand, in making a decision on whether to invest at all in a particular phase of the business cycle, or whether to postpone or increase the investment, businessmen seem most heavily influenced by the movements of the profit rate on sales in the past few quarters. At any rate, there is no reason to doubt that investment behavior is most influenced by recent profit performance of corporations.

THE ACCELERATOR

We have seen that the basis for investment decision making is the expected profit from the investment. But it is difficult to esti- mate expected profits, so economists and businessmen use crude substitutes to make rough guesses. The most widely used index on which to base guesses of the profitability of investments is changes in demand for output.

This approach then investigates the ratio between increased demand for output and increased capital investments. If this ratio is known and stable, we could predict the change in capital (that is, investment) from a change in output demanded. The *ac- celerator* is defined as the ratio between investment decisions and changes in output demanded. In other words, the accelerator is the coefficient by which we multiply a change in output de- manded to predict the level of investment.

Notice that the businessman invests in (net) new machinery only to *increase* his output. So the accelerator coefficient relates investment decisions, not to the level of demand for output, but to the change (increase or decrease) in demand for output. Since the rate of change of demand fluctuates more than the level of demand, this helps explain why investment fluctuates more vio- lently than the level of output.

What is the systematic reasoning that links investment to a change in output? With a given technology, a factory needs a certain amount of capital equipment to produce a certain output. Assume that there is an increase in demand for the factory's prod- ucts, so the factory owner wishes to increase its output beyond the present capacity. If the technology stays the same, he must increase his capital equipment in proportion to the increase in output demanded. Therefore his demand for new capital (net investment) bears a precise relation to the increase in output.

This reasoning is extended to the determination of net investment in the whole economy. The demand for an increase in capital is in some (technologically given) ratio to the decision to increase output. That ratio is by definition the accelerator. Thus, it is said that:

$$\text{accelerator} = \frac{\text{investment}}{\text{change in output demanded}}$$

Remember that this theory claims that the accelerator ratio is some precise and roughly constant number (around 3 in the United States).

There is some truth to this technological relationship in the long run—at least, the ratio of investment required to increase output will change very slowly. In the different phases of the business cycle, however, it is not an accurate or constant relationship for several reasons. First, the time lag between a change in demand and resulting net investment varies from industry to industry and even from phase to phase of the business cycle. A long and complicated process takes place before investment spending actually results. If demand improves, the corporate directors must come to expect increased future demand. But such entrepreneurial expectations may also be affected by noneconomic psychological or political factors. Then the directors must appropriate funds for investment purposes and perhaps arrange outside financing. Next engineers must design new factories or new machines. Even after the construction actually begins, it is some time before all the investment funds are fully spent.[8]

Second, the accelerator assumes that each industry faced with higher demands is already running at full capacity. That is not true, however, in a depression or in the early stages of recovery from a depression. During a depression there is much idle machinery and many empty, unused factories. Therefore in such periods any new demand can be met easily without net investment. Thus the accelerator is notably weaker whenever there is much unused capacity to produce.

Third, the accelerator ignores the physical limitations on the amount of investment or disinvestment in any given period. No matter how much the demand increases at the peak of prosperity, the investment goods industries can produce only so much in a given time. The accelerator assumes unrealistically that these industries have just enough excess capacity to produce the investment goods called forth. Similarly, falling demand in a depression may indicate much disinvestment. But the whole economy can disinvest (or reduce its capital stock) in one year only to the extent of the depreciation of capital in that year. In other words, capital can be reduced in the economy as a whole only as fast as it wears out or becomes obsolete.

Fourth, the simple accelerator ignores the effects of changes in the relative levels of prices and costs. At the peak of prosperity the great demand on the capacity of the capital goods industries may raise the cost of capital goods and thus weaken investment incentives. The level of wage costs also changes systematically over the cycle. Moreover, a firm needs financial capital for investment, which depends mostly on reinvestment of profits; if there is not enough profit, then the firm must borrow in the capital market and must face higher interest costs. On the other side, prices show long-run as well as cyclical fluctuations, which affect expected revenues.

These costs and price changes, which are summarized by profit changes, affect investment as much as or more than the simple amount of output demanded. Therefore, the profits—or the rate of profit—are a better predictor of investment than amount demanded. For both profits and output demanded, the *change* in the indicator may impress investors more than a continuing high or low *level* of that indicator (but the *level* of profits does control how much capital is actually available for investment).

Finally, the accelerator only tries to explain net investment. Since replacement is not automatic, it is gross investment that must be explained. To explain replacement investment—in addition to net investment—and why replacement is sometimes speeded up and sometimes postponed, we must again turn to expectations of profit and available funds from profits.

PSYCHOLOGICAL ATTITUDES

Because investment decisions are based on projections of sales, revenues, and profits into the future, it would be easy to say that fluctuations in aggregate investment are caused by changes in investor confidence about economic conditions. Although it points to a vital aspect of economic behavior, such a formula actually explains nothing. There can be no denying the sensational effects of changes in expectations on real economic conditions in the private enterprise system. Between 1929 and 1932 children did not have enough to eat, men jumped from tall buildings, rich women pawned their fur coats. What caused the trouble? Pessimism?

Certainly there was pessimism in the Great Depression of the 1930s. But what caused the pessimism? In 1929 most indexes of production, new investment, and profits turned down in the summer, but the stock market crash and the collapse of expectations did not occur until autumn. For example, the industrial peak was reached in June 1929, but stock prices did not peak until October 1929.[9] In a competitive, private enterprise economy, especially as it increases in complexity and interrelatedness, a single enterprise cannot accurately predict its future costs and receipts; therefore it tends to keep an optimistic outlook until it encounters obstacles. In fact, the usual order of events in depressions appears to be that production and financial indexes decline first, despite the most extreme optimism. It is only then, because of the change in objective economic conditions, that the optimism changes to pessimism, which reinforces the depression and may postpone the recovery. The reverse process seems to occur in economic expansions, when rises in production and profits are followed by a shift from pessimism to optimism.

Of course, after an expansion begins, it is true that the optimism of businessmen goes beyond a rational response to profit increases, so it carries the expansion far beyond the point that cold calculation would carry it. Such frenzied speculation helps make the peak conditions into a bubble easily burst. Similarly, after a depression begins, pessimistic business expectations (usually overreacting in an irrational manner) cause a much greater decline in business activity than the objective condition warrants. But the ultimate cause of pessimism in businessmen's attitudes is the previous objectively recorded decline in profits or profit rates.

INVESTMENT DETERMINED
BY PROFITS AND PROFIT RATES

In the expansion phase of the cycle, particularly in the early expansion, profits and profit rates rise rapidly. This causes a powerful spurt of investment. At the peak of expansion, profits and profit rates are squeezed by various forces. This profit squeeze causes—via still more pessimistic expectations of future profits—a decline in investment. The decline of investment continues throughout the contraction as profits continue to decline. Toward the end of the recession, profits and profit rates bottom out and expectations become more optimistic. This ending of the profit squeeze (and expected upturn of profits) leads to the beginning of a new investment boom.

Let us see the degree to which the messy facts of the real world bear out that scenario. Figure 4.2 shows the behavior of investment and profits in the 1970–1975 cycle. It is apparent that they are very closely correlated. Profits rise to stage 4, then decline. Investment continues rising to stage 5, then declines. So investment follows profits neatly, with a one-stage time lag.

To be more comprehensive, let us examine the timing and expansion amplitude (increase) of gross investment, corporate profits, and corporate profit rates in the last five cyclical expansions. In order to relate the three indexes, it is convenient to use the profit rate on investment; it should be noted, however, that the profit rate on sales had exactly the same timing and a similar amplitude in every cycle.

Table 4.1 shows the close relationship of investment, profits, and profit rates in each expansion. In the first cycle (1949–1954), investment, profit, and profit rates rose rapidly, then declined in the early part of the business expansion. In fact, in that cycle the profit rate peaked in stage 2 and so did investment. In the next two cycles, profits and profit rates both peaked in mid-expansion and so did investment.

In the fourth cycle (1961–1970), profits reached their peak in stage 4 (when the profit *rate* had already declined a little); while investment—reacting with a time lag—did not peak until stage 5. This delayed reaction of investment to changes in profits and profit rates is normal because it takes businessmen some time to make new plans, and some time to carry out new plans. The same time lag between profits (stage 4 peak) and investment (stage 5 peak) is apparent in the 1970–1975 cycle. The apparent anomaly of profit rates peaking much later (stage 7) in this last cycle resulted from their artificial stimulus by the price-cost controls of the Nixon–Ford administration, even after the downswing had begun.

Moreover, the amplitude of expansion of investment is highest in those three cycles (1949–1954, 1961–1970, and 1970–1975) in which profits and profit rates also expanded the most. Invest-

FIGURE 4.2 INVESTMENT AND PROFITS, 1970–1975

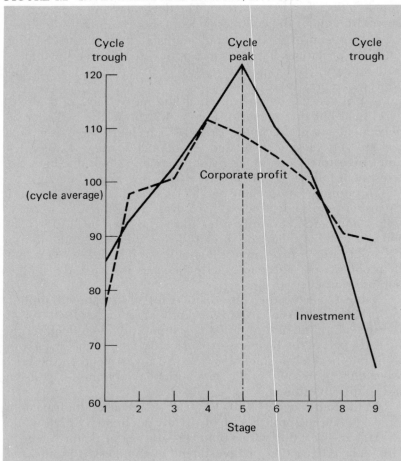

SOURCE: U.S. Department of Commerce, *Survey of Current Business* (August of 1971, 1972, 1973, 1974, and 1975). Data from Table 1.1.

NOTE: Average value for each variable over whole period, 4th quarter 1970 to 2nd quarter 1975, is set at 100. Average value of gross private domestic investment was $121 billion. Average value of corporate profit was $62 billion. All data are in real terms, quarterly, for the United States.

ment expanded the least in the other two cycles, when profits and profit rates also expanded the least. It is reasonable to conclude that investment expansion is stimulated and determined by the rise of profits and profit rates. Investment declines, usually with some time lag, after businessmen have observed that profits and profit rates are being squeezed to lower levels.

The same close relationship of investment to profits and

TABLE 4.1 EXPANSION BEHAVIOR OF INVESTMENT,
PROFITS, AND PROFIT RATES
(quarterly data, deflated into constant 1958 dollars, 1949–1975)

Cycle Expansion (quarters and years)	Expansion Amplitude (Increase from Stage 1 to Specific Peak)			Specific Peak by Cycle Stage		
	Invest- ment	Profit	Profit rate	Invest- ment	Profit	Profit rate
4–49 to 3–53	37	29	45	2	3	2
3–54 to 3–57	23	15	25	3	3	3
2–58 to 2–60	31	28	38	4	3	3
1–61 to 4–69	47	40	49	5	4	3
4–70 to 4–73	36	32	62	5	4	7

SOURCES: U.S. Department of Commerce, *Business Conditions Digest* (October 1974). U.S. Department of Commerce, *Survey of Current Business* (August 1971, August 1972, August 1973, August 1974, August 1975). U.S. Department of Commerce, *National Income and Product Accounts of the United States, 1920–1965.* Federal Trade Commission and Securities and Exchange Commission, *Quarterly Financial Reports of Manufacturing Corporations* (1st quarter 1949 to 2nd quarter 1975). Cycle dates from Table 1.1.

NOTE: Investment is gross private domestic investment. *Profit* is corporate profit and inventory valuation adjustment. *Profit Rate* is profit divided by invested capital, i.e., owners' equity.

profit rates appears in the contractions. The evidence, however, is far murkier because the contractions have been relatively brief in this period. It is only worth noting that investment, profit, and profit rate all reached their troughs in stage 6 of the 1949–1954 (Korean War) cycle. In all the other cycles through 1975, the trough of all three was in stage 9 (except that profit reached its trough in stage 8 of the 1954–1958 cycle). Again, it is reasonable to conclude that investment declines during the whole period of profit squeeze in the contraction. When profit and profit rates bottom out (and at least fall more slowly in stages 8 and 9), then investors regain their confidence and begin to increase investment in the early stages of the next cycle.

REALIZATION OF PROFIT

Investment is a function of profits (and profit rates). What, then, determines how much profit is made in the U.S. economy? In making profits the capitalists face two problems. The first problem is to create or produce a profitable commodity—that is, a commodity that embodies a profit margin above costs at going prices. The second problem is to sell the commodity on the market at the going price—that is, to realize the profit embodied in the commodity.

In formal terms:

$$\$ \text{ sales revenue} - \$ \text{ costs of production} = \$ \text{ profit}$$

The sales revenue depends on the effective or money demand for all commodities, including the demand for consumer goods and services and the demand for investment goods and services. In the last chapter we examined the limitations of consumer demand. If a capitalist has produced a consumer commodity embodying a profit above costs, but there is no consumer demand for it, then the capitalist cannot realize a profit and therefore sustains a loss.

The capitalist may also produce a commodity (such as a machine) designed to meet the demand of investors. If the capitalist sells a machine to other capitalists, just as much profit may be realized from that sale as from the sale of a refrigerator to a consumer. Investment demand, however, is a much smaller part of total demand than consumer demand. It is also partly derived from consumer demand. Therefore, when consumer demand is limited (by income and the distribution of income), investment is also limited. In the last chapter we saw that consumer demand rises more slowly than national income or output; this drastically limits the realization of profits as the expansion progresses.

PRODUCTION OF PROFIT
Before profit can be realized, it must be produced. In the process of production the capitalist buys labor from workers and raw materials and equipment from other capitalists. These human and material inputs must be used to produce a product that will sell (assuming demand does not change) above the cost of these inputs. How does the capitalist usually achieve this magical production of profits above all costs?

If the capitalist pays for labor, machinery, and materials at their long-run market price (averaging out booms and busts), how is a profit made by putting these inputs together and selling their product? Suppose a producer of rubber tires buys the labor power of rubber workers, a quantity of rubber, and some machinery to turn out rubber tires. If the rubber costs a million dollars a year, the producer will put a million dollars value into the rubber tires each year from that source. Assuming there is competition (and no monopoly on either side), the producer must pay the full market value of the rubber; otherwise a competitor will pay a little more. Anyway, we can't explain capitalist profit as a whole by assuming one capitalist cheats another.

The same argument applies to the machinery. Suppose the capitalist buys rubber tire making machinery for $10 million. If the machinery will last for ten years, then one-tenth of its value enters the product each year. Again, competition insures that a capitalist cannot make a profit in the long run by cheating other capitalists.

What about labor? In a precapitalist setting, the same sort of argument shows that competition evens out exchanges according to the labor in them. Suppose one primitive tribe produces rubber taken from trees while another produces deer meat by killing deer. Then a pound of rubber and a pound of deer meat will exchange according to the average number of hours of labor it takes to produce each of these commodities (including the labor in the necessary implements, such as bows and arrows). This will always be the case in the long run, assuming there is no monopoly as an obstacle to competition, because competitors can move from one industry to another. Suppose deer meat is priced too high compared to rubber—in terms of the number of hours of labor required to produce each. Then the rubber-making tribe will start to produce less rubber and begin to kill their own deer meat. Thus, the price of each item exchanged between two tribes (or two members of the same tribe) in a precapitalist economy must roughly approximate the number of hours of labor expended to produce it.

Under capitalism, the same rule must hold in the long run: Every item sold on the market must exchange in approximate relation to the number of hours of labor expended on it, including the hours required to produce the materials and machinery used in its production. So the rubber tire makers buy rubber at a price determined by the labor that went into producing the rubber. And they buy machinery priced according to the labor that went into it. (Of course, these price rules assume competition, no unemployment, and no inflation. These unrealistic assumptions will be dropped as we go along.)

What do the rubber tire enterprises pay for the labor of workers? They must pay according to what it takes to produce a worker—that is, the amount at the present standard of living necessary for food, clothing, shelter, minimal recreation, training and education, and so forth. This is why workers with higher training or education cost more than unskilled workers. Of course, the real wage falls under the long-run average in a depression and rises above it in a boom. Since it is a cultural, not a physical minimum, the wage may rise over time. At any given time, the average wage will be the result of the fierce struggle concerning it between workers and capitalists, unions and monopolies, as well as the degree of unemployment or full employment. Nevertheless, the real wage remains within fairly narrow bounds in any given historical period.

Suppose the total living labor put into rubber tires in one enterprise is 1,000,000 labor-hours. Suppose such a product in rubber tires is valued at $6 million in current prices. Then the total price of the product is equal to the living labor put into it, plus the labor embodied in the depreciated machinery and the labor embodied in the raw materials:

$1 million + $1 million + $6 million = $8 million
(rubber)   (depreciated   (value   (price of
               machinery)   produced   rubber tires)
                               by labor)

But suppose at current prices that the average consumption necessary to each worker at current living standards is achieved at a wage of $3 an hour. Then the one million hours are paid for by $3 million in wages. Therefore, the cost of the rubber tire is:

$1 million + $1 million + $3 million = $5 million
(rubber)   (depreciated   (wages of   (cost of
               machinery)   labor)   rubber tires)

To find the profit, we need only subtract:

$8 million − $5 million = $3 million
(price)   (cost)   (profit on
                               rubber tires)

The mysterious source of profit has now been located. It is the exploitation of the workers. The word *exploitation* here simply means that the workers' product is valued at $6 million, but their wages are only $3 million. For each worker who works an eight hour day, that division means that he or she works four hours to produce the value equal to the wage, and another four hours to produce a surplus product for the capitalist.

WAGE COSTS OVER THE CYCLE

Profits may be expanded by high prices and low costs, or may be squeezed by high costs and low prices. Let us begin by examining one kind of costs—wage costs. If wages rise relatively to prices in some part of the cycle, then profit rates are reduced (all other things remaining constant). If, on the contrary, wage costs fall relative to prices, then profit rates rise if nothing else changes. Finally the rise and fall of profit rates influences the rise and fall of investment.

Several theories of the business cycle, to be examined in the next chapter, do allege that high wages in expansion cut into profits, and therefore cause the downturn. Thus, in this theory, labor is itself responsible for unemployment—again, blaming the victim. But this should mean that there is a shortage of labor causing high wages in each boom. Actually, there is a chronic long-run continuing unemployment in the United States. As we shall see, even at the peak of the boom considerable unemployment continues. Except in wartime, the only authenticated nationwide shortages of labor occurred in one or two railway booms in the nineteenth century. Otherwise, unemployment is the rule in peacetime expansion, so even unions can raise wages only very slowly.

Let us examine the data on cyclical behavior of wages. We saw in Chapter 3 that total profits rose faster than total wages in every expansion, though wages catch up a little near the peak; and that total profits fall faster than total wages during most of the contraction. The individual capitalist firm, however, is not concerned with the relative share of wages and profits in national income. The firm is concerned with its costs in the production process, so we must examine labor costs per unit. It is the labor cost (plus other costs) per unit which, in relation to prices, determines what the margin of profit will be.

Fortunately, an in-depth analysis by Thor Hultgren for the Establishment-oriented National Bureau of Economic Research does furnish some data on costs.

Hultgren's data, shown in Table 4.2, establish that money wages on an hourly basis rose in the average expansion of the 1950s and early 1960s. Because these were cycles with continuing mild inflation, hourly money wages continued to rise—though more slowly—in the contraction phase as well, while real hourly wages declined. The fact that hourly wages rise, however, does not tell us what will happen to labor costs per unit. This depends,

TABLE 4.2 CYCLICAL BEHAVIOR OF HOURLY WAGES, PRODUCTIVITY, AND LABOR COST
(average of 15 U.S. manufacturing industries, average of 3 cycles, 1947–1961)

			Change from Stage to Stage						
		Expansion			Peak		Contraction		
Stages	1–2	2–3	3–4	4–5		5–6	6–7	7–8	8–9
$ Hourly earnings	1.4	2.4	3.0	2.2		1.3	1.3	1.0	0.4
Labor hours per unit	−5.6	−2.8	−1.8	−2.0		2.0	−1.4	−1.0	−0.1
Labor cost per unit	−4.2	−1.0	1.6	−0.2		3.8	0.6	0.3	0.4

SOURCE: Thor Hultgren, *Costs, Prices, and Profits: Their Cyclical Relations* (New York: National Bureau of Economic Research, 1965), Tables 21, 24, and 26. Data reprinted by permission of the National Bureau of Economic Research.

NOTE: Hultgren uses the same nine stage approach to the cycle as was used in several earlier tables in this book. Hultgren, however, does not present the standing at each stage (with cycle average equal to 100). Although he calculates those standings, he presents only the *change* from one stage to the next. This is an appropriate way of concentrating on small increases and decreases.

in addition, on how many labor-hours are necessary to produce each unit.

Hultgren's data reveal that in the average expansion the number of labor-hours required to produce a unit of output declined drastically in early expansion, and continued to decline throughout the expansion. In other words, labor productivity rose in the average expansion. Workers did not, however, receive all the benefit of their higher productivity in higher wages. (Marx would say that the rate of exploitation rose.) Therefore, in three of the four segments of the average expansion—including the rise to the peak—the labor cost per unit actually declined. The combination of rising hourly wages with more rapidly rising productivity reduced one type of production cost. Thus there is no way that rising hourly wages could be held responsible for the profit squeeze in these cycles. On the contrary, lower wage costs per unit were a factor raising unit profits in most of the expansion.

In the average contraction, the situation was very different. Hourly wages rose only very slowly, but in the initial stages of

TABLE 4.3 MONEY AND REAL HOURLY WAGES, 1970–1975 CYCLE (all U.S. nonfinancial corporations, monthly data)

	Change from Stage to Stage:							
	Expansion				Peak	Contraction		
Cycle stages	1–2	2–3	3–4	4–5	5–6	6–7	7–8	8–9
$ Hourly wages	3.7	5.5	5.8	4.7	3.2	4.0	4.5	3.8
Real hourly wages	8.0	3.2	1.3	−0.6	−2.1	−0.6	0.0	0.9

SOURCE: Data for all U.S. nonfinancial corporations from U.S. Bureau of Labor Statistics, *Employment and Earnings* (January 1973, July 1974, September 1975), table C–10. Cycle peak and troughs from Table 1.1.

NOTE: This table follows Hultgren in showing only the *change* from stage to stage. It was derived, as usual, from the absolute standings around the cycle average of 100. Stage 1 levels: wages, 85.0; real wages, 95.8.

each recession productivity fell. Hultgren's data reveal an actual rise in labor-hours per unit of product in the first segment of contraction, with fairly small declines in later segments. This combination of wage increases and productivity decreases led to a large rise in labor costs per unit in the first segment of contraction, and smaller rises thereafter.

Of course, falling productivity in the recession is not explained by lazier workers, nor is rising productivity in expansion mainly explained by speed-up of workers. The main reason for less product per labor-hour in recession is that plants are working far below their optimal capacity. A larger proportion must now be assigned to maintenance of idle machines. Moreover, a large number of white collar workers must be retained for administrative purposes. Finally, because of lack of orders, it is impossible to maintain a smooth, continuous assembly line. In early expansion, on the contrary, all the idle machinery and relatively unproductive workers are put back to work on the assembly line, and many new technological advances also occur at this time.

A similar in-depth study is not available for the 1970s as yet, but there are some interesting data on hourly wages published by the government.

In Table 4.3 hourly wages in money terms rise throughout the cycle, though more rapidly in the expansion than in the contraction. When the money wage is deflated, however, taking into account the rapid price inflation, the hourly wage in terms of real purchasing power does not continuously rise. The real hourly wage fell in 1973 during the height of business expansion; this is very unusual and was caused by Nixon's wage-price controls. The real hourly wage continued to drop until the last segment of the contraction, when it rose a tiny bit. Of course, total real wages fell even further because of rising unemployment (data given in Chapter 3).

TOTAL COSTS OVER THE CYCLE
Costs may be divided in two categories. One category is labor costs, discussed in the last section. A second category includes the costs of material goods bought from other capitalists. This category includes the costs of plant and equipment, which appear as production expenses in the form of depreciation allowances. The other large category of production cost is the price paid for raw materials and intermediate goods used up in production.

The capitalist also counts as costs his payments to other property owners out of the surplus extracted from workers. This includes rent to landlords and interest to money lenders; these are discussed in Chapter 5. There are also tax payments to government, discussed in Chapter 10.

In a careful study of costs and prices, Frederick Mills collected data for many cycles—from the 1890s to the 1930s—on prices of 22 consumer goods, 48 producer goods (i.e., plant and equipment), and 32 raw materials.[10] Mills found that in the average expansion period consumer goods prices rose by only 12 percent of their average value, but producer goods prices rose by 21 percent and raw materials prices rose by 23 percent. Similarly, in the average depression consumer goods prices fell only 18 percent, but producer goods prices fell by 25 percent and raw materials prices by 26 percent. Because of rapid shifts in demand and slow changes in supply, prices of all capital goods (and especially raw materials) rose more rapidly in expansions and fell more rapidly in contractions than did prices of consumer goods.

In recent business cycles, some changes have occurred since costs seldom decline in recessions. Still it appears that nonwage costs, mainly materials, do still rise more rapidly than other prices in expansion, and fall more (or rise less) in recessions. In the expansion from November 1970 to December 1973, the price of finished goods rose by 18 points, but the price of raw materials rose 52 points in the same period.[11] In the contraction from December 1973 to May 1975, the price of finished goods rose by 21 points, whereas the price of raw materials rose only 3 points. In fact, prices of raw materials actually *fell* from stages 6 to 8 (during the contraction in 1974) by 6 points. Thus, the rising costs of raw materials did contribute to the profit squeeze in the expansion in 1973 (when real wages were already falling). Yet the movements of raw material prices actually helped U.S. profit margins in most of the contraction because they fell in 1974 and rose only slightly in 1975.

PROFITS DETERMINED
BY DEMAND AND COSTS

Profits cannot be squeezed from one side alone. The profit squeeze in expansion must be explained by both the limited demand for goods and services (the problem of realizing profit) and the rising costs of equipment and raw materials (the problem of producing profit). In the last chapter we saw that consumer demand is limited in the expansion by a falling propensity to consume among capitalists and a shift in income from workers' wages to capitalist profits. In this chapter we have seen that prices of raw materials, equipment, and other intermediate goods all tend to rise faster than the prices of finished goods, especially consumer goods.

The results of the squeeze by limited demand and rising costs were shown earlier in this chapter as reflected in the declines in total profits and profit rates in the mid and late expansion. Hultgren's data for the 1950s and 1960s illustrate this squeeze.[12] He finds prices rising mildly for most of the expansion and some of the contraction. The profit squeeze came in each cycle because total costs rose even faster than prices at the cycle peak. Since these cycles begin to show inflation phenomena, prices actually fell only in the last two stages of contraction. Total costs, however, fell just as fast as prices in the last stages of contraction, so the profit squeeze ended and recovery began.

The most recent business cycle, 1970 to 1975, reveals the same pattern, modified only by an inflationary trend (which will be explained in Chapters 6 and 8). Table 4.4 shows the pattern of unit costs, prices, and profits derived from official government data for all nonfinancial corporations.

In most of the period of expansion, stages 1 to 4, prices are rising slowly, but costs remain almost constant. Thus, there are enormous rises in the profit margin in this period. Near the cycle

TABLE 4.4 UNIT COSTS, PRICES, AND PROFIT MARGINS, 1970–1975
(all U.S. nonfinancial corporations, monthly data)

	Change from Stage to Stage							
Stages	1–2	2–3	3–4	4–5	5–6	6–7	7–8	8–9
Implicit price deflator	1.7	1.9	2.6	3.1	4.3	4.5	4.4	5.4
Total unit costs	0.4	1.0	1.5	3.6	5.7	4.6	5.6	2.4
Unit profits	12.7	8.0	8.3	−1.0	−1.0	−0.1	−0.9	7.2

SOURCE: U.S. Department of Labor, Bureau of Labor Statistics, *Employment and Earnings* (January 1973, July 1974, September 1975), table C–10. Cycle peak and troughs from Table 1.1.

NOTE: This table follows Hultgren in showing only the *change* from stage to stage. It was derived, as usual, from the absolute standings around the cycle average of 100. Stage 1 levels: prices, 91.4; costs, 93.3; profits, 77.3.

peak, from stage 4 to 5, prices rise a little more, but costs go up still faster, so the profit margin falls.

Throughout most of the 1973–1975 contraction, according to Table 4.4, prices rose even more rapidly than in the expansion period, yet costs rose still more rapidly, so unit profits continued to fall. Only at the end of the contraction period (from stage 8 to stage 9) did the increase of costs slow up very considerably, while prices rose most rapidly. Therefore, in the last segment of contraction, unit profits finally rose again.

The capitalist system was once again temporarily "cured" of its illness by the drastic means of a depression. Although high rates of inflation and unemployment lingered on (keeping millions of people in poverty), the rising profit margins would lead to new investment and new prosperity for business. This completes the description of each of the variables in the business cycle; the next chapter will attempt to tie them together in a full theory of the business cycle.

NOTES

1. All data in this paragraph and the next paragraph are from Wesley C. Mitchell, *What Happens in Business Cycles?* (New York: National Bureau of Economic Research, 1951), pp. 154–157.
2. U.S. Department of Commerce, *Survey of Current Business* (August 1971, August 1972, August 1973, August 1974, August 1975), p. D5.

3. Mitchell, op. cit., pp. 154–155.

4. U.S. Department of Commerce, op. cit., p. D5.

5. See the summaries of several earlier studies plus their own results in the definitive book by John Meyer and Edwin Kuh, *The Investment Decision* (Cambridge, Mass.: Harvard University Press, 1959), pp. 27–29, 134–135.

6. Howard Sherman and Thomas Stanback, Jr., "Cyclical Behavior of Profits, Appropriations, and Expenditures: Some Aspects of the Investment Process," *Proceedings of the American Statistical Association (September 1962), pp. 274–286.*

7. For clarification of these complex relations, see Bert Hickman, "Diffusion, Acceleration, and Business Cycles," *American Economic Review* (September 1959); also see Geoffrey Moore, "Tested Knowledge of Business Cycles," *42nd Annual Report of the National Bureau of Economic Research* (New York: National Bureau of Economic Research, 1962).

8. The timing of investment spending is discussed in Sherman and Stanback, op. cit., pp. 274–285.

9. U.S. Department of Commerce, *Historical Statistics of the United States, 1789–1945* (Washington, D.C.: U.S. Government Printing Office, 1949), p. 345.

10. Frederick Mills, *Price-Quantity Interactions In Business Cycles* (New York: National Bureau of Economic Research, 1946), pp. 132–133.

11. All data in this paragraph are monthly data from U.S. Bureau of Labor Statistics, *Monthly Labor Review* (January 1971 to August 1975).

12. See Thor Hultgren, *Costs, Prices, and Profits* (New York: National Bureau of Economic Research, 1965), tables 10 and 14.

5
UNEMPLOYMENT

This chapter begins with the conservative and liberal theories of cyclical unemployment, then presents a modern radical theory.

CONSERVATIVE NEOCLASSICAL THEORIES

Until the 1930s the main body of neoclassical economic theory did not try to explain, but rather tried to explain away, the business cycle. It was argued that the amount of general unemployment was exaggerated and that there were only partial and frictional fluctuations of production. Moreover, each depression was said to be the last. Indeed, in the 1920s they were said to be gone forever after more than 100 years of business phenomena. In the 1960s conservatives repeated their opinion that "the business cycle has disappeared."

These attitudes are traceable, in the main, to the general social outlook of economists, who supported the status quo. In part, however, they may have resulted from the lack of much theoretical interest in the movements of aggregate demand. Neoclassical economists dealt mainly with demand for particular products based on the subjective utility to individual consumers. Individual desire, however, must obviously be limited and must begin to decline after some given quantity is consumed. Thus a typical neoclassical economist asserts: "It is natural . . . that after the brisk demand of the . . . American public for motor cars in 1922–1923, the intensity of the desire for these articles should fall away."[1] This neoclassical approach leads naturally to thinking of unemployment as a problem of absolute overproduction, of too much production. When, however, the entire economy is examined, and not just each individual product, it becomes clear that the problem in a major depression is not that more is produced than people subjectively desire to consume. On the contrary, there is not nearly enough produced to fulfill the desires or even the minimum health needs of the population; there is too much only relative to effective purchasing power.

As long as most economists accepted Say's law, which insists that there cannot be a general deficiency of effective demand relative to supply, there were only a few logically possible explanations for the fluctuations of aggregate output. One such explanation was that external or noneconomic shocks to the economy may limit supply or bring sudden demands. For example, sunspots may cause bad weather, and bad weather leads to bad harvests; unions may go on strike; governments may foolishly interfere with production activities; wars may stop the flow of raw materials or bring sudden demands for military production; and so forth. Thus one famous economist declares: "Major depressions have been produced by a variety of different types of 'shocks,' not by a regular cycle-producing mechanism."[2]

Certainly such shocks as wars and bad weather do affect the economy; but such occurrences do not always coincide with the major swings in the economy, some of which occur in the absence of any apparent outside shock. Furthermore, noncapitalist economies have reacted quite differently to outside shocks. Therefore we may at least ask what mechanisms in the American economy give rise to cyclical movements as a result of these random shocks. We shall also try to understand how the internal operation of the capitalist economy might produce a business cycle even with no external shocks.

Since conservatives refuse to believe that the private capitalist economy could possibly generate its own depressions, they examine every other accidental or shock explanation with great care. The modern conservative school known as monetarists believes the whole problem is due to government mistakes in handling the monetary system. They argue that fluctuations are not caused by the capitalist system but by the government issuing too much money or too little money.[3] Granted that the U.S. capitalist government makes mistakes in its monetary policies, is it conceivable that the government has made the same mistake every few years for the last 150 years? Such theories of "mistakes" do not explain the systematic behavior of the capitalist economy, in its expansions and contractions, which follow regularly one after the other.

Another conservative notion is that depressions are due to inexplicable waves of psychological pessimism. Such pessimism may cause temporary panics during which money is hoarded and credit is withheld. Typical of these explanations is the statement that "the chief cause of the evil is a want of confidence."[4] The defect of such theories lies in the fact that no one has ever demonstrated cycles of optimism and pessimism in businessmen independent of the economic cycle. In fact, the height of optimism is always reached, as in 1929, at the peak of the business cycle. Only *after* economic conditions have objectively worsened are there irrationally large reactions by businessmen, which intensify the economic downturn. Similarly, irrational optimism may intensify an economic expansion after conditions have objectively improved.

LIBERAL KEYNESIAN THEORIES

The economist whose name is connected with the theoretical revolution of the 1930s is Keynes. As has been seen, Keynes' contribution was the demolition of Say's law. He recognized the possibility that the economy as a whole may be in equilibrium at other than full employment—that is, that more or less may be demanded than is supplied at full employment at the present price level. Yet, one of his most prominent followers comments that "Keynesian economics, in spite of all that it has done for our understanding of business fluctuations, has beyond doubt left at least one major thing unexplained; and that thing is nothing less than the business cycle itself."[5] Keynes' popularity perhaps is attributable to his having said, in a striking manner, the right thing at the right time, for he not only explained the possibility of depressions and inflations but also laid down possible solutions for these problems within the bounds of the private enterprise economic system.

The simplest Keynesian theory of the business cycle was stated by Alvin Hansen and Paul Samuelson.[6] It provides only a bare sketch of reality. The theory consists of just three relationships. First, aggregate demand is composed of planned consumption spending plus planned investment spending. Of course this demand may be greater or less than the full-employment supply of output.

How much income is spent for consumption depends on the second relationship: Consumption is determined by some given propensity to spend out of last year's income, and the average propensity to consume declines as income rises. How much income is spent for investment depends on the third relationship: Investment is determined by the change in income or demand during the previous year (by the so-called accelerator coefficient). If these three statements are accepted as reasonable approximations of reality, what kind of cyclical behavior results?

Assume that national income is expanding in the early expansion phase of the business cycle. The increase in income causes an even greater demand for new capital goods, or net investment. But an initial increase in investment spending causes a further increase in consumer spending and in national income. Then the process continues because the increase in income leads to more investment, which leads to more consumption and income, causing still more investment, and so forth. The consumption and investment relations together thus spell out a cumulative process: An initial expansion in the economy leads to continuing expansion.

Assume now that national income is contracting in the depression phase of the business cycle. The decrease in income causes a large disinvestment of capital. The vast decrease in investment spending means much less income and less consumption. The further decrease in income leads to further disinvestment, which causes a further lowering of consumption, and so forth. Thus the combination of consumption and investment relationships also explains the cumulative process of contraction in the depression. An initial decline leads to continuing decline.

What is more difficult to understand is why the economy ever passes from the process of continuous expansion to the continuous contraction of depression, or, for that matter, how we move from depression back to expansion. The same theory can also explain these turning points, although not as persuasively as it explains cumulative expansion or contraction.

At the peak of expansion it is true that income, consumption, and investment are all increasing. Yet the careful observer can begin to discern strains and even cracks in the impressive facade of prosperity. Consumption increases, but the propensity to consume begins to decline as the proportion of income saved increases. As a result, the aggregate demand out of national income rises more and more slowly. But a smaller increase in national income means, according to the investment relationship, an absolute decline in net investment. A decline in net investment, however, causes a decline in national income, which causes a fall in consumer spending. Thus begins the process of contraction into depression.

Similarly, at the lowest point in a depression (the trough) it is true that income, consumption, and investment are all contracting. Yet as total consumption declines, the propensity to consume rises. As a result, the aggregate demand out of national income falls more and more slowly. But a smaller decline in national income means, according to the accelerator, an absolute rise in the level of investment (or at least less disinvestment). This causes a rise, no matter how small, in aggregate spending. Then the rise in spending means more income and a rise in consumption. Thus begins the process of recovery and expansion. This same fluctuation will continue forever, or as long as we keep the same assumptions. Thus does the simplest theory present a sketch of how the economy produces depression out of expansion and expansion out of depression in a continuing business cycle.

THE UNDERCONSUMPTIONIST
VERSION OF LIBERAL THEORY

Many years before Keynes wrote, the liberal economist, John Hobson, argued that consumer demand is too restricted because wages are too low.[7] He believed unemployment cycles could be cured under capitalism if workers were given higher wages—a theory that appeals to many trade unionists.

Hobson did not say that workers' wages, or even their share of income, are always declining. That could explain how capitalism gets into a depression but not how it gets out of it. What Hobson argued is that while total wages rise in the expansion period, the *share* of wages in national income falls.

Hobson asked, What is the effect on consumer demand of this shift from wages to profits? He argued that profit makers have much higher incomes than wage workers. Therefore they save more and have a lower propensity to consume. Since they now have a larger share of national income, the national propensity to consume will decline.

Hobson concluded that in every expansion period the propensity to consume tends to fall, mainly because of the shift from wages to profits. Hobson thought this was sufficient to explain how inadequate consumer demand at the cycle peak causes a depression, while the opposite process would initiate a recovery.

Critics noted that this argument is not sufficient. Though there may not be enough consumer demand to buy all new production, investor demand may fill the gap. As one conservative economist says, "It will not do to explain insufficiency of investment by the insufficiency of effective demand because effective demand would be sufficient if aggregate investment were."[8] Of course if consumption were not rising at all, more investment could only mean the production of factories to produce more factories to produce more factories, and so on.

The underconsumptionist argument may be buttressed in a modern Keynesian framework by explaining investment with the help of the accelerator principle. As we saw in Chapter 4, the accelerator principle says that investment is determined by the increase in aggregate demand. But consumer demand is the largest component of aggregate demand. When consumer demand rises more slowly at the peak, it means aggregate demand also increases more slowly. When the increase in aggregate demand is less and less, the accelerator principle says investment will actually fall. This sets off a depression. This process is depicted in Figure 5.1.

The opposite process at the bottom of the depression initiates a recovery and expansion. Wages do not fall as rapidly as profits in the contraction. For this reason (and other reasons) consumer demand falls more slowly than income or production. Therefore, aggregate demand reaches a floor and stops falling (or falls very slowly) at the trough of the contraction. When aggregate demand is constant, the accelerator principle says that net investment will stop falling and will actually rise from its negative level to at least become zero. Continued production at this stabilized level sets the stage for a renewed expansion.

Since the problem of a depression, as they see it, is lack of demand, the underconsumptionists argue for higher wages as a solution. Presumably, higher wages would increase consumer demand, allow capitalists to realize more profits, and keep the expansion going forever. They ignore the fact that wages are not only the largest component of consumer demand, wages are also the largest component of costs. If costs rise, the capitalist makes less profit so the solution of higher wages leads to other problems.

FIGURE 5.1 UNDERCONSUMPTION VIEW OF CRISIS AT CYCLE PEAK

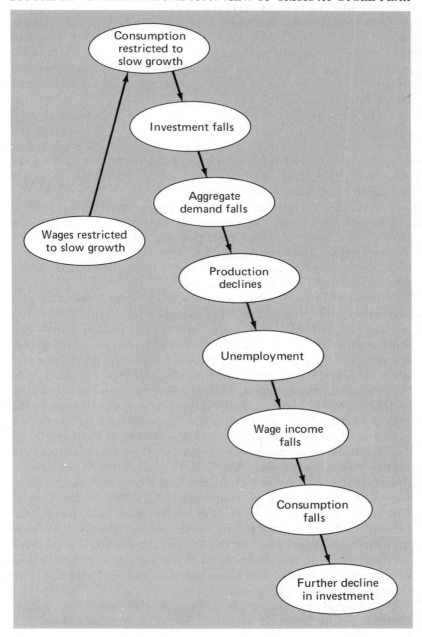

THE CONSERVATIVE
OVERINVESTMENT THEORY

Overinvestment theorists, such as Frederick von Hayek, argue that a crisis arises from high costs.[9] The high level of investment and production leads to a demand for more labor and materials than are available, causing the price of labor and raw materials to rise. Some of Hayek's work also stresses the cost of rising interest rates at the cycle peak.

The heaviest emphasis by overinvestment theorists is usually on the threat to profits from rising wage costs as the economy nears full employment. In wage negotiations employers use this argument to prove that higher wages will lead to less investment and production, and so to unemployment. Therefore, they tell unions to hold down wage requests.

In reality, the argument that high wages in expansion lead to low profits, which leads to a crisis, ignores some crucial facts. As we saw in Chapter 4, labor costs per unit usually fall in most of the expansion, due to rising productivity. Moreover, when labor costs rise somewhat near the end of expansion, they rise less than other more rapidly expanding costs.

Some overinvestment theorists also emphasize that the expansion leads to rising costs of new capital equipment, rising costs of raw materials, and rising interest rates making borrowing more expensive. Assuming that these costs increase faster than the prices of the commodities produced, capitalist profits per unit must decline. When profit rates decline, there is a decline in investment and production, so depression begins. Paradoxically, in this view too high a level of investment leads to high costs, which eventually leads to a crisis characterized by declining investment. This view of the crisis is pictured in Figure 5.2.

To summarize the overinvestment theory: In expansion, rapidly rising demand for labor and investment goods (overinvestment) causes a rapid rise in the cost of these goods to investors. The prices of consumer goods rise more slowly, squeezing profit margins in that sector, and as a result, the increase of total profits proceeds more slowly. Because investment is determined by the increase in profits, less increase in profits causes less investment. Less investment causes less income which causes less consumption, and so forth until the depression is well under way.

The opposite process takes place in the contraction period and eventually leads to recovery. In the contraction, there is a rapidly falling demand for labor and investment goods, so there is

FIGURE 5.2 OVERINVESTMENT VIEW OF CRISIS AT CYCLE PEAK

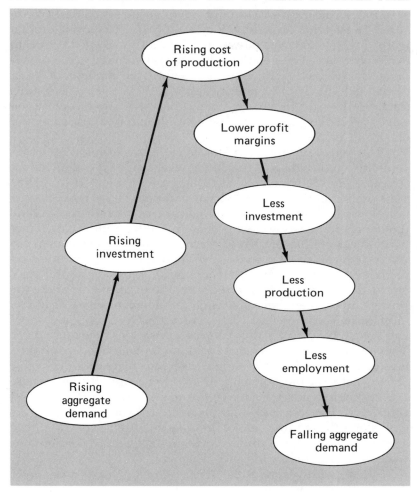

a fall in the cost of these goods to investors. Since the prices of finished goods fall more slowly (or rise more rapidly if there is an inflation in the midst of recession), the profit margin eventually improves. This improvement of the profit margin then leads to more investment and a new expansion.

Since the problem causing the depression is a profit reduction due to higher costs, these theorists argue the position that the government could cure the problem by taking appropriate steps. The steps they urge, however, are the exact opposite of the underconsumptionist suggestions. Their solution—which is pleasing to business—is to hold down costs, particularly wage costs. Those who emphasize the rising costs of labor claim that more employment can only come by cutting wages. A recent textbook says: "The general solution to involuntary unemployment is a reduction in real wages until the amount of labor demanded equals the amount supplied."[10] The Nixon administration followed this advice by putting very strict controls on wages, while keeping very loose controls on prices (discussed in detail in Chapter 10).

The notion of solving unemployment by cutting wages conveniently ignores the fact that lower wages mean less demand for consumer goods, which makes it harder for capitalists to realize their profits. Both Marx and Keynes emphasized this fact.

Nevertheless, some radicals join conservatives in blaming the depression crisis on low profits caused by high wages. Thus, two radicals, citing the *Wall Street Journal* as their source, say "Knowledgeable observers of the labor scene have pointed directly to an increasingly obstreperous labor force as an influence on the decline in productivity during the expansion."[11] Like the conservatives, they argue that high employment levels lead to a militant or "obstreperous" labor force that forces higher wages and lower productivity, thus causing a crisis by squeezing profits. They do not seem to recognize that, on the one hand, capitalists must produce profits by forcing workers to create a surplus value above costs; on the other hand, however, capitalists must also realize their profits by sales in the market, which require high consumer demand and high wages. In simpler terms, the criticism is that a thing cannot be squeezed from only one side at a time. The capitalists' dilemma is that they would like both low wage costs and high consumer demand.

Other overinvestment theorists, who emphasize rising costs of capital and capital goods, advocate other policies to cut costs. Most would lower costs of capital to investors through government influence on interest rates. Specifically, they would have the Federal Reserve System manipulate money and credit supplies so as to lower interest costs (for details of this procedure, see Chapter 6). Even though the costs of buying physical capital goods would be unaffected, investors could borrow money capital more cheaply. Therefore, their own profits would be higher; investment would be stimulated, and the economy would recover.

The theme that higher costs, particularly wage costs, cause

lower production and lower investment, is repeated over and over again by conservative economists and the business press. In October 1974 an economist wrote in the *Wall Street Journal:*

> *The cost of labor is soaring. . . . One reason many analysts view the trend as "ominous" is that it could soon begin to erode company profits sharply and trigger increasing layoffs. So far, corporations generally have managed to boost their prices even more rapidly than labor costs have risen. . . .*[12]

This article admits that prices had actually risen faster than labor costs in the year from September 1973 to September 1974. In fact, we saw in the last chapter that real wages were falling while corporate profit rates were still rising in that period. This article is merely worrying that *maybe* corporate profits could soon begin to fall, not that they had already.

Propaganda from Wall Street has even convinced a few radical economists that "The overal profit rate of U.S. corporations has been falling since at least 1965."[13] A look at the data in Table 5.1, taken from equally conservative sources, indicates that that claim is totally false. Profit rates—both before and after taxes—of all manufacturing corporations did fall in the recession of 1969–1970. Then, however, profit rates rose steadily during the next expansion, and continued to rise in the inflation-in-recession year

TABLE 5.1   PROFIT RATES ON STOCKHOLDERS' EQUITY, U.S., 1965–1974

Year	Petroleum (after taxes)	All Manufacturing (after taxes)	All Manufacturing (before taxes)
1965	11.9%	13.9%	21.9%
1969	11.9	12.4	20.1
1970	11.0	10.1	15.7
1971	11.2	10.8	16.5
1972	10.8	12.1	18.4
1973	15.6	14.8	21.6
1974	19.9%	15.4%	23.4%

SOURCES: Profit rates after taxes from First National City Bank, cited in Labor Research Association, *Research in Economic Trends*, vol. 1 (September 1975), Number 3, p. 6. Profit rates before taxes from Federal Trade Commission and Securities and Exchange Commission, *Quarterly Financial Reports of All Manufacturing Corporations* (Washington, D.C.: Government Printing Office, 1st quarter 1965 to 4th quarter 1974).

of 1974. Petroleum profit rates behaved the same, except that their after tax profit rate rose unbelievably to almost 20 percent in 1974!

It is somewhat more scientific to test the proposition that profit rates are falling by examining the average for entire cycles of boom and bust periods. Table 5.2 shows that profit rates have fluctuated enormously, but have shown no trend. Profit rates were very, very low in the 1930s during most of the Great Depression. Profit rates rose greatly in World War II, but were held down somewhat by wartime controls. When controls came off, profit rates rose again. They reached their height in the Korean War, when only minimal controls existed. Profit rates then fell for two cycles. They were revived again by the Vietnam War and thus rose in the last two cycles.

The old overinvestment theorists argued that at the peak of the cycle rising costs squeeze profits, which lowers investment and causes a depression. The newer conservatives stress a longer run view that rising costs are pushing profit rates lower continuously, so the lower rates reduce incentives to invest, while the lower amounts of profit reduce the capital available for investment for long-run growth. For example, "the total amount of new investment capital that will be needed for continued economic

TABLE 5.2 PROFIT RATES ON STOCKHOLDERS' EQUITY, 1933–1975 (all U.S. manufacturing corporations)

Cycle	Average Profit Rate	Events
1933–1938	3.8%	Great Depression
1938–1945	16.2	World War II
1945–1949	17.8	Recovery from war
1949–1954	24.3	Korean War
1954–1958	21.0	Continuing cold war
1958–1961	17.3	Lessening cold war
1961–1970	19.3	Vietnam War
1970–1975	19.5%	Vietnam War, wage-price controls

SOURCES: 1933 to 1949, annual data from U.S. Internal Revenue Service, *Statistics of Income, Corporate Income Tax Returns* (Washington, D.C.: Government Printing Office, 1935–1951). 1949 to 1975, quarterly data from U.S. Federal Trade Commission and Securities and Exchange Commission, *Quarterly Financial Report of Manufacturing Corporations* (Washington, D.C.: Government Printing Office, 1st quarter 1949 to 4th quarter 1975).

growth between 1974 and 1985 has been set at $4.7 *trillion* by a recent New York Stock Exchange study."[14] A very similar estimate by the Ford administration's Commerce Department is cited by the U.S. Treasury Department as a basis for arguing that present levels of corporate profits after taxes are insufficient to fill these immense capital needs.[15] Treasury Secretary William Simon then drew the conclusion (which all this was leading toward) that the corporate tax rate should be lowered, perhaps to zero![16] He also favored lower tax rates on capital gains based on the same argument.

The conservative arguments about lack of profits leading to lack of capital for investment, both in depressions and over the long run, have several things wrong with them. First, it was shown above that profit rates in the United States have not fallen in the long run. Similarly, a careful British study found that the same conservative propaganda about a profit crisis in their economy is mythical, that in fact the share of profits after taxes in the United Kingdom has been stable from 1950 to 1973.[17]

Second, profits do drop in each recession or depression, but that does not mean that there is a lack of capital. In a depression, there is a surplus of capitalist saving with no profitable place to invest it. For example, Treasury Secretary Simon made his statement which cried about lack of capital for investment in June 1975. But according to the government's own figures, in May 1975 fully 25 percent of all U.S. plant and equipment was standing idle.[18] How can the problem be lack of capital when 25 percent of existing physical capital is not utilized?

Finally, it is clear that all this mythology is designed to justify either controls on wages or lighter taxes on corporations. Moreover, a congressional investigation shows that corporations are already paying very little in taxes because of the loopholes in the law.[19] Although the corporate rate is supposed to be 48 percent, in 1974 the actual rate paid by 142 major corporations was only 23 percent. Eighteen of these corporations (including Chase Manhattan, Mobil Oil, and Bank of America) paid 10 percent or less; and eight of the corporations (including Ford Motor Company, with $351.9 million adjusted net income) paid no taxes at all. Representative Charles Vanik, chairman of the congressional investigation, concluded: "If U.S. corporations are already paying little or nothing in federal income taxes, it makes no sense to give them tax relief in an effort to stimulate investment capital."[20]

A GENERAL (RADICAL)
THEORY OF THE BUSINESS CYCLE

Although the liberal underconsumption and conservative overinvestment theories appear superficially opposed, the radical view treats them as two different aspects of a more general process.[21] At the peak of prosperity, the limited consumer demand and the rising cost per unit act together to squeeze profits and choke off economic circulation. At the trough of the depression, the end of decline in consumer demand and the falling costs per unit increase profits and stimulate economic activity.

The theory that depression is caused by both limited demand (underconsumption) and high costs (overinvestment) is a radical one because it shows that cycles of expansion and depression are inevitable under capitalism. Some liberals believe they could prevent depressions by giving higher wages to increase demand, but that ignores the cost problem. Some conservatives would prevent depressions by lowering wages and interest rates, but that ignores the demand problem. Actually, most traditional economists now agree with radicals that cycles of boom and bust are inherent in unregulated capitalism. They have fallen back to the second line of defense: that depressions can be prevented by the monetary and fiscal policies of the U.S. government (an issue discussed in Chapter 10).

The general radical theory may be stated here, very briefly, within the same framework we used earlier. Demand for output consists of consumption plus investment. Cost of output consists of wages plus plant, equipment, and materials used up. Total profit is the difference between the value of output demanded and the cost of output produced.

Almost all economists agree that the crisis leading to a recession or depression is caused by a profit squeeze. Anyone doubting this should reexamine the data in Chapter 4 on profits and profit rates. In the cycles of the 1950s and early 1960s, both profits and profit rates rise to mid-expansion (stage 3), then begin to fall. In the cycles of the late 1960s and early 1970s, profits peak in late expansion (stage 4) and then begin to fall. The question is only: What causes the profit squeeze? Limited revenue or rising costs or both?

Conversely, both total profits and rates of profit fall enormously in the early stages of the contraction. Then in the trough of the contraction, profits and profit rates are almost constant at a low level. These trends set a floor to the recession and prepare for a recovery. The question is only: What ends the profit squeeze? Rising revenue or lower costs or both?

In the early expansion, prices rise very slowly (actually declining in the first stages of some cycles). The reason goes back to the fact that aggregate wages, and therefore consumer demand are rising very slowly (and the propensity to consume is falling). Fortunately for the capitalists, cost per unit is rapidly declining in this period. The reason is that rapidly rising productivity creates falling labor costs per unit. In other words, the product is getting larger and capitalists are keeping a higher percentage of it. Since costs are falling while prices are slowly increasing, the result is a great increase in the profit rate.

At some point in the expansion (whether mid-expansion or late expansion), the situation becomes quite different. This new situation does not occur suddenly: It is the result of a slow but inexorable process. On the one side, costs per unit decline more slowly or begin to rise in mid-expansion, finally rising considerably in late expansion. Prices, after declining or rising slowly in early expansion, pick up speed in mid-expansion, then rise more slowly at the peak (as demand weakens). As a result, profits already show very little increase in mid-expansion and usually decline toward the end of the business cycle expansion.

Why does demand weaken in late expansion? Total wages rise considerably, but the share of labor is below its cycle average (though the share did rise a little in the late expansions of some cycles in the 1950s and 1960s). Therefore, aggregate consumer demand rises, but the propensity to consume is still below its long-run average. Thus, the price increase is limited by the limits of effective demand under capitalism.

Why do costs rise more rapidly than prices in late expansion? This is due partly to the fact that labor costs per unit rise because of falling productivity. The main reason for the cost rise, however, is that nonlabor costs, especially raw materials, rise much faster.

Since costs are rising more rapidly than prices (because of limited demand), profit is squeezed. If profit is squeezed in mid-expansion, then investment declines soon after. If profit declines in late expansion, then investment declines soon after (at the peak). Whether investment declines in mid or late expansion, its decline is decisive. Falling investment leads to an eventual decline in income, which causes a further decline in demand, leading to falling production and unemployment.

From the viewpoint of the capitalist system, are wages and salaries too high or are they too low? On the one hand, since in most expansions labor costs per unit are slowly rising (though Hultgren actually found them declining a little at the peak), wages are cutting into the production of capitalist profits, so they are too high. On the other hand, since consumer demand is not rising rapidly enough to raise prices faster than costs, aggregate wages—the main support of consumer demand—are too low. Remember that the *ratio* of aggregate wages to profits is lowest in early expansion; and, although it rises a bit in late expansion, it is still below the cycle average (so the propensity to consume is still below its cycle average). In this sense, wages are both too high and too low. The system cannot be saved from crisis by lowering wages because this weakens demand and prevents realization of profits. The system cannot be saved from crisis by raising wages because this reduces the rate of profit created in production.

Schematically, the profit squeeze at the cycle peak may be depicted as in Figure 5.3, which shows only the essentials. The profit squeeze at the peak is caused by both rising costs and restricted demand. This profit squeeze leads to less investment, which leads to a contraction. During the ensuing contraction, the profit squeeze first worsens, then begins to ease. In the recent cycles, with continuing inflation, prices are still rising in the early stages of contraction. Yet total costs rise more rapidly. Therefore, the profit squeeze continues and deepens. In this period, the share of labor does rise, but only because profits are falling. The statistical fact that their percentage share of income is rising cannot comfort workers much when their own real income is dropping.

In later contraction, the situation begins to ease somewhat for the capitalist. Prices decline a little, or at least rise a little less rapidly. Costs per unit, however, rise very little in the mid-contraction and actually decline at the depression trough. Since the profit rate finally stops declining (and may even rise at the trough), capitalists see a ray of hope on the horizon. Therefore, they start some investment, increase current production, and the recovery begins.

FACTORS INTENSIFYING
CYCLICAL UNEMPLOYMENT

We have now stated the basic theory of business cycles, but it is still quite abstract. To get closer to reality we must examine many other factors that do not cause, but do seem to intensify,

FIGURE 5.3   PROFIT SQUEEZE AT CYCLE PEAK

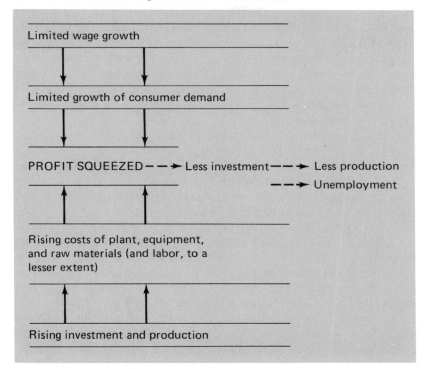

cyclical upswings and depressions. Among these factors are (1) monopoly rigidities in the economy, (2) irrational optimism and pessimism, (3) foreign trade and investment, (4) postponement or hurrying of major inventions and innovations, (5) depreciation and replacement cycles, (6) panics and expansions in money and credit, (7) some kinds of government intervention, and (8) inventory cycles. The effects of business optimism and pessimism were discussed earlier in this chapter. Monopoly power is discussed in Chapters 7 and 8, government intervention is examined in Chapter 9, and international relationships are discussed in Chapter 10.

Inventions

One factor intensifying the business cycle is the postponement of major inventions and innovations in depressions and their hurried introduction in periods of expansion. An invention is a new discovery; an innovation is the industrial use of that invention.

There is no apparent reason to assume that the whole mass of investors should have ideas in bunches.[22] Of course one major invention is likely to lead to many others in that field or in closely related fields, but unusual inventive activity in one area may be canceled on the average by unusual lack of activity in some other area. There would still be some random variation in the rate of invention, but it would be within moderate limits around the given rate, certainly not enough by itself to set off a major depression or recovery.

However, the rate of invention may be influenced by the state of the economy. In a period of prosperity, increased demand for output means increased desire for better technology with which to expand output rapidly. And more funds may be available for research. By contrast, research expenditures dropped in the severe depression of 1929–1933.

The rate of innovation (putting inventions to an economic use) does have its random movements. But the only movements great enough to cause significant intensification of the business cycle are the declines in innovation registered after depressions have begun and the rise in innovations registered after expansions have begun. It thus appears that changes in the rate of innovation are determined mostly by changes in business conditions; so innovations are not shocks from outside that initiate business cycles. Since, however, most innovations are made in expansions and are postponed in depressions, they are a factor intensifying the business cycle.

Replacement

Another intensifying factor is the postponement or hurrying of investment to replace depreciated capital equipment, which is normally more than 50 percent of all investment.[23] If replacement spending is greater or less than current allowances for depreciation, then total demand is greater or less than it would have been. Furthermore, most changes in the difference between replacement and depreciation are not random with respect to the business cycle. During a depression, when there is no desire to maintain a high level of output, many necessary replacements may be postponed. Yet depreciation allowances continue, and thus this source of saving may be far greater than the replacement investment during such a period. In fact, because depreciation is related to aggregate capital accumulated in many previous years, it declines only very slightly except in very long depressions.[24]

Replacement expenditures are often postponed because they

are not needed during depressions, so the continued saving of funds for eventual replacement of depreciated machinery means a net loss of demand. This reduction of demand intensifies the depression. On the other hand, when a long period of prosperity begins, firms spend replacement funds sooner than necessary; the latest innovations are made as replacements long before the old machinery has finished its useful life. This extra investment demand then adds fuel to the expansion under way.

Inventories

Still another intensifying factor is the rise and fall of inventories. Inventories are stocks of goods held by producers, wholesalers, or retailers. Cycles are caused partly by fluctuations in investment in producers' equipment and factories but also by fluctuations in investment in inventories. Changes in inventory investment play a very important role in most business cycles. For example, in the five business cycles from 1919 through 1938, the average change in inventory investment accounted for 23.3 percent of the average rise in GNP in expansions and 47.5 percent of the decline in GNP in contractions. In the same period, changes in construction and producers' durable equipment together accounted for an average of only 20.5 percent of the rises and 37 percent of the declines in GNP.[25] This finding was confirmed for the 1945–1960 period when changes in inventories again constituted very large percentages of the cyclical changes in GNP.[26] If the longer and more severe major depressions or expansions are examined, it appears that much of the decline or rise occurs in investment in plant and equipment. Examination of the shorter, less severe, minor recessions or expansions reveals, however, that most of the decline or rise of investment is in inventory investment.

In the upswing of the cycle, when sales are rising and businessmen are optimistic, there is a high level of inventory investment. Businessmen try to keep their inventories in some desired ratio to sales but are never able to keep enough on hand during rapid expansions. Moreover, their optimism leads them to overexpand inventories. The high and rising level of investment in inventories is one more factor pushing demand upward during the expansion.

Only after the peak of the cycle is passed and a depression begins do business inventories finally catch up with sales expectations. Then, as sales are falling and businessmen become pessimistic, they soon start to lower the level of inventory investment. Businessmen lower their inventory investment just to keep the same ratio of inventories to sales, but then they lower it even further because of pessimistic expectations. By the trough of the cycle, businessmen believe they have far too many goods on hand to sell in a reasonable time, so they frantically try to reduce their inventories by not buying new goods. Then inventory investment becomes quite negative—that is, it is less than what is sold. Thus inventory investment reacts to the same factors as plant and equipment investment (falling consumer demand, relatively high costs), and the precipitous decline in inventory investment makes the depression that much worse by further lowering the demand for goods.

Money and Credit

The final intensifying factor considered here is the use of money and credit in a capitalist economy. Monetary panics have often closed and bankrupted hundreds of banks, as in 1907 and 1932. In every contraction, the flow of credit is disrupted, to some extent further restricting both consumer and investor demand. The stock market crash of 1929 also drastically contracted the funds available for investment.

A closely related factor is the credit policies of financial institutions. They charge high interest rates at the peak of the crisis, pushing many small businesses to the wall. On the other hand, they are free and easy with credit during expansion, encouraging much speculation, which usually goes beyond reasonable sales prospects. Therefore, expansion of money and credit supplies during expansion intensifies the boom, while collapse of money and credit in crises worsens depressions. So money and credit, like the other factors just discussed, do not cause depressions by themselves, but their reactions can turn mild downturns into awful depressions.

In spite of government regulations and controls on the monetary system, this problem is not ancient history. In 1975 two radical economists wrote:

> The specter haunting today's capitalist world is the possible collapse of its financial institutions and an associated world economic crisis. . . . The banking and credit community is showing increasing signs of weakness. Thus, in the span of one year the United States witnessed the two largest bank failures in its history (U.S. National Bank in San Diego and Franklin National Bank in New York). In addition, . . . more than a dozen European banks reported big losses or failed in 1974.[27]

TABLE 5.3 BORROWING BY U.S. CORPORATIONS

	All Corporations		All Nonfinancial Corporations	
Year	Long term debt bonds and mortgages (in $billions)	Long term debt as percent of stock investment	Bank loans (in $billions)	Bank loans as percent of GNP originating in nonfinancial corporations
1950	$ 66	70%	$ 18	12%
1955	98	87	26	12
1960	154	110	38	14
1965	210	130	61	16
1970	$363	181%	$103	20%

SOURCE: Various U.S. government publications, reported in Harry Magdoff and Paul Sweezy, "Banks, Skating on Thin Ice," *Monthly Review* (February 1975), pp. 3–4; reprinted in the excellent collection by David Mermelstein, *The Economic Crisis Reader* (New York: Vintage Books, 1975).

Of course, 1974 was a recession year, but data on long-run trends indicate an increasing problem of weakness in the credit area that is likely to exacerbate any future U.S. crisis. There is a trend toward more and more corporate borrowing from banks. This results from the constant drive of corporations to increase their profits by borrowing capital (say, at 6% interest) to invest it and get a return higher than the interest rate (say, a profit rate of 15%). This long-run trend is quite clear in Table 5.3.

By the first half of 1974 nonfinancial corporations owed banks an amount equal to 25 percent of the GNP originated by these corporations. In addition, they owed other financial institutions an amount equal to 5 percent of their product. This means an enormous burden of interest payments. It is easy to meet these payments during a profitable business expansion. In a depression, however, these interest payments (and return of principal, since loans will not be extended) may lead to disaster.

On the other side, banks make the most profits themselves by expanding loans as far as possible; if the bank pays depositors 5 percent, but lends the money for 10 percent, the profit is considerable. The trick is not to let deposits sit idle, but to lend as much as possible. In an expansion, when corporations look like very safe bets to return both principal and interest on time, banks rush

TABLE 5.4 LENDING BY LARGE COMMERCIAL U.S. BANKS

Year	Loans ($billions)	Deposits ($billions)	Loans as Percent of Deposits	Cash plus U.S. Treasury Bonds and Notes as Percent of Deposits
1950	$ 32	$ 88	36%	54%
1955	48	105	46	43
1960	72	127	56	35
1965	120	182	66	22
1970	189	267	71	18
1974	$319	$389	82%	14%

SOURCE: Various U.S. government publications, reported in Harry Magdoff and Paul Sweezy, "Banks, Skating on Thin Ice," *Monthly Review* (February 1975), pp. 3–4; reprinted in the excellent collection by David Mermelstein, *The Economic Crisis Reader* (New York: Vintage Books, 1975).

to lend them money. The long-run trends toward less safe lending positions are visible in Table 5.4.

The long-run trend in large commercial U.S. banks has been to lend out a larger and larger percentage of deposits. At the same time, their liquid reserves of cash and U.S. treasury bonds and notes are becoming a smaller and smaller percentage of their deposits. This makes them big profits in a boom, when most loans are repaid with interest. In a depression, however, many corporations and many consumers cannot repay their loans, let alone pay interest. The banks, therefore, are faced with falling profits and are caught in a bind for cash. They may not be able to meet withdrawal demands of depositors (which usually increase in a depression), so some banks will fail and go bankrupt, thereby intensifying the depression.

NOTES

1. D. H. Robertson, *Banking Policy and the Price Level* (Clifton, N.J.: Augustus M. Kelley, 1949), p. 10.
2. James S. Duesenberry, *Business Cycles and Economic Growth* (New York: McGraw-Hill, 1958), p. 11.
3. William Mitchell, John Hand, and Ingo Walter, *Readings in Macroeconomics* (New York: McGraw-Hill, 1975), pp. 271–272.
4. Alfred and M. P. Marshall, *The Economics of Industry* (New York: Macmillan, 1881).

5. J. R. Hicks, *The Trade Cycle* (New York: Oxford University Press [Clarendon Press], 1950), p. 1.

6. See Paul Samuelson, "Interactions Between the Multiplier Analysis and the Principle of Acceleration," *Review of Economic Statistics,* May 1939, pp. 75–78.

7. For an exhaustive description of the many varieties of underconsumption theory, see Gottfried Haberler, *Prosperity and Depression* (Cambridge, Mass.: Harvard University Press, 1960).

8. William Fellner, "The Capital-Output Ratio," *Money, Trade, and Economic Growth: Essays in Honor of John Henry Williams* (New York: Macmillan, 1951), p. 121.

9. For an exhaustive description of the many varieties of overinvestment theory, see Haberler, op. cit.

10. Richard Leftwich and Ansel Sharp, *Economics of Social Issues* (Homewood, Ill.: Irwin, 1974), p. 249.

11. Raford Boddy and James Crotty, "Class Conflict and Macro-Policy," *Review of Radical Political Economics,* vol. 7 (Spring 1975), p. 8. A similar view is given in Andrew Glyn and Bob Sutcliffe, *British Capitalism, Workers, and the Profit Squeeze* (Baltimore: Penguin Books, 1972).

12. Alfred Malabre, Jr., "Real Cost of Labor Outpaces Pay Gains As Productivity Lags," *Wall Street Journal* (October 31, 1974).

13. Andrew Zimbalist, "Limits of Work Humanization," *Review of Radical Political Economics,* vol. 7 (Summer 1975), p. 55. He cites as his source an editorial of the *Wall Street Journal* (Feb. 20, 1975).

14. Bill Wycko, "The Work Shortage," *Review of Radical Political Economics,* vol. 7 (Summer 1975), p. 16. A few radicals support this outrageous conservative propaganda on the basis of a dogmatic interpretation of certain statements of Marx about a tendency of profit rates to fall in the early nineteenth century.

15. See "A Shortage of Capital," *Riverside Press-Enterprise,* Riverside, Calif., (June 20, 1975), p. A–3.

16. See *Riverside Press-Enterprise* "Lower Corporate Taxes," (June 20, 1975), p. A–3, and (July 9, 1975), p. A–3.

17. M. A. King, "The United Kingdom Profits Crisis: Myth or Reality?" *The Economic Journal,* vol. 85 (March 1975), pp. 33–54.

18. U.S. Department of Commerce, *Survey of Current Business* (July 1975). Their data is an understatement because it does not include plants that are 100 percent idle.

19. All data in this paragraph from an investigation by a taxation subcommittee of the House Ways and Means Committee chaired by Representative Charles Vanik, reported in "Corporations Evade Taxes," *Riverside Press-Enterprise* (October 8, 1975), p. 1.

20. Representative Charles Vanik quoted in *ibid*.

21. The radical view was first developed by Karl Marx in various works. Its history since Marx is given in Paul Sweezy, *Theories of Capitalist Development* (New York: Monthly Review Press, 1958). It is further developed in Michal Kalecki, *Theory of Economic Dynamics* (New York: Monthly Review Press, 1968). Also see John Strachey, *Theory of Capitalist Crisis* (New York: Covici-Friede, 1935).

22. For the opposite argument, that inventions and innovations inevitably tend to appear in waves and that business cycles "are due to the intermittent action of the 'force' of innovation," see Joseph A. Schumpeter, *Business Cycles* (New York: McGraw-Hill, 1939), p. 175.

23. See Simon S. Kuznets' data, discussed in R. A. Gordon, "Investment Opportunities in the United States," in *Business Cycles in the Post-War World* (New York: Oxford University Press, 1952), p. 293.

24. See Wesley Mitchell, *What Happens During Business Cycles* (New York: National Bureau of Economic Research, 1946), p. 142.

25. See Moses Abramowitz, *Inventories and Business Cycles* (New York: National Bureau of Economic Research, 1950), p. 5.

26. See Thomas Stanback, Jr., *Post-War Cycles in Manufacturers' Inventories* (New York: National Bureau of Economic Research, 1962), p. 6.

27. Harry Magdoff and Paul Sweezy, "Banks: Skating on Thin Ice," *Monthly Review* (February 1975), p. 1.

APPENDIX A
Marx on
Cyclical Economic Crises

Some economists swear by Marx; others swear at him. There have been many interpretations of the views of Karl Marx on the cyclical economic crises of capitalism, but the various interpretations disagree violently.[1] Here, a few quotes are given from Marx just to get the flavor of his views for those who are interested. Remember that Marx defined "surplus value" as that value of the product extracted from the workers by the capitalist beyond all wage costs and other costs. It is the source of all profit, rent, and interest.

Marx points out that making profits requires not one step, but two. First, the capitalist must extract surplus value from the workers by holding down wages; but, second, the capitalist must sell the goods that embody the surplus value.

> *The creation of . . . surplus value is the object of the direct process of production. . . . But this production of surplus value is but the first act of the capitalist process of production. . . . Now comes the second act of the process. The entire mass of commodities . . . must be sold. If this is not done, or only partly accomplished . . . the laborer has been none the less exploited, but his exploitation does not realize as much for the capitalist. . . . The realization of surplus value . . . . is not determined . . . by the absolute consuming power, but by the consuming power based on antagonistic conditions of distribution, which reduces the consumption of the great mass of the population to a variable minimum within more or less narrow limits.[2]*

Profits, therefore, may be and are squeezed from two directions at the peak of expansion: (1) by rising costs of production, which may prevent creation of surplus value, and (2) by limited demand, which may prevent realization of surplus value.

Sometimes Marx emphasized the limited demand resulting from the exploitation of workers. "The ultimate cause of all real crises always remains the poverty and restricted consumption of the masses."[3] Expansions are brought to an end by the limits imposed by class structure:

> *The epochs in which capitalist production exerts all its forces are always periods of overproduction, because the forces of production can never be utilized beyond the point at which surplus value can be not only produced but also realized; but the sale of commodities, the realization of the commodity capital and hence also of surplus value, is limited not only by the consumption requirements of society in general, but by the consumption requirements of a society in which the great majority are poor and must always remain poor.*[4]

On the other hand, Marx criticized and ridiculed the naive underconsumptionists of his day. He insisted that wages do not remain constant; wages rise in total and in hourly rates in the typical expansion.

Marx also acknowledged that, in some extraordinary cases, capitalist investment could be so rapid as to cause a shortage of labor. This shortage leads to high wages, cutting into the rate of profit, and causing a crisis. "If the quantity of unpaid labor supplied by the working class, and accumulated by the capitalist class, increases so rapidly that its conversion into capital requires an *extraordinary* addition to paid labor, then wages rise, and all other circumstances remaining equal, the unpaid labor diminishes in proportion."[5] (Italics added.) He goes on to say that this fall in the rate of profit leads to a depression, which causes wages to fall again.

Note, however, that Marx calls this an extraordinary rise in wages. He also says that such cases have only occurred in exceptional periods, such as the U.S. railway boom of the nineteenth century. Marx emphasized that in most periods of normal capitalist expansion, there is a rising rate of exploitation, that is, profits are rising faster than wages. Marx makes the point very clear:

> *The falling tendency of the rate of profit is accompanied by a rising tendency of the rate of surplus value, that is, the rate of*

FIGURE 5.4A MARX'S VIEW OF THE CYCLE

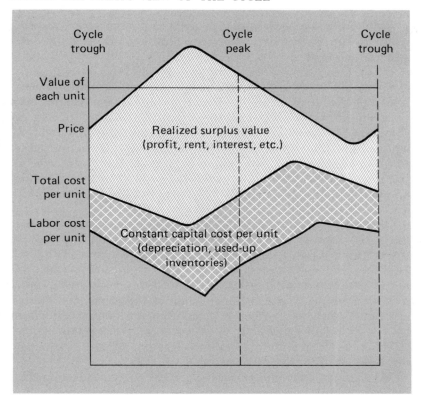

exploitation. *Nothing is more absurd, for this reason, than to explain a fall in the rate of profit by a rise in the rate of wages,
although there may be exceptional cases when this may apply.*[6]

If rising wages were not the cause of the profit squeeze, what
was? One side of the squeeze was the rising cost of capital goods,
including plant, equipment, and raw materials. Marx points out
that the rising cost of capital goods is a normal occurrence as
capitalists accelerate their demand in an expansion:

*The same phenomenon (and this as a rule precedes crises) can occur
if the production of surplus capital takes place at a very rapid rate,
and its retransformation into productive capital so increases the
demand for all the elements of the latter that real production*

cannot keep pace, and consequently there is a rise in the prices of all the commodities which enter into the formation of capital.[7]

The other side of the profit squeeze is the inability to realize profits in the market because of limited demand caused by the exploitation of workers with wages rising slowly. Marx's statements on this point were already presented above.

Figure 5.4A illustrates a rough approximation of Marx's view of the business cycle. The line showing value is constant because the cycle is first analyzed on the simplifying assumption of no change in the available labor force, no change in capital, and no change in technology. The line showing price is far below value in the depression, but rises above value near the cycle peak so that price equals value only in the long-run. The line showing labor cost per unit falls in early expansion because wages are still held down by unemployment and because of rapidly improving productivity. Near the peak the labor cost line rises, both because wages rise somewhat and because bottlenecks begin to reduce productivity; it falls again toward the end of recession. The total cost line falls even faster in very early expansion because of falling constant capital costs per unit, then rises even more rapidly at the peak with rising constant capital costs, and finally falls rapidly in late contraction as constant capital costs decline rapidly. Remember that Marx defined the costs of constant capital to include costs of worn out or depreciated plant and equipment plus costs of used up raw materials.

As a result of the movements of price and cost, the amount of realized surplus value per unit expands rapidly in the expansion, then begins to shrink somewhere in late expansion. After the peak it shrinks very rapidly. The amount of realized surplus value begins to recover only at the very end of contraction.

APPENDIX A NOTES

1. See Howard Sherman, "Marx and the Business Cycle," *Science and Society,* vol. 31 (Fall 1967), pp. 488–504.
2. Karl Marx, *Capital* (Chicago: Charles Kerr, 1907), vol. 3, p. 286.
3. Ibid., p. 568
4. Ibid., vol. 2, p. 363, footnote.
5. Karl Marx, *Capital* (New York: International Publishers, 1967), vol. 1, p. 620.
6. Karl Marx, *Capital* (Chicago: Charles Kerr, 1907), vol. 3, p. 281.
7. Karl Marx, *Theories of Surplus Value* (New York: International Publishers, 1952), p. 371.

APPENDIX B
A Radical Model

A formal mathematical model in economics, consisting of a group of independent equations describing economic relationships, is merely a convenient summary of things already known. Mathematics is a tool and should be neither worshiped nor despised.

To be comprehensible a model must be relatively simple, so models are always very abstract and far from reality. The following model abstracts all the intensifying factors, such as psychological expectations or innovations. The model does not include government or international relations, nor is it explicit on the role of monopoly. It assumes that all the parameters (such as the accelerator coefficient) remain constant. It assumes very simple and constant time lags in each relationship.

With all these warnings, here is the model. We begin with the statement: If there is equilibrium, the gross national income (Y) will equal consumption spending (C) plus gross investment spending (I).

$$Y_t = C_t = I_t \tag{1}$$

The subscript t indicates a time period. This Keynesian formulation is equivalent to Marx's proposition that aggregate value of the nation is produced in department I, investment goods, and department II, consumer goods. This model is inspired by Marx, but will use the usual Keynesian symbols because they are familiar to all Anglo-American economists and most students of economics. For those who prefer it, I have elsewhere written a similar, but more complex, model in Marxist symbols and terminology.[1]

It is also true, at equilibrium, that the gross national product
(Y) will equal wage income (W) plus profit income (P) (including
all property income, rent, interest, etc.) plus depreciation of
capital (D).

$$Y_t = W_t + D_t + P_t \qquad (2)$$

This Keynesian formulation is roughly similar to Marx's proposition that the aggregate value of commodities equals variable
capital (wage costs) plus constant capital (costs of depreciated
plant and equipment and used up inventories of raw materials)
plus surplus value (profits, rent, and interest extracted from
workers).

Consumption is determined, according to the facts in
Chapter 3, by the propensity to consume out of capitalist profits
($a + bP$) plus the propensity to consume out of workers' wages
(all of W). There is some time lag between receipt of income and
consumer spending.

$$C_t = a + bP_{t-1} + W_{t-1} \qquad (3)$$

where a and b are constants, and b is between zero and one. This
formulation stresses, as Marx did, that there are different
propensities to consume by different classes. Thus the distribution of income between classes is crucial to the determination of
aggregate consumer demand.

We must, therefore, specify the distribution of income in this
model. According to the facts in Chapter 3, the percentage of
national income going to labor (the wage share) declines in every
expansion. This is shown in the following equation where c and d
are constants, and d is between zero and one.

$$W_t = c + dY_t \qquad (4)$$

In Marx's terminology there is a rising rate of exploitation, that is,
a declining ratio of wages to surplus value in every expansion.

From Chapter 4, it appears that capitalist investment demand is a function of recent and past profits.

$$I_t = v(P_{t-1} - P_{t-2}) \qquad (5)$$

where v is a constant, a kind of accelerator coefficient. Since investment is based here on profit rather than output demanded, it automatically reflects costs as well as revenue. In Marx's terminology, profit is determined both by the production of surplus value above costs and by the realization of surplus value in the market.

Consumer demand was already determined in equation (3) and wage costs in equation (4). Therefore, both the revenue or realization side of profit and the cost or production side of profit will be fully determined as soon as we determine material costs. These nonwage costs, or constant capital costs, include depreciation of plant and equipment as well as the using up of raw material inventories (all represented by the symbol D in equation (6)). According to Chapter 4 data, these costs of machinery and raw materials rise faster than prices of all other output. This is stated mathematically in our final equation.

$$D_t = -n + mY_t \tag{6}$$

where n and m are constants. The more rapid rise of material costs than wage costs is roughly the same as Marx's rising *organic composition of capital,* which measures the ratio of constant capital costs to labor costs. As in Marx's system, if it is not offset, it results in a declining rate of profit.

This model is radical in that every business expansion is inexorably ended because the rising costs and limited demand squeeze profit. Even if it is still increasing, a slower rate of increase of profit will lead to declining investment. Thus, this model will result in periodic declines in output and income. As output declines, the model slowly reverses itself. Eventually, as material costs fall more rapidly than prices and consumer demand falls more slowly than output, profit declines more slowly and bottoms out. Then investment picks up again and a new expansion begins.

Mathematically, there are six variables and six equations. By substitution, these may be reduced to one equation in one variable (such as Y). It will relate Y_t to Y_{t-1} and Y_{t-2} and, given the initial value of Y (national product), we can determine its path over time. Given the usual values of the constants (reflecting consumption propensities of workers and capitalists, accelerator, rate of exploitation, and organic composition of capital), the national product will show a cyclical time pattern. Other mathematical details are not relevant here.[2]

APPENDIX B NOTES

1. See Howard Sherman, "Marxist Models of Cyclical Growth," *History of Political Economy* vol. 3 (Spring 1971), pp. 28–55.

2. For details of solution, see note 1, above. Also see H. Sherman, "Comparison of Keynesian and Marxist Dynamic Models," *UCR Economics Working Papers*, number 13 (Riverside, Calif.: Department of Economics, University of California at Riverside, April 1976).

6
INFLATION

Chapter 1 examined the human misery and economic _____tion that may result from high rates of inflation as well as u.nemploy- ment. Chapter 2 explained briefly how the Keynesian approach finds that inflation results when the aggregate demand for all commodities is greater than their supply by a fully employed labor force. The *aggregate supply* is the total amount of goods and services at present prices; inflation causes these prices to rise. The *aggregate demand* is the total amount of money that con- sumers, investors, and government plan to spend at the pres- ent time. Both Marx and Keynes stressed that only a demand in money terms is an effective demand under capitalism; mere de- sire or need without money is not included in aggregate demand.

With these qualifications, the Keynesian explanation of inflation boils down to the idea that inflation results when aggregate demand is greater than aggregate supply. It must also be understood that the aggregate monetary or effective demand includes, not just coins and paper money and demand deposits, but all the forms of credit in the economy—in short, demand includes anything that allows an individual or business or gov- ernment to purchase goods and services now, whether they pay now or later. This has the important effect that demand may be expanded to some extent by banks and financial institutions and/or by government manipulation of the financial system.

We shall find that this Keynesian explanation of inflation by aggregate demand, including credit, is adequate to explain most of the inflations of past U.S. capitalist history up through the 1940s. In the 1950s, however, traces of a new kind of inflation emerged that were confusing in Keynesian terms. Moreover, the inflation of the late 1960s and early 1970s is definitely a new variety that the usual Keynesian model cannot explain; it is inflation at a time of deficient aggregate demand. We begin this chapter with a look at those types of inflation that a simple Keynesian model can explain; then we turn to the present type which it cannot explain. The possibilities and the inadequacies of present governmental monetary policy are also examined.

NORMAL INFLATION
IN BUSINESS EXPANSIONS

In most, but not all, business expansions in the United States prices have risen. In most, but not all, U.S. business contractions prices have fallen. The best index of U.S. wholesale prices reveals that, in 23 of the 26 cyclical expansions and contractions between 1890 and 1938, prices moved in the same direction as business activity and production.[1]

In Keynesian terms, prices usually moved up in expansions because effective demand for all products was moving upward faster than the physical supply of products. In contractions, prices usually moved down (e.g., by about 50 percent in the Great Depression) because effective demand for all products was moving downward faster than the physical supply of products was decreasing. Higher prices took up part of the increased demand in expansion, while lower prices were part of the reaction to decreased demand in contraction.

Why does the flow of aggregate demand in money terms rise so rapidly during a period of expansion? On the one hand, the money supply expands because banks give credit (in the form of demand deposits). Businesses want to borrow in order to take advantage of profitable opportunities, and banks want to lend because it appears that businesses can easily repay the loans with interest. Therefore, the money supply in circulation will increase rapidly.

Not only is there more money in circulation, but it turns over faster because consumers and businesses both spend more rapidly. In Keynesian terms, the level of consumption and investment both rise. Consumers wish to get bargains before prices rise further and also because they feel assured of future income. Businesses likewise dig into their hoarded savings—and borrow more on credit—to make the investments that appear attractive. In times of expansion everyone wishes to spend in order to buy goods rather than to hoard money.

In a depression, on the other hand, the flow of money demand usually decreases even faster than the transactions with the national product. Banks call in their loans and businesses do not want to make new loans; therefore, the money supply rapidly declines. Furthermore, individuals and businesses hoard their savings for the rainy days ahead, especially because there are no attractive opportunities for investment. As a result, money circulates more slowly and hoarding increases considerably in a depression. For these reasons, during most of U.S. history, depression was normally a time of price deflation.

INFLATION IN WARTIME

The usual inflation experienced during peacetime prosperity has been very slow and very slight compared with the rapid and spectacular inflation stimulated by wartime spending. Just how closely price inflation is correlated with war may be seen in Figure 6.1. Very rapid price inflation accompanied the Revolutionary War, the War of 1812, the Civil War, and World War I. We shall see later that there was also rapid price inflation in World War II, the Korean War, and the Vietnam War.

During wartime there is little production of consumer goods or private producer goods. At the same time there is full employment, with high wages and profits. All of the increased goods and services are in the military sphere, and are all bought by the government—which finances most of its purchases by printing money or by borrowing, with only limited tax increases. Therefore, civilians have relatively high incomes and high monetary demand, but the amount of available civilian goods and services is very limited. Furthermore, as prices begin to rise rapidly, people rush to buy goods before prices rise further, thus increasing the spending flow even faster than income rises because their propensities to consume and invest are rising.

THE MONEY SUPPLY
AND THE FEDERAL RESERVE

The present money supply consists of coins and paper currency outside of commercial banks and checking accounts (de-

FIGURE 6.1 WAR AND INFLATION IN U.S. HISTORY (WHOLESALE
PRICE INDEX, 1770–1929)

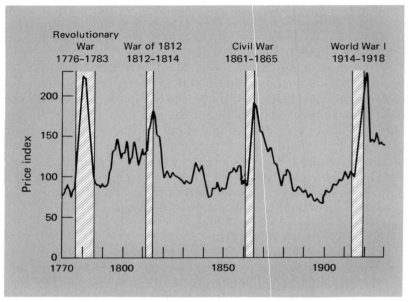

SOURCE: U.S. Department of Commerce, *Historical Statistics of the United States, 1789–
1945* (Washington, D.C.: GPO, 1949).

mand deposits) in commercial banks. In July 1973 the total U.S.
money supply was $264.5 billion, $56.8 billion in currency and
$205.1 billion in demand deposits. Demand deposits, which ac-
count for a fairly constant percentage of the money supply (76.4
percent in 1947 and 77.2 percent in 1973), are the debts of commercial banks. When we say banks "create" money, we refer to
the fact that banks have the ability to create demand deposits.

The business of bankers consists of taking the money deposited with them, on some of which they pay interest, and lending
it out at higher rates of interest. Money deposited in time or
savings accounts pays interest to the depositor, but it must stay
frozen, or on deposit, for some definite time before the interest is
paid (thus it is counted only as *near money*). Money deposited in
checking accounts available on demand (and therefore counted
as part of the *money supply*) pays no interest. In order to pay the
interest on savings accounts, bankers must get higher interest
rates on the money they lend to others.

Bankers are torn between two objectives. On the one hand,
they want to make as much profit as possible by lending out as

TABLE 6.1 CONSOLIDATED BALANCE SHEET FOR THE
BANKING SYSTEM OF THE UNITED STATES
ON OCTOBER 27, 1971

Assets (in millions)		Liabilities and Capital (in millions)	
Gold certificates (held by Federal Reserve)	$ 10,500	Total deposits	$571,000
		Capital owned by stockholders	70,200
Treasury currency	7,600		
Loans	489,300		
U.S. government bonds	133,800		
Total assets	$641,200	Total liabilities and capital	$641,200

SOURCE: *Federal Reserve Bulletin*, November 1971, p. A19.

much as they can (and the riskiest loans pay the highest interest rates). On the other hand, they want safety; they want to be able to pay off easily all depositors who demand their money. Technically bankers are said to seek *liquidity*. The most liquid assets are those most easily available in cash to pay off depositors. Thus the most liquid asset is money in paper currency and coins (or even gold), which pay no interest to the banker. The next most liquid assets are government notes and bonds, sometimes called near money, which pay low interest but can be cashed immediately (although at variable prices if cashed before maturity). Least liquid are risky private loans, which may pay high interest but cannot be cashed for a long time and may never be paid back if the individual goes bankrupt. The precise way in which the entire American banking system holds its assets is indicated in Table 6.1.

Bank liabilities consist mainly of deposits, or the amount that is owed to their depositors. The assets of the whole banking system include gold (held only by the government's Federal Reserve Bank), currency (a very small item), and U.S. government bonds. By far their largest assets, however, are the loans that banks will someday get back from individuals and businesses. For purposes of analysis we shall often classify all assets merely as *reserves* of money and near money or as *loans* to businesses, individuals, and governments. We shall soon discover that modern banks are required by the government to keep a certain ratio of their deposits in the form of reserves, which limits their power to make loans.

THE FEDERAL RESERVE SYSTEM

On December 23, 1913, President Woodrow Wilson signed the Federal Reserve Act establishing the Federal Reserve System (Fed). It was the government's answer to the banking failures and monetary panics of the early 1900s. The Fed is the central bank of the United States, corresponding to the Bank of England or the Bank of France. Its original purposes were to give the country a currency flexible enough to meet its needs and to improve the supervision of banking. Today, however, these form only a part of broader and more important objectives, which include maintaining price stability and fostering a high rate of economic growth.

Federal Reserve functions are carried out through 12 Federal Reserve Banks and their 24 branches, but there is also central coordinating by the Board of Governors in Washington. The Board of Governors consists of seven members appointed by the president and confirmed by the Senate. One of the board's duties is to supervise all Fed operations. The board participates in all of the principal monetary actions of the Fed. It has full authority over changes in the legal reserve requirements of banks (within the limits prescribed by Congress). The board reviews and determines interest rates of the individual Federal Reserve Banks. And the members of the board constitute a majority of the Federal Open Market Committee, which buys and sells government bonds in the open market. In addition, it is responsible for the regulation of stock market credit, and it has the authority to establish the maximum rates of interest member banks may pay on savings and other time deposits.

The Federal Reserve controls the money supply in order to achieve its purposes. The real bases of the value of the nation's money supply are the goods produced and confidence in the government. Until recently, however, the money supply of the United States had as its legal base the country's gold stock, which stood at $11.8 billion on August 26, 1970. Congress had required the Federal Reserve to hold an amount equal to 25 percent of its liabilities in the form of gold, but this was purely a congressional whim. The requirement was removed in 1968 with no significant effect on the efficiency with which money has performed its functions.

Although the Federal Reserve Banks still hold gold certifi-

TABLE 6.2 RESERVE REQUIREMENTS OF MEMBER BANKS
(as percentage of deposits)

| Date | Demand Deposits (checking accounts) | | Time Deposits (saving accounts) All Banks |
	City[2] Banks	Country[2] Banks	
Dec. 1948	22.0%	16.0%	7.5%
July 1954	18.0	12.0	6.0
Apr. 1958	16.5	11.0	5.0
Oct. 1962	16.5	12.0	4.0
Mar. 1967	16.5	12.0	3.0
Aug. 1970	17.5	12.5–13[1]	3.0
July 1973	18.5%	8.0–13%[1]	3.0%

Limits Set by Congress Within Which the Federal Reserve May Set the Requirements.			
Minimum	10.0%	7.0%	3.0%
Maximum	22.0	14.0	10.0

SOURCE: *Federal Reserve Bulletin*, August 1973, p. A9.

[1] The reserve requirement increases with size of bank.
[2] Any bank with over $400 million in deposits is a "city" bank; any other smaller bank is a "country" bank.

cates, this is merely one of several types of assets. Gold certificates need bear no relationship to Federal Reserve liabilities (i.e., they bear no necessary connection to the U.S. money supply). The other principal types of assets are government securities and loans to the member banks. The principal liabilities are Federal Reserve note currency, which constitutes most of the paper currency held by the public, and member bank reserves, which, as will be seen, form the basis for the creation of credit money by the banking system.

The Federal Reserve specifies exactly how much reserve each member bank must hold in relation to its deposits. Recently required ratios are given in Table 6.2. Bank reserves of money or "checking accounts at the Fed" may be kept either in the bank vault or in the nearest Federal Reserve Bank. If it is kept as a deposit in a Federal Reserve Bank, the member bank may even earn a small interest on its money reserves. Country banks are given a lower required reserve ratio, apparently on the theory that they may also fall back on loans from the larger city banks.

The first purpose of the reserve system is, of course, to ensure

that the bank has sufficient funds to meet its depositors' with-
drawals. Yet in the Great Depression thousands of banks failed
because runs on the banks by depositors exhausted their reserves. This purpose is now more fully met by the Federal Deposit Insurance Corporation (FDIC), which guarantees all deposits up to $40,000. The more important purpose that the Fed
now serves is to control the money supply as a tool of general
economic control.

HOW BANKS MULTIPLY MONEY

Exactly how much money can banks create with a given
amount of new deposits? Obviously this depends in large part on
what reserve ratio the Federal Reserve requires them to hold.
Part of each new deposit must be held in reserve, and part may
be lent out. For convenience assume that the Federal Reserve
ratio is set at 20 percent for all kinds of deposits in all kinds of
banks. Then if a bank receives a $1000 deposit, it deposits the
$1000 at the Federal Reserve Bank, thus increasing its reserves
by $1000. The reader may imagine that this would permit the
bank to make new loans totaling $4000 and thereby created
$4000 in new money. Its new reserves of $1000 would be 20
percent of the original $1000 deposit and the $4000 in new deposits created by the loans. It might thus appear that a single
bank could expand the money supply by a multiple of each new
deposit it receives.

This is not the case, however. Something called *adverse
clearing balances* prevents this. Assume that recipients of the
$4000 in new loans write checks, totaling $4000, drawn on their
newly created demand deposits. Now, assume (for simplicity of
analysis) that these checks are all deposited with another bank.
This second bank will immediately deposit these checks in the
account it maintains at the Federal Reserve Bank, which increases the reserves of the second bank by $4000 but simulta-
neously charges these checks against the reserve account of the
original bank. This reduces the original bank's reserves by $4000.

The Federal Reserve Bank then sends the checks back to the
original bank on which they are drawn. The bank reduces by
$4000 the demand deposits of the writers of the checks. Thus the
bank finds its reserves reduced by $4000 and its demand deposits
reduced by $4000. Because it had reserves equal to 20 percent of
its demand deposits and because it is required to maintain this
ratio of reserves to demand deposits, it can afford to lose only 20
percent as much in reserves as it loses in demand deposits.

When the bank lost $4000 in demand deposits, this permitted it to lose only $800 (20 percent of $4000) in reserves. Thus it has lost $3200 in reserves that it could not afford to lose. Obviously it over-extended its loans by $3200. If the bank had lent only $800 instead of $4000, it would not have experienced this difficulty.

To avoid these adverse clearing balances with the Federal Reserve Bank, a bank must restrict its loans to its *excess reserves.* When the bank received its new deposit of $1000, it was required to hold only $200 of it in reserves. This means it had excess reserves of $800 (the original $1000 it received minus the $200 it must hold as reserves). Thus it can be concluded that if a single bank received a new $1000 deposit, it must keep $200 in reserve but could lend out $800. It lends money by giving its customers a new demand deposit of $800, thus creating money.

Yet a single bank may reasonably claim it adds nothing to the money supply. When the customer actually uses the loan, he draws his deposit down to zero, while the bank merely pays out the $800 in cash. It is when the whole banking system is considered that a new deposit will generally lead to a multiple expansion of the money supply. How this expansion works can be seen in Table 6.3.

When the $800 loan from Bank A (in Table 6.3) is spent, it becomes new deposits in Bank B, which are the basis for new reserves of $160 and new loans of $640. In the case of the whole banking system, the process will continue until all of the original new deposit ($1000) becomes required reserves in various banks. Because the new required reserves are then $1000 (or 20 percent of all new deposits), the new loans are $4000 (or 80 percent of all new deposits). Based on an initial new deposit of $1000 in money, the banking system has thus created a total increase in deposits of $5000 (assumed to be demand deposits and therefore counted as money).

For our analysis we use the concept of the money multiplier. The *money multiplier* may be defined as follows:

$$\text{money multiplier} = \frac{\text{total increase in deposits}}{\text{initial new deposit}}$$

A simple formula for deriving the money multiplier is

$$\text{multiplier} = \frac{1}{\text{required Federal Reserve ratio}}$$

TABLE 6.3 HOW THE MONEY MULTIPLIER WORKS

---

1. *Assume an initial increase in deposits of $1000.*
2. *Assume a required Federal Reserve ratio of 20 percent.*
3. *Assume that banks are always fully loaned out.*

Bank	Increase in Loans	Increase in Deposits (or Money Supply)	Increase in Reserves (Required)
Bank A	$ 800 (3)	$1000 (1)	$ 200 (2)
Bank B	640	800	160
Bank C	512	640	128
Bank D	410	512	102
Bank E	328	410	82
Bank F	262	328	66
—	—	262	—
—	—	—	—

	Total Increase in Loans	Total Increase in Deposits (or money supply)	Total Increase in Reserves (required)
All banks	$4000	$5000	$1000

Assuming that each banker has to keep 20 percent of his deposit liabilities in the form of cash, the money supply can be expanded to five times the amount of cash that the banking system holds:

$$\text{multiplier} = \frac{1}{0.20} = 5$$

Thus the initial new deposit of $1000 is multiplied by 5 to get a $5000 total increase in deposits (or in the money supply).

The analysis does not yet take into account several kinds of leakage that may occur in varying degrees over time. The assumption that banks are always fully loaned up is not consistent with the facts. There are often some excess reserves—that is, reserves above the legal requirement. Therefore the volume of expansion of deposits does depend on the degree to which bankers decide to make the maximum loans on their reserves. It also depends on the degree to which businessmen wish to accept these loans. Finally, the whole process takes time, and only a certain amount of the predicted expansion will occur in any given period.

It is nevertheless generally true that banks lend in some multiple of their reserves and that total expansion of the money supply will be greater, the smaller the required Federal Reserve Ratio.

MONETARY POLICY

One of the long-standing ways in which government has influenced the economy has been through the use of policies designed to expand or diminish the flow of money and credit. The main idea is that in a depression an increased flow of money and credit will combat unemployment by increasing purchases of both consumer and investment goods. In times of expansion, restriction of money and credit will reduce inflationary pressures by reducing the flow of demand. Monetary policy works mainly through its effects on the price for renting the commodity called money—that is, the rate of interest on loans. If the government can increase or reduce the supply of money while the demand for it remains constant, then interest rates may be lowered or raised. If spending plans are financed by borrowed funds, and if these plans react in any way to changes in the rate of interest, it follows that changes in the supply of money for loans will have some effect on total spending.

Exactly how should monetary policy be applied in an inflationary situation and how effective is it? The supply of money and credit may be restricted by monetary policy through three major controls: (1) raising the Federal Reserve requirements for bank reserves, (2) raising the interest rate that the Federal Reserve charges banks, and (3) through the sale of government bonds by the Federal Reserve. Let us see how each of these controls is supposed to work.

First, in order to restrict credit the Federal Reserve may raise the ratio of money reserves that banks are required to hold against their deposits. Furthermore, as soon as one bank decreases its loans, the effect on all banks may be several times as great by virtue of the money multiplier. Thus, in theory, the raising of the Federal Reserve ratio from 10 to 20 percent would lower the multiplication of money by banks from tenfold to only fivefold. If all banks were fully loaned out, this would cause a great decrease of loans. A reduction in the volume of loans may then mean less money available for consumer and investor spending, thus reducing inflationary pressures.

Second, the Federal Reserve may also raise the interest rate banks must pay if they wish to borrow from the Federal Reserve Banks. A bank will then either have to charge higher interest rates on loans to its customers, or reduce the amount it lends in order to avoid borrowing reserves from the Federal Reserve. Either way, less money may be available for further consumption and investment spending, which may reduce demand and thus lead to a lower rate of price inflation.

Finally, the Federal Reserve may sell more government bonds to banks or rich individuals. The money to pay for the bonds must come from bank reserves or from individual bank deposits. In either case the ability of banks to make loans is reduced (manyfold, according to the money multiplier). Again, consumer and investment spending may be decreased and inflationary pressures reduced.

These methods of reducing money spending in an inflation encounter certain obstacles. First, each assumes banks had already made loans up to their maximum ratio of deposits to reserves. But banks often keep extra reserves above even the highest possible required reserve ratio and thus can keep lending until these reserves are exhausted. Second, these monetary controls assume that corporations must borrow from banks all the money they need for new investments. But corporations often keep their own internal savings, which they may decide to use regardless of bank policies. Third, in cases when the government succeeds only in getting banks to raise their interest rates (by lowering money supply), there may be little effect on demand. If expected profit rates are rising even faster than interest rates, corporations may still be willing to borrow and invest more rapidly. In all of these cases the government may be able to restrict the money supply, but the propensity to spend the present money supply may increase even more rapidly.

Despite these weaknesses, monetary policy, if applied with extreme harshness, *may* be able to choke off a general inflation. Of course, too severe a remedy may cause instability in the bond and stock markets, loss of confidence by domestic and foreign investors, and a business downturn. Finally, it should be noted that *general monetary tools are of little help in an inflation caused by monopolistic price setting in particular industries.* Monetary deflationary policies may even lower aggregate economic activity and increase unemployment if the inflation occurs together with some amount of general unemployment (as appeared to be the case in the early 1970s in the United States).

   In a depression exactly the opposite monetary policy may be applied. The supply of money and credit may be expanded by (1) lowering the required Federal Reserve ratio, (2) lowering the interest rate the Federal Reserve charges banks, or (3) the purchase by the Federal Reserve of government bonds in the open market to put more cash into the hands of individuals and banks. These measures are designed to increase the volume of borrowing and, thus, the volume of spending by increasing the supply of money for loans and by lowering interest rates.

   Obstacles to monetary policies intended to combat depression include most of those met by counterinflationary policies and a few that are different and more difficult to surmount. First, the interest rate cannot go below zero, and in actual practice lenders will not go below a floor that is somewhat above a zero rate. Yet during a depression it may require a zero or even negative interest rate to stimulate borrowing. Second, most investors do not seem much stimulated to borrow by slightly lower interest rates. Businessmen apparently consider the pessimistic outlook for smaller profits, or even losses, to be quantitatively much more important in investment decisions.

   You can lead a businessman to the river of loans, but you cannot force him to drink. The government may increase the banks' supply of money, but consumers and businesses may reduce their propensities to borrow and spend even more rapidly. In short, monetary policies may have some effect in minor recessions, but when pessimistic expectations become general in a depression, monetary policy may be able to do little or nothing to expand the volume of spending. Thus, the Federal Reserve system is generally impotent to stop a contraction.

INFLATION IN THE
MIDST OF UNEMPLOYMENT

   Notice that government monetary policy—a favorite tool of conservatives—can help a little against ordinary inflation, very little against depression and unemployment, and not at all against inflation in the midst of a depression with large scale unemployment. (In Chapter 9 other government policies will be explored.) Here, it is first necessary to see the course of recent inflation and to begin to ask how it has been caused.

   Table 6.4 and Figure 6.2 record an initial large drop in prices during the Great Depression of 1929–1933. Then, with the recovery of demand, there was a price rise until 1937. The recession of 1938 caused a price drop which was followed by the slow rise

TABLE 6.4   PRICE MOVEMENTS IN THE UNITED STATES, 1929–1975 (wholesale price index for all commodities, 1967 = 100)

Year	Index	Year	Index
1929	49	1953	87
1930	45	1954	88
1931	38	1955	88
1932	34	1956	91
1933	34	1957	93
1934	39	1958	95
1935	41	1959	95
1936	42	1960	95
1937	45	1961	95
1938	41	1962	95
1939	40	1963	95
1940	41	1964	95
1941	45	1965	97
1942	51	1966	100
1943	53	1967	100
1944	54	1968	103
1945	55	1969	107
1946	62	1970	110
1947	77	1971	114
1948	83	1972	119
1949	79	1973	135
1950	82	1974	160
1951	91	1975	175
1952	89		

SOURCES: U.S. Bureau of Labor Statistics, *Handbook of Labor Statistic 1974* (Washington, D.C.: Government Printing Office, 1975), p. 325, and U.S. Bureau of Labor Statistics, *Monthly Labor Review* (March 1976), p. 85.

of prices during World War II. This rise would have been much more rapid except that price control held down inflationary pressures. Immediately following World War II, however, the vast demand for consumer and investment goods burst the dam and flooded the market with purchasing power, resulting in the rapid price rises of 1946–1948. A recession lowered prices in 1949, then the Korean War caused a second major round of inflation in 1950–1951. Another recession lowered prices at the end of the Korean War, after which they rose steadily until 1960. Prices fell slightly in the brief recession of 1961, remained fairly stable in the early 1960s, but rose sharply from 1965 to 1971 because of the Vietnam War.

FIGURE 6.2 RECENT PRICE MOVEMENTS IN THE UNITED STATES
(WHOLESALE PRICE INDEX, 1929–1970; BASE: 1957–1959 = 100)

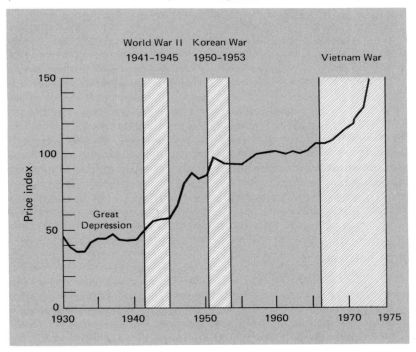

SOURCE: U.S. Department of Commerce, *Statistical Abstracts of the United States*,
1964 (Washington, D.C.: GPO, 1964), p. 351; and *Federal Reserve Bulletin* (August
1973), p. A-66.

    The surprising point is that the price index rose rather than
declined in the recessions of 1958, 1969, and 1974. During these
recessions the prices of industries with monopolistic power actually rose in the face of declining aggregate demand.

    It is such evidence that forces us to distinguish the inflations
of the late 1950s, 1969, and 1974 from the ordinary *demand-pull
inflation* which is caused by the upward pull of aggregate demand. Here, instead, prices apparently are pushed upward by
individual firms and industries. It is called *cost-push inflation* to
indicate the belief that prices are pushed upward by either
higher profit margins or higher wage costs. Many conservative
economists argue that monopoly or oligopoly power of firms is *not*
responsible for spiraling prices. On the contrary, they argue that
the bargaining power of labor unions pushes wages upward and
that prices only follow wages. The opposite view, held by most

radicals, is that prices are pushed up by monopolies to make higher profits, that wages mostly lag behind prices, and that wage increases are merely bemoaned as an excuse for higher prices.

The truth is that in almost every inflation on record there is massive redistribution of income from the poor to the rich. Capitalist owners of businesses push up their prices rapidly; therefore, profit margins remain constant or rising in most inflations. On the other side, workers' wages lag behind prices in most inflations (as proven by the data in Chapter 1 and 3), so the real buying power of wages declines. If, as alleged, the main cause of the present inflation is the monopoly power of business, then there is an even more drastic shift of income from workers and consumers into the hands of the owners of the monopoly corporations.

To settle these issues, Chapter 7 will examine in detail the changing degree of business monopoly power and union power in the United States. Chapter 8 will then relate monopoly power to price behavior and to the performance of corporate profits— only then can we explain how inflation can occur in the midst of large-scale unemployment.

NOTE

1. Frederick Mills, *Price-Quantity Interactions in Business Cycles* (New York: National Bureau of Economic Research, 1946).

7
MONOPOLY POWER

The world of numerous, small competitive capitalist enterprises, which Adam Smith thought would produce the best result for all concerned, is gone forever (if it ever existed). Since the period of the 1890s and early 1900s, western Europe and the United States have been characterized by the domination of a relatively few giant firms. This new stage of monopoly has not ended capitalism, but it has intensified many old qualities and added some entirely new and unpleasant features.

In the monopoly stage of capitalism the setting of prices and outputs is quite different than under competition, and the profit result is equally different. The amount of waste, manipulation of the consumer, limitation of the worker's wages, and conflict between profit seeking and social needs (such as the need for a decent environment) exist on entirely new scales. If Adam Smith's harmony-of-interests theory ever had a grain of truth, it is surely not applicable to the monopoly stage of capitalism.

THE TREND OF CONCENTRATION

In a purely competitive economy each competing business unit would be so small that its actions taken alone could not appreciably influence the quantity of goods or the price in the market. Such, more or less, was the U.S. economy during the early nineteenth century. Small farms and small businesses produced most of the output, and there were no giant corporations dominating an entire industry (though there were many local monopolies). As late as 1860, there were still no incorporated business firms in many of the major urban industrial centers. Since that time, the picture has changed drastically.

The size of corporations rose rapidly in the post-Civil War period. By 1900 the share of manufacturing output produced by corporations had grown to two-thirds. Some of the big corporations developed by virtue of rapid internal growth; others arose through mergers of formerly independent firms.

Mergers have come in waves. The first massive movement, which lasted from the early 1890s to the outbreak of World War I, was characterized by *horizontal* mergers, in which a big corporation absorbed other corporations that were its direct competitors. The result of such mergers was, of course, industries dominated by fewer and much larger corporations. The second wave came in the 1920s. It was characterized by *vertical* mergers, which occurred between firms producing goods in sequence, as when a giant corporation absorbs its suppliers or absorbs the firms to which it sells its output. The 1960s witnessed a third and unique wave. Most of these mergers were of the *conglomerate* variety, in which a giant corporation absorbs other corporations that have no relation to it. The aim is simply to establish a colossal corporate empire that will give its controllers immense economic and political power.

From 1950 through 1959, there were an average of 540 corporate mergers a year. From 1960 through 1967, the average was 1100 a year. In 1968, there were 2655 mergers. More and more of these were conglomerate mergers between two giants in different industries. From 1948 through 1953, conglomerate mergers accounted for 59 percent of the total. From 1960 through 1965, they comprised 72 percent of the total. In 1968, conglomerate mergers accounted for 84 percent of all mergers.[1]

The enormous size and power of the 100 largest conglomerates may be seen in the data on how many large firms in each separate industry are under their control. "In more than half of the 1014 product classes in manufacturing as a whole, at least one of the 100 largest was among the 4 largest producers, and in 31 percent at least 2 came from the 100 largest. It is thus obvious that the 100 largest companies are not limited in their operations

TABLE 7.1 DISTRIBUTION OF CORPORATE ASSETS
(all U.S. corporations, 1969)

Size (in assets)	Corporations (percent in size group)	Assets (percent owned by group)
$ 0–100,000	58%	1%
100,000–500,000	30	5
500,000–5,000,000	10	9
5,000,000–250,000,000	2	30
250,000,000 and over	0.07	55
Total	100.00%[1]	100%

SOURCE: U.S. Internal Revenue Service, Statistics of Income, Corporation Income Tax Returns for 1969.

[1] Data add to more than 100% because of rounding.

to only a few large-scale industries but rather are broadly represented among the largest producers of manufacturing products throughout most of the wide spectrum of U.S. industry."[2]

Today there still are millions of very small industrial enterprises, but a few hundred corporate giants hold most of the wealth and do most of the producing. Table 7.1 reveals the extremely high concentration of corporate assets in a comparatively few firms. At the bottom, a large number of small corporations (890,000, or 58 percent of the total) held a minuscule portion of total corporate assets ($30 billion, or 1 percent). At the top, a few giant corporations (1,041, or just 0.07 percent) held a majority of all assets ($1.218 trillion, or 55 percent). That some 1,000 U.S. corporations would hold more than $1 trillion in assets is incredible; that amount is more than the total value of all western European assets. Among those 1000 corporations, there is still a great concentration within just the top 200 or 300 corporations.

The figures for all corporations average out differences in various sectors. In the important sector of banking alone, for example, there are approximately 13,775 commercial banks, but a mere 14 of them hold 25 percent of all deposits, and the 100 largest banks hold 46 percent of all deposits.[3]

Another function of banks is to hold assets in *trust* for individuals and corporations. Banks exercise the voting power for these stocks, which gives them immense power without having legal ownership. Forty-nine of the largest banks hold over 5 percent of the common stock in 147 of the 500 largest industrial corporations in the United States. They also hold at least 5 percent of the common stock in 17 of the largest companies in the fields of merchandising and transportation. These banks are represented in the boards of directors of the majority of the largest corporations in the fields of manufacturing, merchandising, utilities, transportation, and insurance.

Finally, let us turn to the decisive sector of manufacturing taken alone. In the general category of manufacturing enterprises, there were 180,000 corporations and 240,000 unincorporated businesses in 1962.[4] Ninety-eight percent of all manufacturing assets were owned by the corporations. Of the 420,000 manufacturing firms, the 20 largest (not 20,000, but 20!) owned 25 percent of total assets of manufacturing firms. The largest 50 firms owned 36 percent, and the largest 200 owned 56 percent. If adjustment is made for giant firms that are owned by even larger giants (i.e., if their ownership is added together), we arrive at a much higher percentage of control. The fact is that, after adjustment for ownership of subsidiaries, a mere 100 firms owned 58 percent of the net capital assets of all the hundreds of thousands of manufacturing corporations. Another index of the imbalance of economic power is the fact that the largest 20 manufacturing firms owned a larger share of the assets than the smallest 419,000 firms combined.

When profits earned are examined, the contrast is even more striking. The net profits of the 5 largest corporations were about twice as large as those of the 178,000 smallest corporations combined. In order to appreciate the size of these giants, consider just one of them, General Motors. "General Motor's yearly operating revenues exceed those of all but a dozen or so countries. Its sales receipts are greater than the combined general revenues of New York, New Jersey, Pennsylvania, Ohio, Delaware, and the six New England states. . . . G.M. employees number well over 700,000 and work in 127 plants in the United States and 45 countries spanning Europe, South Africa, North America, and Australia. The total cash wages are more than twice the personal income of Ireland."[5]

If the individual industries which are the arenas of most direct competition are examined, the picture of economic concentration may be even more sharply drawn than in the aggregate data. Let an *industry* be defined so that there is easy substitution among the products of all firms within it, and very little possible substitution with products of outside firms. In most industries, just three or four giant monopolistic firms control most of the production, and most of these top firms, as shown above, are part of the 100 largest super-giant conglomerates. Many small firms also exist in most industries, but altogether they produce a small percentage of the total output. U.S. government data for 1963, adjusted slightly for more precise market definition, showed that 39.6 percent of all industries were highly concentrated, that is, had 50 percent or more of their product sold by four companies.[6] Another 32.1 percent of all U.S. industries were moderately concentrated, that is, had 25 percent to 49 percent of their product sold by four companies. Only 28.3 percent of all industries were somewhat competitive, that is, less than 25 percent of their product was sold by four companies.

Moreover, among the top companies are many interlocking directorates. In 1965, the 250 largest corporations had a total of 4,007 directorships, but these were held by just 3,165 directors.[7] Among these, 562 men held 2 or more directorships, and 5 men held six each! Other studies have traced control to eight main groups: three that each held large blocs of stock in several corporations were Rockefeller, Mellon, and DuPont; two that used financial control over several corporations were Morgan-First National and Kuhn-Loeb; three were groups known for their local control in the cities of Boston, Chicago, and Cleveland. In addition, as seen earlier, there is now formal control by large conglomerates (themselves usually part of one of the major interest groups) of top corporations in each of several industries.

INCREASING BUSINESS CONCENTRATION

The size and power of the largest firms keep increasing, even as a percentage of the immense and increasing U.S. total capital. Table 7.2 shows that the percentage of all U.S. manufacturing assets owned by the 200 largest rose by 3 percent points in the Great Depression. It fell a little in World War II as small and medium-sized firms expanded even more rapidly than the giants to meet the unlimited government demand. The share of assets of the 200 largest rose again by 13 whole percentage points from 1949 to 1968. The share of value added in manufacturing (another measure of concentration) produced by the 200 largest corporations also rose 12 percentage points from 1947 to 1967 and rose another percentage point from 1967 to 1972.[8]

Since 1950, 1 out of every 5 of the 1,000 largest manufacturing companies has been swallowed by an even larger giant. Since 1959, big business has been absorbing other business firms with

TABLE 7.2 SHARE OF 200
LARGEST MANUFACTURING
CORPORATIONS

Year	Percentage of Total Manufacturing Assets
1929	45.8%
1939	48.7
1949	47.1
1959	54.8
1968	60.4%

SOURCE: Federal Trade Commission, reported and discussed in John Blair, Economic Concentration (New York: Harcourt Brace Jovanovich, 1972), p. 64.

$10 million or more in assets at a rate exceeding 60 a year. In 1966, 101 companies, each with assets of more than $10 million, were absorbed by other companies; in 1967, the number was 169; in 1968, it was 192. Obviously oligopolistic business giants are far from satisfied with the immense size and power they already have. There is nothing to lead us to believe that these mushrooming industrial empires are about to discontinue merging. Furthermore, the few large firms control most research and thus will continue to grow more rapidly. A 1960 survey showed that just 4 firms accounted for 22 percent and 384 firms accounted for 85 percent of all industrial research and development.[9] Finally, it is worth noting that much of the increase in concentration comes during depressions. In every depression millions of small businesses are driven to the wall and go bankrupt. Then the big fish eat the little fish, buying up most assets for a song. The result is that each recession or depression further increases monopoly power.

The economy of the United States has thus changed from a predominantly competitive to a predominantly monopolistic production situation. The monopolies are still growing through conglomerate mergers of giants in different industries. The apparent degree of concentration may not change in each industry, but the same conglomerate may now control a large firm in each of many industries. Thus the data on particular industries, which indicate that the shares of the 3 or 4 largest have not increased

much for several years, severely understate the trend toward concentration of power in the 100 largest manufacturing firms.

THE REASONS FOR MONOPOLY

One fundamental cause of the emergence of the giant corporation is the economy of scale that can be derived from large
production units that turn out cheaper goods by using more specialized machinery, more specialized workers, and mass production assembly lines. Small firms are driven out of business by the
cheap goods produced through large-scale applications of
technology. The large firm gains a monopoly by selling at a lower
price while making more profit.

In addition to improved technology based on the economies
of scale, there are other reasons for the greater profitability of
huge firms like General Motors. These firms grow internally or
via merger far beyond the technologically necessary minimum
because they wish to exercise monopoly power over the market.
With small competitors eliminated or dominated, the few remaining giant firms can restrict output and set higher prices to
make higher profit rates.

The huge firms try to gain monopoly control of a whole industry to escape what they call the "rigors of competition" or
"cut-throat competition"—meaning that they want the freedom
to set their prices wherever they please without fear of competition. Their behavior and excuses are ironic because they tell
everyone else how great the free, competitive market is.

The giant monopolistic firms attempt to eliminate risk and
uncertainty, not only controlling their own industry's output, but
also (1) buying out raw material suppliers, (2) buying out dealers
and outlets for the finished product, (3) using vast nationwide
advertising, and (4) linking up with banks and other financial
sources. With these motivations there is no clear upper limit to
desirable size. The motto seems to be "the bigger the better."

PRICES AND PROFIT MAXIMIZATION

What is the effect of monopoly on the price structure? The
essence of the monopolist's position is the ability to keep competitors out of the market by means of greater efficiency, control
of natural or financial resources, control of patents, or any other
legal or illegal methods. Thus prices can be as high as the market
will bear, and there is no competitive mechanism to bring the
higher profit back down to the average rate of profit in industry as
a whole.

Although the monopolist can make a higher than average rate of profit, profit cannot be made out of thin air. Total profits still remain within the limits of total revenue minus costs. To some extent monopoly does not affect aggregate prices or aggregate profits but only redistributes aggregate profits. From a given amount of aggregate profits monopolists may take away part of the profits of small businessmen and farmers by competing for the consumer's dollar. They may also increase their share of profits through their power to buy raw materials and food at low prices and sell finished goods at high prices to these small entrepreneurs. However, monopolists may also increase total profits by using their power to raise prices or to restrict money wages in order to lower the workers' real wages.

Monopoly price and quantity of production are set by monopolists as they see fit. In order to maximize profits, however, they can only set the quantity at the point of greatest difference between total revenue (determined by demand) and total cost (determined by the cost of labor plus material costs). Once the quantity is set, even a monopoly can sell only at a price determined by the demand at that point. The difference between this and the competitive situation is that under monopoly the quantity supplied is set lower so that the price is higher. Therefore the short-run rate of profit is higher than the average under competition. The long-run rate of profit remains higher because capital cannot freely enter the industry.

Contrary to this view, many economists claim that modern businessmen do not always attempt to maximize profits. The capitalist today, however, is not the individual businessman but the corporation. Whether the businessman is rational and calculating in private life is essentially irrelevant to the functioning of the system. In corporate decisions there can be no doubt that the making and accumulating of profit hold as dominant a position today as they ever did. Like the individual enterprise of an earlier period, the giant corporation is an engine for maximizing profits, but it is not used merely as an enlarged version of the personal capitalist. There are two differences: (1) The corporation has a much longer time horizon, and (2) it is a much more rational calculator.[10]

Having said that much, it is important to avoid a dogmatic notion that every corporate decision is made in terms of immediate dollars and cents returns. Certainly corporate management may sacrifice short-run profits to ensure the security of their market control, to spur company growth, and even to act as dictated by the somewhat vague concept of prestige. Thus prices are not always set as high as the market will bear. It could be said that management maximizes a multiple set of objectives. Equally well (because the difference is only semantic), it could be emphasized that each of the other objectives is merely a rational way to achieve maximum long-run profits, which are the real sole objective.

WHO CONTROLS THE CORPORATION?

Liberals agree that monopoly is an evil aspect of capitalism, but they believe a remedy short of doing away with capitalism is possible. Some rely on stricter enforcement of antitrust laws. Others admit that these laws have clearly proved inadequate and advocate stricter laws. Still others claim that a process of internal change in giant corporations is automatically eliminating most of its negative qualities. John Kenneth Galbraith is the leading spokesman of the latter view.

Galbraith maintains that there is a great contradiction between the notion that the modern corporation is controlled by the management and the fact that it nevertheless ruthlessly tries to maximize profits for its stockholders. Furthermore, he argues that the most important factor of production is no longer capital but the specialized talent of scientists and technologists, and that real power passes from stockholders and top management to the members of the *technostructure* (i.e., the technical personnel, including scientists and technicians). According to Galbraith, the members of the technostructure do not get the profits they are supposed to maximize. Because the technostructure supplies talent, not capital, why should they worry about the return of capital? He says that the modern corporation has the capacity to shape society, but its resources are used to serve the deeper interests or goals of the technostructure, which possesses the real power.[11]

Galbraith agrees that a few hundred giant corporations control the market, regulate output and prices, and exercise enormous political control. Yet with a wave of his hand he eliminates the corporate executive and puts the control of the corporation in the hands of scientists and technically skilled workers. He then finds that the technostructure really manages the corporation and that, for their own reasons, they manage it in the best interests of all society. In other words, Galbraith is very critical of capitalism, especially of the tremendous centralization of the means of production, but nevertheless is apologetic in the sense that he concludes that the industrial system has actually solved (or is solving) its problem.

The radical view is that Galbraith ignores the real position of modern corporate management. In the first place, the fact that so many top executives hold stock means their motivations cannot possibly be inconsistent with profit seeking. For example, in early 1957, 25 managers of General Motors owned an average of 11,500 shares each.[12] They might not be able to affect policy even with that amount of stock in General Motors, yet each owned roughly $500,000 in the company, so it is improbable that any manager was indifferent to profits. Further, among stockholders there are more managers than representatives of any other group, and a larger proportion of managers own stock than in any other group.

Galbraith, of course, argues that it is not the motivation of the managers but the motivation of the technostructure that is decisive. Radicals counter that the goals of the technostructure would be the same as those of the managers: survival of the firm, growth, independence from outside control. All these demand profit-making activity. More important, it flies in the face of reality to believe that the technicians control the corporations. The managers hire and fire the technicians, not vice versa. In the end it is the boss rather than the hired hand who makes the decisions (and will use expert advice only to make more profitable decisions).

MONOPOLY PROFIT RATES

The monopoly structure of American capitalism has been examined and the price-setting behavior of its management investigated. How do monopolistic structure and behavior affect the performance of American capitalism? In this section the effect on profit rates is reviewed. First the sources, in theory, of monopoly profit are briefly recapitulated; then the facts of monopoly profit are presented.

The whole point of monopoly control of markets is, of course, to restrict output and charge higher prices. All consumers are hurt by higher monopoly prices. Workers may have a constant wage in dollars, but as prices rise their buying power falls. If we reduce the figure for money wages by the percentage of price increases, the result is called the *real wage*. For example, if money wages stay at $100 while prices rise by 7 percent, the real wage declines. Therefore, if money wages stay constant, we may say that price increases by monopolies lower real wages and thereby increase their profits.

Purchasers of producer goods also suffer from monopoly

prices, so the profits of small businesses and farmers are lowered. Some large firms also have extra market power as large buyers of commodities from small business, forcing down the prices of these small suppliers.

The giant firm also has extra power in the labor market, so it may add to its profits by buying labor at a rate lower than the average wage. This factor may, of course, be somewhat offset by trade union action. In the modern world of monopoly, wages are not determined simply by automatic market supply and demand. They are determined by the bargaining strength of capital and labor, with monopoly capital usually in the stronger position. Workers are thus squeezed from both sides by monopoly. On the one hand, the monopolies can pay lower money wages by exerting their power in the labor market. On the other hand, monopolies can charge workers higher prices as consumers.

Additional monopoly profits come from lucrative government military contracts, which are financed from the workers' tax money, thus again increasing total profits (see Chapter 9). Extra-high returns from foreign investments abroad also add to monopoly profits; that is, profits are extracted from workers in foreign countries (see Chapter 10). In summary, monopolies, or oligopolies if there are more than one large firm controlling the industry, make profit far above the average rate in several ways: (1) selling at higher prices to consumers, thereby lowering the real wage, (2) selling at higher prices to small business and farmers, (3) buying at lower prices from small business and farmers, (4) buying labor power at lower wages from workers, (5) selling to the government at higher prices, and (6) buying labor power and materials at lower prices in foreign countries. Through these relatively high prices and low costs (always relative to a competitive firm in the same situation), the monopoly or oligopoly firms extract more profits from worker-consumer-taxpayers here and abroad; they also transfer some profits from small business and farmers to themselves.

Turning to the facts, we may investigate first how the profit rates of an enterprise are affected by its absolute size. The size of a business is indicated by the total amount of its assets, and the profit rate is the total profit divided by the capital investment of all the stockholders. Profit rates by asset size for all corporations since 1931 are given in Table 7.3.

In an economy of pure and perfect competition, all profit rates should be equalized in the long run. As Table 7.3 demonstrates, in the U.S. economy the long-run profit rate is not the

TABLE 7.3 LONG-RUN PROFIT RATE, BY
CORPORATE SIZE
(all U.S. corporations, 1931–1961, excluding the
war years 1940–1947)

Size (in assets)	Profit Rate (profit before taxes divided by stockholders' capital)
$ 0–50,000	−7.1%
50,000–100,000	4.1
100,000–250,000	5.9
250,000–500,000	7.4
500,000–1,000,000	8.3
1,000,000–5,000,000	9.3
5,000,000–10,000,000	9.7
10,000,000–50,000,000	10.4
Over $50,000,000	10.4%

SOURCE: U.S. Treasury Department, Internal Revenue
Service, *Statistics of Income, Corporation Income Tax
Returns, 1931–1961* (Washington, D.C.: Government
Printing Office, 1934–1965); discussed in Howard Sherman,
Profit Rates in the United States (Ithaca, N.Y.: Cornell
University Press, 1968), p. 41.

same for all corporations. On the contrary, the smallest corporations have low or even negative profit rates, and the profit rate
rises with the scale of the corporation, although the differences
are quite small among the largest-size groups. This is a proof of
the existence of monopoly power and imperfect competition.

Economic concentration, however, has another important aspect. The indicator of market power is a firm's relative size and
importance in its own industry. A *concentration ratio* in each
industry may be defined as the percentage of sales controlled by
the eight largest corporations in the industry. Several studies
have found a definite relationship between an industry's concentration ratio and its profit rates. Some evidence is presented in
Table 7.4.

The very high concentration of production that exists in
many industry groups reflects the fact that in the majority of U.S.
industries the bulk of production is concentrated in a few giant
corporations, with hundreds of smaller companies producing
very little. Moreover, inspection of the table reveals a considerable rise in profit rates as the degree of concentration rises. Thus

TABLE 7.4 PROFIT RATES AND CONCENTRATION RATIOS,
BY INDUSTRY GROUP
(all U.S. manufacturing corporations in 1954)

Industry Group	Concentration Ratio (percent of sales by eight largest sellers)	Profit Rate (profit before taxes divided by stockholders' capital)
Motor vehicles and parts	98.1%	27.1%
Tobacco	91.5	20.3
Transportation equipment except motor vehicles	75.6	29.8
Rubber	74.2	17.8
Primary metals	70.8	13.0
Chemicals	63.3	19.9
Electrical machinery	60.8	20.7
Petroleum and coal	57.7	7.7
Instruments	56.1	23.9
Stone, clay, glass	55.0	19.9
Food and beverages	45.7	14.4
Machinery, except electrical	44.4	16.2
Fabricated metal	40.3	15.6
Paper	39.4	17.3
Textile mill	37.1	5.1
Leather	33.7	11.4
Furniture	23.8	12.8
Printing and publishing	21.5	15.1
Apparel	20.5	7.6
Lumber	15.5%	12.2%

SOURCE: Concentration ratios from U.S. Senate, Committee on the Judiciary, *Concentration in American Industry* (Washington, D.C.: Government Printing Office, 1957); profit rates from U.S. Treasury Department, Internal Revenue Service, *Statistics of Income, Corporation Income Tax Returns for 1954* (Washington, D.C.: Government Printing Office, 1957); discussed in Howard Sherman, *Profit Rates in the United States* (Ithaca, N.Y.: Cornell University Press, 1968), p. 85.

in the 10 industry groups over the 50 percent concentration level, the average rate of profit is 20 percent; it is only 13 percent in the 10 industry groups under the 50 percent concentration level. The conclusion is that the giant corporations, with larger size and greater market power, have higher rates of profit than the small competitive firms.

This analysis may be extended to the trend of aggregate profits under capitalism. It appears that the giant corporations have steadily reduced production costs per unit and that there have been powerful impulses toward innovation. Yet monopoly cannot be considered a rational and progressive system because although it reduces costs, it continues to set extremely high prices. Moreover, its increased productivity does not benefit everyone but only a few. Profit rates increase, and the share of profit in national income rises. Contrary to the nineteenth-century economist's version of falling rates of profit, under monopoly the rate tends to rise.

MONOPOLY AND WASTE

To some extent, large firms are more efficient because of economies of scale. Production cannot reach optimum efficiency below a certain point, or quantity of output. Thus the fact that large firms account for most U.S. output means that most of the economy has the ability to produce at lower costs than ever before. Studies of cost data reveal the possibility of high efficiency at a fairly constant level beyond the necessary minimum sacle of production.[13] Of course, because the very large firms also have disproportionately larger research facilities and control a very large percentage of all unexpired patents, they have the greatest potential for increasing efficiency. Moreover, many investment projects require resources beyond the means of small firms.

But the large, entrenched firm stands to lose most from the obsolescence of present machinery and from product improvements that reduce the number of units the customer need buy—for example, a longer-lasting light bulb. Therefore if the large firm has an oligopoly position and faces no serious competitive pressure for improvement, it may develop, patent, and not use important inventions. Monopoly power has paradoxical effects on innovation. Giant firms have a rapid rate of technological progress, but they retain a large amount of technologically obsolete equipment.

Monopoly power may also be used to restrict supply in order to raise prices. Thus, as will be seen in the next chapter, monopoly power is one of the principal causes of inflation. Monopolies will expand production as rapidly as possible only in extraordinary periods of unlimited demand. This usually occurs only when government demand skyrockets, as in World War II. In wartime, monopolies can cease restricting output but still charge prices as high as the government will allow.

Moreover, as is also shown in the next chapter, the existence of economic concentration may have increased the severity and

possibly the number of depressions because of (1) its destabiliz-
ing effects on remaining small businesses and (2) its lowering of
workers' ability to consume. It would seem that this is another
reason why the net effect of monopoly may be to lower the rate of
economic growth.

On the other hand, breaking up large firms into smaller units
would probably not increase economic growth. Reducing the
American economy to small firms would certainly cause a major
decrease in economic efficiency because of the loss of economies
of scale—and most likely would have negative effects on investment. It is impossible to go backward to a competitive small
business economy; the only answer seems to be to go forward to
public and workers' control of the giant corporations.

The rate of growth (and waste) under monopoly is also affected by the fact that the sales effort has greatly expanded. Once
a relatively unimportant feature of the system, sales effort has
become one of its decisive nerve centers. The impact of advertising and related expenditures on the economy is outranked only
by that of militarism. In all other aspects of social existence, the
influence of advertising is second to none. In an economic system
in which competition is fierce and relentless but in which the
small number of rivals rules out price cutting, advertising becomes to an ever increasing extent the principal weapon of the
competitive struggle. There is little room under atomistic competition for advertising; in monopoly it is the most important factor
in the firm's survival.

Relatively large firms are in a position to exercise a powerful
influence on the market for their output by establishing and maintaining a pronounced difference between their products and
those of their competitors. This differentiation is sought chiefly
by means of advertising, trademarks, brand names, distinctive
packaging, and product variation. If successful, it leads to a condition in which consumers believe the differential products can
no longer serve as close substitutes for each other.

Advertising involves a massive waste of resources, a con-
tinual drain on the consumer's income, and a systematic destruction of the consumer's freedom of choice between genuine alter-
natives. Furthermore, advertising in all its aspects cannot be
meaningfully dealt with as some undesirable excrescence on the
economic system that could be removed if we would only make
up our minds to get rid of it. Advertising is the very offspring of
the monopoly form of capitalism, the inevitable by-product of the
decline of price competition; it constitutes as integral a part of

the system as the giant corporation itself. The economic importance of advertising lies partly in its causing a reallocation of consumers' expenditures among different commodities. Even more important, however, is its effect on the magnitude of aggregate effective demand and thus on the level of income and employment. In other words, it generates useless expenditures by consumers, which soak up part of its overproduction by getting consumers to spend money beyond their direct needs.

Advertising affects profits in two ways. The first effect is the fact that part of advertising and other selling expenses are paid for through an increase in the prices of consumer goods bought by productive workers. Their real wages are reduced by this amount, whereas total profit is maintained by the higher prices. The other, more complicated, effect is that the profits and wages some capitalists and workers make from the business of advertising constitute an expense for other capitalists. This component of the outlays on advertising and sales effort does not constitute an increase in total profit but does cause its redistribution. Some individuals living off profit are deprived of a fraction of their incomes in order to support other individuals living off profit, namely those who derive their incomes from advertising itself.

Furthermore, in making it possible to create the demand for a product, advertising encourages investment in plant and equipment that otherwise would not take place. The effect of advertising on the division of total income between consumption and saving is not measurable, but is clear in direction and probably very large. The function of advertising, perhaps its dominant function today, is to wage a relentless war on behalf of the producers and sellers of consumer goods against saving and in favor of consumption.

Actually much of the newness with which the consumer is systematically bombarded is either fraudulent or related trivially, and in many cases even negatively, to the function and serviceability of the product. Moreover, other products are introduced that are indeed new in design and appearance but that serve essentially the same purposes as old products they are intended to replace. The extent of the difference can vary all the way from a simple modification in packaging to the far-reaching and enormously expensive annual changes in automobile models.

In addition, most research and development programs, which constitute a multibillion-dollar effort in the United States, are more closely related to the production of salable goods than to their much touted mission of advancing science and technology. For example, if monopoly profit and dealers' markups were excluded, then the real cost of production of the 1945 automobile, built with the technology of 1975, would have been far less than it was in 1945. The big three in auto making have always spent enormous sums on changes in automobile styles each year, which are of no use to consumers, but help sell more cars. Thus the total amount of waste from all the time and effort devoted directly and indirectly to selling products under monopoly must considerably lower the rate of economic growth.

Not only does monopoly greatly increase the waste of capitalism but it also raises pollution and environmental destruction to a new level. In the competitive model, apologists could claim that consumer preference dictated what was produced and therefore that pollution was merely an unfortunate by-product of the demands of the public. The apologists argued that these unfortunate by-products of public preference could be handled by some minor public action in beautifying the environment. Under monopoly, such apologetics are no longer possible; it is clear that consumer preference is manipulated and directed toward whatever products are most profitable to produce, and therefore "environmental damage becomes a normal consequence of the conflict between the goals of the producing firm and those of the public."[14]

So far, only the civilian wastes and peacetime pollution caused by monopoly have been considered. The next chapter discusses the effects of monopoly on unemployment and inflation. Its full effect, however, cannot be appreciated until its political power and militarist trend, as well as its international spread, are analyzed (as will be done in chapters 9 and 10).

UNION POWER

In the next chapter, the monopoly power of big business will be exposed as the major cause of the present pattern of inflation persisting even in the midst of high unemployment. But many people have alleged that this inflation may be equally or primarily caused by the monopoly power of unions. There is no question but that the power of a union in an industry—and perhaps in all industry—can keep wages higher than they would be if individual workers faced the giant corporations alone.

The point to be explained, however, is not why wages and prices are at some given level. The question is one of inflation, increasing prices (and increasing wages, usually at a lesser

TABLE 7.5 UNION MEMBERSHIP, 1945–1972
(Union Members as % of all Employees in
Nonagricultural Employment)

Year	Percent Unionized	Year	Percent Unionized	Year	Percent Unionized
1945	35.5	1954	34.7	1963	29.1
1946	34.5	1955	33.2	1964	28.9
1947	33.7	1956	33.4	1965	28.4
1948	31.9	1957	32.8	1966	28.1
1949	32.6	1958	33.2	1967	27.9
1950	31.5	1959	32.1	1968	27.9
1951	33.3	1960	31.4	1969	27.1
1952	32.5	1961	30.2	1970	27.5
1953	33.7	1962	29.8	1971	27.2
				1972	26.7

SOURCE: U.S. Department of Labor, Bureau of Labor Statistics, *Handbook of Labor Statistics 1974* (Washington, D.C.: Government Printing Office, 1974), p. 366.

speed)—and why U.S. capitalism has the new phenomenon of inflation during depression. This new condition did not exist at all before the 1950s and got much worse in the 1969 and 1974–1975 depressions. Therefore, this new situation must be explained by some new variable or by a large and continuing increase in some old variable.

This chapter has demonstrated that the monopoly power of business is not only high, but has drastically increased since 1950. What about the power of unions? Has it increased? Probably the best indicator of union power in the economy is the percentage of workers who are in unions. If unions represent 90 percent of all workers, they are undoubtedly more powerful than if they represent 10 percent of all workers. The available data is presented in Table 7.5 and Figure 7.1.

These data show that, excluding agriculture, in which unions have had few members, the percentage of unionized workers was at a low of about 12 percent in the Great Depression. The militant organizing drive of the CIO (Congress of Industrial Organizations) rapidly raised union membership in the late 1930s and in World War II to a high of 35.5 percent in 1945. The CIO organized many millions of unskilled and semiskilled workers that the AFL had always ignored.

FIGURE 7.1   UNION MEMBERSHIP AS A PERCENT OF TOTAL LABOR
FORCE AND OF EMPLOYEES IN NONAGRICULTURAL ESTABLISH-
MENTS, 1930–1972 (EXCLUDES CANADIAN MEMBERSHIP)

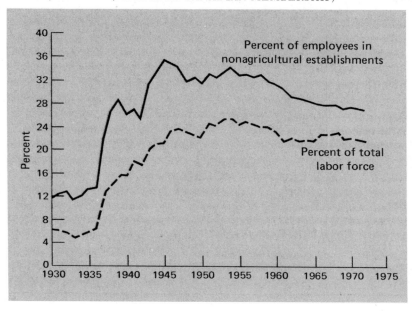

SOURCE: U.S. Bureau of Labor Statistics, *Handbook of Labor Statistics, 1974* (Washington, D.C.: GPO, 1974).

After 1945, union leaders became less militant (and some
were corrupted by power or bribes), so the drive by labor diminished. Moreover, in the repressive period of the 1950s, labor
was split by redbaiting and the left-wing unions driven out, with
some destroyed. Finally, under the pressure and leadership of
business, a reactionary Congress passed the Taft-Hartley Act,
which was designed to accomplish—and did accomplish—a
chaining down and further weakening of labor. For these reasons,
and others, union membership dropped from 35.5 percent of the
nonagricultural labor force in 1945 to only 26.7 percent in 1972.

Of course, unions are stronger in the manufacturing sector
than in the rest of the economy. The manufacturing sector, however, has declined in importance relative to other sectors, especially service industries. Moreover, union power has been declining even in the manufacturing sector. The changes in percent of
unionization in manufacturing are shown in Table 7.6.

Table 7.6 shows that union strength declined by 5.3 percentage points in all manufacturing from 1958 to 1972. When man-

TABLE 7.6 UNIONIZATION IN MANUFACTURING BY INDUSTRY
(union members as percent of employees on payrolls)

Industry	1958	1972	Change in Percentage Points from 1958 to 1972
All Manufacturing	52.4	47.1	−5.3
Food, beverages and tobacco	55.1	53.4	−1.7
Clothing, textiles and leather	50.1	41.6	−8.5
Furniture, lumber, wood and paper	50.3	50.1	−0.2
Printing and publishing	39.7	32.7	−7.0
Petroleum, chemicals and rubber	39.6	34.7	−4.9
Stone, clay, and glass	44.6	48.0	+3.4
Metals and machinery	52.3	47.1	−5.2
Transportation equipment	78.7	59.1	−19.6

SOURCE: U.S. Department of Labor, Bureau of Labor Statistics, *Handbook of Labor Statistics, 1974* (Washington, D.C.: Government Printing Office, 1975), p. 367.

ufacturing is divided into eight industrial groups, the percentage of workers in unions rises slightly in only one group, while it fell in seven groups.

The loss of bargaining strength, with a lower percentage of the labor force enrolled in unions, helps explain the weakening position of labor versus capital. The increased monopoly power of business helps explain the present trend of price inflation.

NOTES

1. All data in this paragraph are from the Federal Trade Commission and were cited in Federal Reserve Bank of Cleveland, *Economic Commentary* (May 12, 1969), p. 3.

2. John Blair, *Economic Concentration* (New York: Harcourt Brace Jovanovich, 1972), pp. 53–54.

3. The figures on concentration in banking are taken from the Patman Committee Staff Report for the Domestic Finance Subcommittee of the House Committee on Banking and Currency, *Commercial Banks and Their Trust Activities: Emerging Influence on the American Economy* (Washington, D.C.: Government Printing Office, July 1968), p. 5.

4. The data that follow are taken from Willard F. Mueller, "Economic Concentration," in hearings before the Subcommittee on Antitrust and Monopoly of the Committee on the Judiciary, United States Senate, 88th Cong., 2d Sess., *Part 1: Overall and Conglomerate Aspects* (Washington, D.C.: Government Printing Office, July 1964), pp. 111–129.

5. Richard Barber, *The American Corporation* (New York: Dutton, 1970), p. 20.

6. All data from Census Bureau, *1963 Census of Manufacturers* adjusted by Blair, op. cit., p. 14.

7. All data in this paragraph from Blair, op. cit., p. 76.

8. U.S. Department of Commerce, "Concentration Ratios in Manufacturing," *1972 Census of Manufacturing* (Washington, D.C.: Government Printing Office, 1975), SR 2–4, Table 1.

9. See John K. Galbraith, *The New Industrial State* (Boston: Houghton Mifflin, 1967), p. 23.

10. In this respect, see James Earley, "The Impact of Some New Developments in Economic Theory: Discussion," *American Economic Review* (May 1957), pp. 333–335.

11. Galbraith, op. cit., chapters 5, 6, 7, 8.

12. Gabriel Kolko, *Wealth and Power in America* (New York: Praeger, 1962), p. 13.

13. See J. S. Bain, "Price and Production Policies," in Howard S. Ellis, ed., *A Survey of Contemporary Economics* (New York: McGraw-Hill, 1948), p. 140.

14. John K. Galbraith, "Economics as a System of Belief," *American Economic Review*, May 1970, p. 477.

8

MONOPOLY AND STAGFLATION

Stagflation was defined earlier as the condition of price inflation in the midst of stagnant or falling production and heavy unemployment. This is a new phenomenon in the United States. As also mentioned earlier, in 23 of 26 cycles before World War II prices rose in the expansion, but fell in the contraction. Similarly, in the cycle that peaked in 1948, prices rose in the expansion and fell in the contraction. In all of these cycles, of course, unemployment declined in the expansion phases and rose during the contractions.

On the basis of such data, traditional economists found a relation between prices and unemployment. These economists argued that wages and prices always rise in periods of falling unemployment, that is, in economic expansion; while wages and prices always fall when unemployment rises, that is, in economic contraction. It is probably still true that a catastrophic rate of unemployment, such as in the depths of the Great Depression when a fourth to a third of the labor force was unemployed, would bring lower prices or deflation. But it is no longer true that any significant unemployment—short of a catastrophic rate—will actually lower prices. Higher unemployment may slow the rate of inflation, but even that is not clear in recent experience.

TABLE 8.1 UNEMPLOYMENT AND PRICES, U.S., 1970–1975
(Level in each stage of cycle, with cycle average = 100)

	Expansion				Peak	Contraction			
Stages	1	2	3	4	5	6	7	8	9
Unemployment	101	103	98	85	86	89	99	143	154
Consumer price index	89	91	94	99	100	103	109	113	115
Wholesale price index	82	81	88	100	107	113	134	129	130

SOURCE: Derived from monthly data in U.S. Department of Commerce, *Survey of Current Business* (August 1971, August 1972, August 1973, August 1974, August 1975).

The new situation is most dramatically revealed in the most recent cycle. Table 8.1 and Figure 8.1 show that unemployment declined as usual in the expansion of 1970 to 1973, and rose as usual in the contraction of 1973 to 1975. The wholesale price index rose in the expansion, but continued to rise almost as fast in the contraction. The consumer price index rose in the expansion, but rose even faster in the contraction.

If earlier cycles are examined, it becomes clear that this phenomenon has existed since the 1950s, but has intensified in the most recent cycles. The expansion still shows the usual relation between unemployment and prices. Table 8.2 reveals that the unemployment rate declines in every cyclical expansion, though it didn't decline very much in 1970–1973. Prices rose in every expansion; they rose least in the very mild expansion of 1958–1960; they rose most in the Korean War expansion and in the last two expansions under the influence of the Vietnam War.

It is when we turn to recent recessions that the picture changes from the old pattern. The new pattern is shown in Table 8.3.

Unemployment has increased drastically in every one of these contractions, though least in the mild recession of 1961. Consumer prices, however, did not fall in any of these five contractions. They rose very slightly in the 1961 recession, rose more in the 1958 recession, still more in the 1970 recession, and rose most in the 1973–1975 depression! Wholesale prices stayed almost constant in the 1954 and 1961 recessions, rose a little in 1958, a little more in 1970, and showed an astounding rise in the 1973–1975 depression.

FIGURE 8.1 UNEMPLOYMENT AND CONSUMER PRICES, UNITED
STATES, 1970–1975

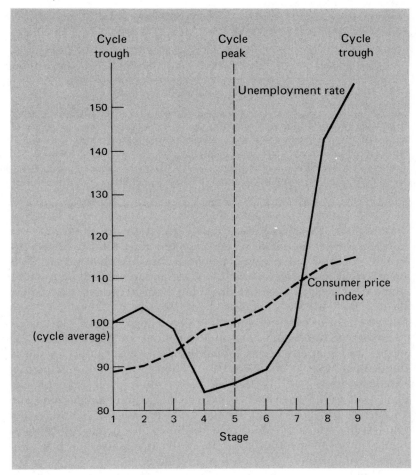

SOURCE: Derived from data in U.S. Department of Commerce, *Survey of Current Business*
(August of 1971, 1972, 1973, 1974, and 1975).

NOTE: Average value for each variable over whole period, November 1970 to May
1975, is set at 100. Average rate of unemployment was 5.9 percent. Average level of
consumer price index (1967 = 100) was 134. All data is monthly.

LABOR UNIONS AND INFLATION

There is no evidence that labor unions obtain such high
wages as to cause inflation. The most important fact to stress is
that real wages decline in each depression or recession. In other
words, although money wages have risen somewhat in recent

TABLE 8.2 UNEMPLOYMENT AND PRICES IN
CYCLICAL EXPANSIONS
(change from stage 1 to stage 5 of cycle, where level at each stage is
set so that cycle average = 100.)

Expansion	Unemployment Rate	Consumer Price Index	Wholesale Price Index
Oct. 1949–July 1953	−109	+12	+11
Aug. 1954–July 1957	−39	+5	+18
Apr. 1958–May 1960	−32	+2	+1
Feb. 1961–Nov. 1969	−69	+23	+13
Nov. 1970–Dec. 1973	−14	+11	+25

SOURCE: Derived from monthly data in U.S. Department of Commerce, *Survey of Current Business* (August 1971, August 1972, August 1973, August 1974, August 1975).

contractions, they have risen much less than prices. We saw in Chapter 3 that aggregate wages rose less than total revenue. We saw in Chapter 4 that wages per hour rose less than prices. This means that inflation during the contraction periods cannot be blamed on wages because they lag behind prices. In human terms, the worker's standard of living declines in each depression-plus-inflation.

Nor can price inflation in expansions be blamed on high wages. In Chapter 4 it was shown that labor cost per unit actually declines in most of the expansion. Therefore, the cost of paying wages cannot possibly be the cause—though it may be the excuse—for higher prices in most of the expansion period. The slight rise in labor costs in the later expansion period is not enough for wages to catch up with the earlier productivity rises. Again, these wage increases are only an excuse for price increases, and are not the determining factor.

Finally, it was shown in Chapter 7 that union strength in most industries has been declining. The percentage of workers unionized reached a peak in 1945 and has declined drastically since then. Declining labor unions can hardly be used to explain more rapid inflation (especially in contractions with high unemployment)—except that the weakness of unions has helped business monopolies in their economic and political domination. Of course, it is true that the industries with business monopolies also have the strongest unions. The reason is that the large size of most of the monopoly corporations means that more workers are concentrated in one place and are therefore easier to organize.

TABLE 8.3 UNEMPLOYMENT AND PRICES IN
CYCLICAL CONTRACTIONS
(change from stage 5 to stage 9 of cycle, where level at each stage is
set so that cycle average = 100.)

Contraction	Unemployment Rate	Consumer Price Index	Wholesale Price Index
July 1953–Aug. 1954	+84	0	0
July 1957–Apr. 1958	+65	+2	+1
May 1960–Feb. 1961	+27	+1	0
Nov. 1969–Nov. 1970	+49	+6	+3
Dec. 1973–May 1975	+68	+15	+23

SOURCE: Derived from data in U.S. Department of Commerce, *Survey of Current Business* (August 1971, August 1972, August 1973, August 1974, August 1975).

Yet even in the concentrated industries the percentage of union membership has declined, so it is hard to believe that unions have had much to do with inflation in these industries.

To the extent that unions may contribute to inflation in the concentrated industries, two facts are worth noting. First, in the aggregate for all workers in all industries, labor costs per unit still decline in expansions, and real wages still decline in the contractions. Second, to the extent that the monopolies do more easily grant wage increases, and then use them as excuses to raise prices even further, these increases go to a rather small, select group of workers. There is a great deal of data showing that the more concentrated, high wage, more unionized industries mainly use a white male labor force.[1] The more competitive, low wage, less unionized industries exploit a labor force that has a very high percentage of minority workers and women workers. So any wage increases in the concentrated industries have only resulted in a little redistribution of income to the better-off workers, while workers as a whole have definitely lost from the inflation process. Moreover, it is worth repeating that the degree of unionization has declined even in the more concentrated industries.

MONOPOLY POWER
AND ADMINISTERED PRICES

In the Great Depression of the 1930s (and in the smaller depression of 1938), Gardiner Means found what he called *administered prices* in the monopoly sector.[2] In these more concentrated industries, Means found that prices were not set in a competitive market, but were carefully administered or set in the best interests of the monopolies. He found that the competitive prices changed frequently, but the administered or monopoly prices changed very seldom.

More specifically, Means found that the prices in the competitive sector registered large declines in the depression contractions; but the administered prices in the monopoly sector declined very little. Means defines the competitive sector as the 20 percent least concentrated industries, while the monopoly sector is defined as the 20 percent most concentrated industries. From 1929 to 1932, prices in the more competitive sector fell 60 percent, but prices in the monopoly sector fell only 10 percent.[3] A few prices in the monopoly sector even rose a little in the face of the Great Depression.

In the expansion of 1933–1937 competitive prices rose by 46 percent, while monopoly prices rose only 10 percent. In the depression of 1937–1938 competitive prices fell again by 27 percent, while monopoly prices fell only 3 percent! Monopoly prices are clearly more stable and are very resistant to the decline of demand in depressions. It will be shown that the stability (or increase) of monopoly prices is achieved at the expense of large price declines for small and competitive business, lower purchasing power for consumers, and high unemployment of workers.

Table 8.4 shows that the industries with great monopoly power lowered their prices very little; but they kept prices from going down more only by reducing their production by very large percentages. The more competitive sectors had no choice but to let their prices be forced down by lack of demand, while their production declined less because of greater demand at the lower prices. The monopoly sector thus held up its prices and profit per unit at the expense of great decreases in production and large-scale unemployment. The competitive sector lowered production less, fired fewer workers, but suffered much greater declines in prices and profits per unit. A highly monopolized economy is thus more apt to produce high rates of unemployment in every decline.

Data for more recent contractions show similar patterns, becoming only more dramatic in the latest depression. The competitive sector is defined in Table 8.5 as all those industries where concentration of sales by eight firms is under 50 percent. The monopoly sector is defined as all those industries where concentration of sales by eight firms is over 50 percent. This table on the

TABLE 8.4 PRICE AND PRODUCTION BEHAVIOR
IN DEPRESSION, 1929–1932

	Decline (in percent of 1929)	
	Prices	Production
Motor vehicles	12	74
Agricultural implements	14	84
Iron and steel	16	76
Cement	16	55
Automobile tires	25	42
Leather & leather products	33	18
Petroleum products	36	17
Textile products	39	28
Food products	39	10
Agricultural commodities	54	1

SOURCE: U.S. National Resources Committee (under the direction of Gardiner Means), *The Structure of the American Economy*, (Washington, D.C.: Government Printing Office, 1939), p. 386.

TABLE 8.5 COMPETITIVE AND MONOPOLY CONTRACTIONS
(changes in price indexes from cyclical peak to trough)

Dates of Cycle Peaks and Troughs	Changes in Competitive Prices	Changes in Monopoly Prices
Nov. 1948–Oct. 1949	−7.8%	−1.9%
July 1953–Aug. 1954	−1.5	+1.9
July 1957–Apr. 1958	−0.3	+0.5
May 1960–Feb. 1961	−4.0	+0.1
Nov. 1969–Nov. 1970	−3.0	+5.9
Dec. 1973–May 1975	+1.8%	+27.0%

SOURCES: Price changes for 1948–1949, 1953–1954, and 1957–1958 from Robert Lanzillotti, Hearings before the Joint Economic Committee of the U.S. Congress, *Employment, Growth and Price Levels* (Washington, D.C.: U.S. Government Printing Office, 1959), p. 2238. Price changes for 1969–1970 from John Blair, "Market Power and Inflation," *Journal of Economic Issues* (June 1974). Price changes for 1960–1961 and 1973–1975 calculated by author from U.S. Department of Labor, *Wholesale Prices and Price Index* (Washington, D.C.: U.S. Government Printing Office, April 1961 and August 1975). Cycle peak and trough dates from Table 1.1.

behavior of prices in the monopoly sector and prices in the competitive sector is perhaps the most important in this book.

Table 8.5 reveals that the pattern for the 1948 recession was the same as in the 1929 and 1937 depressions. In all three cases, monopoly prices declined a little, while competitive prices declined an enormous amount. In the 1954 and 1958 recessions, we see the first indications of the new stagflation behavior. Competitive prices decline as usual, though by a small amount. But monopoly prices actually rose in the recessions, though again by a small amount. The new situation is very clear in the 1970 recession, in which competitive prices decline by a significant amount, while monopoly prices reveal a considerable rise. A finer division indicates still stronger price declines in the more competitive industries. Whereas prices in all industries under 50 percent concentration fell 3.0 percent, prices in industries under 25 percent concentration fell by 6.1 percent.

Price data on the 1973–1975 depression indicate that monopoly prices rose in the depression by an astounding percentage. This very large price increase throughout the now dominant monopoly sector caused even competitive prices to show a slight rise in the depression for the first time on record. This undoubtedly caused great disruption in the competitive sector, decreased production, increased bankruptcies, and increased unemployment.

PRICES OF AUTOS, OIL, AND FOOD

Before giving a systematic analysis of such price behavior, it is worth looking at three of the most important examples of monopoly pricing and restriction of production. The most obvious is the auto industry, in which the big three control over 90 percent of U.S. domestic production. The largest, General Motors (GM), is usually the price leader. In the early part of the 1973–1975 depression, from the third quarter of 1973 to the third quarter of 1974, demand for autos fell rapidly and GM sales were down 22 percent. Yet GM did not lower its prices as traditional economics would predict. Rather, GM raised its prices by $900 to $1000; the lower sales were met by further restriction of production and firing thousands of GM workers.[4]

Oil prices rose dramatically during the 1973–1975 depression. The companies blamed the price rises on the Arab oil producers. But the fact is that the U.S. companies artificially restricted oil production for many years before that time. Internationally, almost all oil in the Arab countries was owned by

Anglo-U.S. companies, who carefully controlled the flow (and made profit rates that were over 100 percent every year from 1950 to 1970 on the oil from that region).[5] In the United States, with immense oil deposits of its own, the oil companies have not built a new refinery since 1965 and they have cut back exploratory drilling by 60 percent since 1956.[6] Even during the so-called shortage, the U.S. oil companies held immense amounts of oil off the market in reserve holding areas. So it is the U.S. oil companies who caused the shortage, who raised U.S. prices, and who made enormous profits from it.

Finally, U.S. consumers have been badly hurt by rising food prices and restricted food production. Yet myth has it that food production is a purely competitive area, so the high prices could not possibly be the result of monopoly. Thus, the argument is that high food prices must be due to Russian wheat deals (a very small percentage of the crop) or to a bad anchovy harvest off Peru or some other random factor, but not to monopoly because there is none. The fact is that the number of small farmers is shrinking while the number of giant agribusiness corporations is rising. On the supply side, farmers must buy most of their implements and fertilizers from monopolies, such as International Harvester. On the selling side, Campbell sells 90 percent of soups, four firms sell 90 percent of breakfast cereals, Gerber sells most baby food, Del Monte sells most canned fruits and vegetables, and just 20 supermarket chains sell 40 percent of all food.[7]

The power of the monopolies in food sales was accurately summed up by one investigator of the high prices of our Thanksgiving meals: "The Smithfield ham comes from ITT, the turkey is a product of Greyhound Corporation, the lettuce comes from Dow Chemical Company, the potatoes are provided by the Boeing Company, and Tenneco brought the fresh fruits and vegetables. The applesauce is made available by American Brands, while both Coca Cola and Royal Crown Cola have provided the fruit juices."[8] In the 1973–1975 depression, prices received by farmers dropped, but these middlemen (canners, packers, and distributors controlled by conglomerates) increased their share of the food dollar to 60 cents, so retail prices actually rose!

EXPLANATION OF PRICE BEHAVIOR
In all recessions before the 1950s, prices fell. That behavior was predictable and easily explained by traditional economic theory. Neoclassical theory leads us to expect that falling demand will cause both output and prices to decline. By reducing supply

and also reducing prices to sell more of the supply, the amount of output supplied is brought back into equilibrium with the demand in each industry.

Similarly, in the aggregate, Keynesian theory predicts that an excess supply will lead to falling production, unemployment, and falling prices. If there are institutional rigidities or monopoly power, then there will be stable prices. Keynesian theory predicts price inflation only when there is an excess demand above the supply at full employment.

Neither neoclassical nor Keynesian theory predicts price inflation in the face of falling demand and unemployment. Yet that has been the fact in the monopoly sector in the recessions of 1954, 1958, 1970, and 1975. Of course, traditional theory would admit that firms with monopoly power can always set prices higher if they wish to restrict their supply enough to do so. But why, in the face of falling demand, should monopolies find it profitable to reduce their production so drastically as to actually increase prices?

Only a few economists, mostly in the Marxist and institutionalist tradition, have provided some answers to this question.[9] In most of the monopoly sector a single large firm in each industry sets prices; other firms just follow this price leader. These large firms mostly follow a policy of setting the price as a certain margin of profit added on to their cost level. This procedure of *cost-plus pricing* by the large corporations has been confirmed by a large number of empirical investigations.[10]

The giant corporations do *not* maximize their short-run profit by setting prices as high as possible at any given moment. Rather, they set prices with a profit margin that will insure their maximum long-run growth—and maximum long-run profits. This profit margin must, therefore, be enough to fully meet their expected needs for growth and expansion. Each corporation sets a *target profit level* based on its previous earning record and the record of the leaders in its industry.

What happens if a giant corporation finds its sales revenue falling in a recession or depression? The firm will try to regain enough revenue to reach its target profit by higher price markups on the remaining sales. This process has been illustrated very well in an arithmetic example in an excellent article by Wachtel and Adelsheim, who write:

> For example, say a firm operating in a concentrated industry has
> direct costs (raw material and labor) of $200 per unit of output and

sets its profit markup above direct costs of 20 percent, therefore selling the product for $240 per unit and making a profit of $40 per unit. Let us say the firm has a target level of profits of $40,000; to realize this profit level it will have to sell 1,000 units at $240 per unit. Now we have unemployment and a recession which causes the volume of sales to fall, say, to 950 units. But if the firm still has a target profit level of $40,000, which it wants to attain, it will have to raise its prices to slightly over $242 per unit from the previous level of $240 per unit. It does this by raising its percentage markup over costs to 21 percent compared to the previous 20 percent. Having increased their profit per unit, the firm now achieves its target profit level, but the resultant manifestation in the economy is the simultaneous occurrence of inflation and unemployment.[11]

This illustration assumes little or no further decrease in demand when the price is marked up. But Wachtel and Adelsheim point out that their conclusion—that monopolies will raise prices in a recession by implementing these policies—holds true even if the price increases cause some further decline in demand. Of course, even the tightest monopoly, in reality, will lose a few customers from any price rise, but most of them have a strong enough market control—and a strong enough image from advertising—that they won't lose many customers. Just how high a price they can set is a function of their degree of monopoly power—a power that is roughly reflected in their high degrees of industrial concentration.[12]

More specifically, their degree of monopoly power over price has three main constraints.[13] First, if the industry raises its price (led by the price leader), how many customers are willing or able to switch to a substitute product? Second, if the price is raised and if this leads to a higher profit margin, how many new firms will be able to enter the industry, or how high are the barriers to such new entrants? Third, what is the realistic likelihood of any government intervention if the price gouging becomes too obvious to be overlooked?

It follows from this cost-plus behavior that such oligopoly firms do not change their prices as frequently as competitive firms. Even if there is rapid inflation of prices and costs, these firms usually keep one price for quite a while, then raise it to the new level dictated by their usual profit margin above costs. Thus, there is considerable evidence that in periods of business expansion and rapid inflation, it is the prices of the more competitive firms that rise more rapidly and change from day to day.

In a recession, however, the small, competitive firms are immediately forced to drop their prices as demand falls (since no one of them can restrict the industry supply), regardless of the effect on their profit rates. Not so the large, oligopoly firms. In the recession, if their costs per unit remain the same (as they do in physical terms over a wide range of output), then they can and will adjust their prices so as to maintain total profits as near constant as possible. Of course, that entails extra reduction of production and unemployment of many more workers than in a similar competitive industry, but that is not their worry.

Indeed, if, as in recent recessions, costs per unit actually rose in the early part of recessions (with declining productivity), they will actually raise prices as far as they believe necessary to maintain profit rates. Productivity per unit declines at first because the corporations hesitate to fire excess workers (at the lower production levels) since the decline may be only temporary. When the recession deepens and they realize it may be lengthy, the large corporations make very drastic employment cuts to be efficient at a much lower output.

MONOPOLY AND
STABILITY OF PROFIT RATES

According to this cost-plus explanation of monopoly price and output behavior, the monopoly sector should show much more stable profit rates than the competitive sector. And indeed they do. Table 8.6 reveals the average rise and fall of profit rates according to the degree of industrial concentration.

Profit rates on sales (and the same is true for profit rates on stockholders equity) rise almost twice as fast in the competitive sector as profit rates in the monopoly sector in the average expansion. But profit rates in the competitive sector also fall almost twice as fast as profit rates in the monopoly sector in the average contraction. The conclusion is that monopoly profit rates are far more stable than competitive profit rates.

Table 8.7 presents similar data on cyclical fluctuations in corporate profit rates according to the size of the corporation. These data on profit rate fluctuations by size are interesting because most large corporations have monopoly power, and most monopolized industries contain very large corporations. The extent of monopoly power is reflected in the table in the fact that average profit rate increases with size. Table 8.7 also shows that the profit rates of the larger corporations rise less in expansions and fall less in contractions than the profit rates of the smaller corporations. Therefore, it may be concluded that the profit rates

TABLE 8.6 MONOPOLY POWER AND STABILITY OF PROFIT RATES
(profit on sales, all U.S. manufacturing corporations,
3 cycles, 1947–1965)

Group	Percent of All Sales of Each Industry Made by 8 Largest Firms in Industry	Average Percentage Change in Profit Rates in Expansions	Average Percentage Change in Profit Rates in Contractions
Monopoly sector (*average* of eleven most concentrated industries)	66	+27	−30
Competitive sector (*average* of nine least concentrated industries)	31	+52	−58

SOURCE: U.S. Federal Trade Commission, *Quarterly Financial Reports of Manufacturing Corporations* (Washington, D.C.: Government Printing Office, 1947–1965); discussed in Howard Sherman, *Profits in the United States* (Ithaca, N.Y.: Cornell University Press, 1968), p. 171. Motor Vehicles industry omitted for technical reasons.

of large monopoly corporations are far more stable than those of small competitive corporations.

Why do the large monopoly corporations have more stable profit rates in boom and bust? First, they attempt to set their prices so as to maintain a stable profit rate. Second, their monopoly power allows them to set their prices at those levels. They maintain those prices in contractions by restricting their production and employment. In expansion, they raise prices only slowly while rapidly increasing their production and employment to obtain or keep a high share of the expanding market. Third, the costs of the largest corporations may rise a little at lower output levels, but nowhere near the cost increase per unit of the small corporations in each contraction. The unit costs of small corporations rise rapidly when they go below optimum capacity. Fourth, the effective interest burden of small corporations is greater than in large corporations both because they pay higher interest rates and because they borrow a higher percentage of their capital. Fifth, and very important, the small corpora-

TABLE 8.7   CORPORATE SIZE AND PROFIT RATE ON SALES, 1970–1975

Asset Size	Change in Expansion	Change in Contraction	Average Value of Profit Rate Over Whole Cycle
0–$1 million	+87	−22	4%
1–5 million	+36	−24	5
5–10 million	+22	−13	6
10–50 million	+27	−18	7
50–100 million	+29	−10	7
100–250 million	+12	−5	7
250–1 billion	+13	−8	8
over $1 billion	+22	−5	9
All	+25	−12	8%

SOURCE: Federal Trade Commission, *Quarterly Financial Reports of Manu-facturing Corporations* (4th quarter 1970 through 2nd quarter 1975). Expansion from 4th quarter 1970 to 4th quarter 1973; contraction from 4th quarter 1973 to 2nd quarter 1975; cycle peak and trough dates from Table 1.1.

NOTES: Quarterly data, all U.S. manufacturing corporations. Average value set equal to 100 points. Expansion change measures rise in point standing from initial trough to cycle peak. Contraction change measures fall in point standing from cycle peak to final trough.

tions have all their eggs in one basket (with no reserves), while the large conglomerates are very diversified with some invest-ments in industries that may happen to grow in spite of a contrac-tion. The conglomerates can shift reserve capital from strong to weak areas.

There is also some evidence that crises hit the small competi-tive firms long before they hit the large monopoly firms. In the business expansions in the period from 1947 to 1963, the profit margins of the competitive industries (defined as those below 50 percent concentration of sales by 8 firms) turned down 6.7 months before the expansion peak on the average. Yet the profit margins of the monopoly industries (defined as those over 50 percent con-centration of sales by 8 firms) did not feel the squeeze for another 4 months, turning down on the average only 2.2 months before the expansion peak. It appears that the increased monopolization of the economy produces a more stable sector of high monopoly power, but further destabilizes the competitive sector. And the instability of the competitive sector is the prime factor setting off each new crisis of overproduction and contraction.

RETROSPECT AND PREVIEW

Chapters 2, 3, 4, and 5 proved that the cycle of boom and bust, with periodic high levels of unemployment, is inherent in capitalism. In every expansion, demand is limited by the poverty of the masses of worker-consumers, while costs of new equipment and raw materials rise as capitalists in these areas find supply always below the rising demand. In every contraction the excess supply, or overproduction relative to effective demand, is cured by wiping out many smaller capitalists, with the monopolies buying their capital cheaply; by drastic reduction of all supply; by unemployment lowering labor costs; and by stagnation lowering the costs of raw materials and equipment.

Chapters 6, 7, and 8 showed that the phenomenon of inflation appears in recessions now because of the vast increase in concentrated monopoly power. In several recessions of the 1950s and 1960s, while competitive prices dropped in each contraction, monopoly prices rose. In the depression of 1973–1975 general inflation increased competitive prices a little, while monopoly prices soared. As a result of the monopolists' control over prices—as well as some other factors associated with absolute size—the monopoly profit rates are relatively stable, declining very little in recession or depression. The small competitive firms, however, bear the full burden of the depression profit decline, though workers shoulder an even bigger burden through reduced real wages. Hence, increasing monopoly has caused greater declines of production and unemployment, while raising prices through that very restriction of supply.

Monopoly, however, is not the only factor whose increase has led to both more inflation and greater unemployment. First, the capitalist government of the United States is influencing the economy more strongly than ever before and is in part responsible for the current stagflation. This aspect of the U.S. economy is discussed in Chapter 9. Second, the international scene has shifted against U.S. capitalism, so as to intensify these problems. These international changes are investigated in Chapter 10.

NOTES

1. See Barbara Deckard and Howard Sherman, "Monopoly Power and Sex Discrimination," *Politics and Society*, vol. 4 (Fall, 1974), pp. 475–482.

2. Gardiner Means, "Inflation and Unemployment," in John Blair, ed., *The Roots of Inflation* (New York: Franklin, 1975), pp. 1–15. Also see the summary of Means' findings in John Blair, *Economic Concentration* (New York: Harcourt Brace Jovanovich, 1972), part 4.

3. Means, op. cit., pp. 8–9. Means' methods and findings are criticized by the conservative economists, George Stigler and James Kindahl (cited and themselves criticized in Blair, *Economic Concentration,* p. 465). Means is upheld against Stigler and Kindahl by Douglas Bohi and Gerald Scully, "Buyers Prices, Sellers Prices, and Price Flexibility," *American Economic Review* vol. 65 (June 1975), pp. 517–526.

4. Richard Edwards, "The Impact of Industrial Concentration on the Economic Crisis," in David Mermelstein, ed., *The Economic Crisis Reader* (New York: Random House [Vintage Books], 1975), pp. 217–218.

5. Farouk Akhdar, "Multinational Firms and Developing Countries: A Case Study of the Impact of the Arabian-American Oil Company (Aramco) on the Development of the Saudi Arabian Economy" (Ph.D. dissertation, University of California, Riverside, 1975), pp. 85–95.

6. See Bennett Harrison, "Inflation by Oligopoly: Two Case Histories," *The Nation* (August 30, 1975), pp. 145–148.

7. William Robbins, "The American Food Scandal," in Mermelstein, op. cit., p. 326.

8. William Robbins, "The American Food Scandal," in Mermelstein, op. cit., p. 325.

9. The basic theory was first stated in Michael Kalecki, *Theory of Economic Dynamics* (New York: Monthly Review Press, 1968), Chapter 1. It is applied to the present situation in John Blair, "Market Power and Inflation," *Journal of Economic Issues* (June 1974), pp. 90–115; and in Alfred Eichner, "A Theory of the Determination of the Mark-up Under Oligopoly," *Economic Journal,* vol. 83 (Dec. 1973), pp. 1184–1199.

10. See the citations in Eichner, op. cit., p. 1184.

11. Howard Wachtel and Peter Adelsheim, "The Inflationary Impact of Unemployment: Price Markups During Postwar Recessions, 1947–1970," U.S. Congress Joint Economic Committee, *Hearings* (Washington, D.C.: Government Printing Office, forthcoming).

12. See this concept in Kalecki, op. cit., Chapter 1.

13. See these concepts in Eichner, op. cit., pp. 1190–1191.

9
GOVERNMENT AND STAGFLATION

Economic power lies in the hands of a few thousand owners and executives of the major corporations. In this chapter, we shall explore the degree to which their vast economic power gives disproportionate political power to that same relatively small number of top corporate owners and executives. Then we shall see how the resulting government affects economic inequality via taxation, welfare, farm subsidies, antitrust laws, and education. Finally, government policies, particularly military spending, will be considered in relation to unemployment and inflation.

HOW ECONOMIC INEQUALITY
PRODUCES POLITICAL INEQUALITY

In spite of our formal political democracy, money talks in politics as elsewhere. Thus it is no surprise that many writers, not all radical, have alleged that those with economic power are dominant in U.S. politics. While he was president of the United States, Woodrow Wilson wrote: "Suppose you go to Washington and try to get at your Government. You will always find that while you are politely listened to, the men really consulted are the men who have the biggest stake—the big bankers, the big manufac-

turers, the big masters of commerce, the heads of railroad corporations and of steamship corporations. . . . The masters of the
Government of the United States are the combined capitalists
and manufacturers of the United States."[1]

How far can Wilson's hypothesis be substantiated by the
facts? Do the large number of low-income workers or the few
high-income, upper-class capitalists dominate U.S. politics? The
economics of class structure were examined in Chapter 3. Now
we must ask about consciousness of class background because
this will affect political behavior. A careful study conducted in
1964 found, contrary to the myth of an all middle-class America,
that 56 percent of all Americans said they thought of themselves
as working class. Some 39 percent considered themselves middle
class. (It is true, though, that 35 percent of all those questioned
said they had never thought of their class identification before
that moment.) One percent said they were upper class, and only 2
percent rejected the whole idea of class.[2]

An individual's political behavior is strongly influenced by
class background. But that leads to a puzzle. If a majority identify
with the working class, and everyone has one vote, why do parties favorable to the working class not win every election? Why
do government policies usually favor, as Woodrow Wilson asserted, not working-class interests but those of the wealthy
capitalist class? More precisely, given formal democracy and
capitalism, exactly how does our extreme economic inequality
tend to be translated into inequality of political power?

In the first place, there is the simple fact that the degree of
political participation tends to vary with class background. "The
average citizen has little interest in public affairs, and he expends
his energy on the daily round of life—eating, working, family
talk, looking at the comics [today, TV], sex, sleeping."[3] More
exactly, 86 percent of those identified in another 1964 study as
middle class voted, but only 72 percent of the working class
voted. Similarly, 40 percent of the middle class had talked to
others about voting for a party or candidate, but only 24 percent
in the working class had talked about it. Among the middle-class
people interviewed, 16 percent gave money to a political cause,
14 percent attended political meetings, and 8 percent worked for
a party or candidate; in the working class, figures on the same
activities were only 3 percent, 5 percent, and 3 percent, respectively.[4]

Thus political participation of all kinds increases with income. Some of the reasons are obvious. Lower-income workers

have less leisure, less money above minimum needs, more exhausting jobs. Furthermore, detailed studies show that because workers have less education and less access to information, they have less knowledge of the importance of various issues, which accounts, in part, for their lower participation. The same studies show more cross-pressures on workers—for example, the racial antagonisms that conveniently divide and weaken their working-class outlook.[5]

Unequal political power is also achieved through control of the news media. Even if the average worker "had an interest in politics, he would have great difficulty getting accurate information; since the events of politics unfold at a great distance, he cannot observe them directly, and the press offers a partial and distorted picture."[6] Even the quantity of news is limited. Although 80 percent of Americans read newspapers and 88 percent have television sets, only 2.8 percent of total newspaper space and even less television time is devoted to political news.[7]

If the quantity of political news is deplorable, its quality is abysmal or worse. The first problem is that only one view is available to most people because of increasing concentration of television and newspaper ownership. In 1910, some 57 percent of American cities had competing daily papers; but in 1960, only 4 percent had competing dailies. Furthermore, news media tend to have a conservative bias because (1) they do not want to offend any powerful interests; (2) they especially do not want to offend major advertisers, all of which are big businesses; and (3) most important, "since the media of communication are big businesses, too, the men who control them quite naturally share the convictions of other businessmen."[8]

Economic power also worsens the substantial inequality of political power available to different pressure groups. Thus a standard political science textbook points to *status* as the most important factor in determining the influence of a pressure group. After listing other sources of status, it concludes: "Finally, since status is so closely tied to money in the United States, the group with greater status will almost automatically be able to command greater financial resources. And it costs money to engage in pressure politics. . . ."[9]

The fact of economic power weighs all the more heavily because advertising is now a vital component of politics. "Pressure groups . . . are now spending millions of dollars every year on *mass propaganda*. Not only broad groups like the National Association of Manufacturers, but even individual companies maintain elaborate bureaucracies to sell 'correct' ideas on general policy questions along with favorable attitudes to the company."[10]

The vast amount of business advertising reinforces the general ethos of capitalism. What is its message? Ours is a lovely country; material luxuries represent the ultimate goal; everyone can have these material luxuries. A certain percentage of business advertising is devoted to specifically political issues. Yet the government permits all business advertising to be counted as a cost, which can be deducted from income when taxes are computed. Of course labor unions are not allowed this tax deduction for political advertising.

WATERGATE AND THE PRESIDENT

There is no great mystery about how economic power gains dominance over the president. Money, big money, is required for presidential campaigns. For example, just in the few months of primary campaigns in 1972, Edmund Muskie spent about $2 million. It is estimated that President Nixon spent $29 million in the 1968 campaign and about $55 million in the 1972 campaign. Two traditional political scientists admit that "because campaigns are exceedingly costly, the wealthier a person is, the more strategic his position for bringing pressure to bear on politicians."[11]

In return for the money showered on him, Nixon appointed conservative businessmen to most cabinet and subcabinet positions; to almost all committees and agencies; to most high posts in the Republican party; and to many ambassadorships (including 16 of the 19 in western Europe). Obviously these positions are desired and used in furthering the interests of these individual businessmen and of all business; one example is the business favors done by Nixon's friend, John Mitchell, who became attorney general. This process, by which the president is elected by economic power and then appoints economically powerful people to positions from which they can further extend and defend economic power, may be called a feedback mechanism. In later sections we shall look at how the political feedback mechanism operates on education, farm subsidies, tax loopholes, military spending, and so forth.

More direct feedback mechanisms to influence the political process itself include police to stop demonstrations, the use of the CIA and FBI to attack "radicals" (meaning anyone opposed to the administration), and the use of the president's prestige in TV and press announcements to promote big-business policies. Last but not least, the Watergate scandal exposed the joint use of economic power and the president's political power to do political espionage, possibly so extensive as to prevent the opposition party from winning an election. If it could be used to such an astounding degree against liberal Democrats, how much must it be used against socialist radicals? Notice that Watergate involved economic power in several ways. On the one hand, at least $2 million was required for the actual conspiracy, of which about $800,000 apparently came from Texas oil men anxious to be given presidential favors. On the other hand, it reflects all the money that went into electing Nixon the first time.

One more word on Watergate. It mirrors the fact that when conservatives talk about "law and order", they define it to be primarily the protection of private property here and abroad—by any means available. Thus, letting the police shoot a black or Chicano unemployed worker in the back because he stole a $5 item is law and order; breaking into and bugging the Watergate Democratic headquarters (or breaking into and robbing a psychiatrist's office in the Pentagon Papers case) is law and order because it protects the administration that protects private property; bombing Cambodia—even though it is unconstitutional because Congress did not authorize it—is law and order because it protects the friends of capitalism abroad. Thus the conservative view of law and order is always to protect property (or the so-called national security, which is the same thing) but not people. This function of so-called law and order (or protection of private property) is the main function of the U.S. government.

CONGRESS AND ECONOMIC POWER

Congress, too, is not immune to the lure of economic power. Congressmen need money to get elected and reelected; they need it to pay for TV advertising, to pay air fares, and for many other basic necessities of political life. Lincoln is said to have spent only 26 cents on his campaign, but in the 1950s congressmen spent about $15,000 to $25,000, and in the 1970s many congressmen were spending over $100,000 on each campaign. In the 1970 Senate race in New York alone, Goodell spent $1.3 million, Buckley $2 million, and Ottinger $4 million.

The Republican and Democratic parties together spent about $140 million in 1952, $155 million in 1956, $175 million in 1960, $200 million in 1964, $300 million in 1968, and $425 million in 1972.[12] One investigation found that the Democratic party's money comes about 55 percent from corporations, 20 percent from big labor, 15 percent from racketeers and gangsters,

and 10 percent from middle-class Americans in small contributions. The Republicans usually collect about twice as much in
total, most of which comes from big business. Conservative
Senator Russel Long guesses that "about 95 percent of congressional funds are derived from businessmen."

Congressmen are also indirectly affected by economic power
through the strong influence of the president. Furthermore, big
business can threaten to open or close plants in a particular congressional district. Business can give a congressman free time on
radio or TV or a free plane ride. In addition, there are about 5000
full-time lobbyists in Washington, about 10 for each congressman
(and many are ex-congressmen or good personal or business
friends of congressmen). Except in emergencies, lobbyists do not
directly buy votes. They merely serve as the main channel for the
largest campaign contributions, buy lunches and dinners, and
supply petty cash, credit cards, profitable investment opportunities, legal retainers to congressmen (most of whom are lawyers),
lecture fees, poker winnings (congressmen *always* win), vaca-
tions, and fringe benefits ranging from theater tickets to French
perfume. The two largest lobbies are the oil interests (which
make billions in special tax loopholes) and the military armaments industry. All this power is so strong—and so necessary for
election—that even liberals like Senators Fulbright, Mansfield,
and Pastore will be found voting consistently for the direct needs
of business interests in their districts, no matter how they may
vote on broader issues. Thus one friendly senator, Boies Penrose,
said to a meeting of businessmen (back in 1900, when such things
were said more frankly): "I believe in a division of labor. You
send us to Congress; we pass laws under . . . which you make
money . . . and out of your profits you further contribute to our
campaign funds to send us back again to pass more laws to enable
you to make more money."[13]

ECONOMIC BACKGROUND
OF POLITICAL LEADERS

Most congressmen need no pressure to get them to vote as
economic power desires because that is already their natural
inclination; most are white, male, and affluent. Upper-income
members of the capitalist class hold a disproportionate percentage of the top political positions. From 1789 to 1932,
the fathers of U.S. presidents and vice presidents were 38 percent professionals, 20 percent proprietors and officials, 38 per-

cent farm owners, and only 4 percent wage earners or salaried workers. Similarly, from 1947 to 1951, the fathers of U.S. senators were 22 percent professionals, 33 percent proprietors and officials, 40 percent farm owners, and only 4 percent wage earners or salaried workers. Finally, from 1941 to 1943, the fathers of U.S. representatives were 31 percent professionals, 31 percent proprietors and officials, 29 percent farm owners, and only 9 percent wage earners or salaried workers.[14]

Data for 1970 show that 266 of the 435 members of the House of Representatives (about three-fifths) had outside financial interests providing over $5,000 in income per year beyond their congressional salaries.[15] This figure may be an underestimation because income of wives and children was not listed (nor was income under $5,000 listed). To make $5,000 a year from stocks and bonds requires at least $70,000 or $80,000 in holdings. The congressmen were not required to reveal the extent of their holdings; some voluntarily disclosed this information. Very wealthy men, with fortunes ranging from many tens of thousands of dollars up to the figure of slightly under $3 million listed for Representative Pierre Du Pont, sit in Congress.

What are the sources of their wealth? A total of 102 congressmen held stock or well paying executive positions in banks or other financial institutions; 81 received regular income from law firms that generally represented big businesses. Sixty-three got their income from stock in the top defense contractors; 45, in the giant (federally regulated) oil and gas industries; 22, in radio and television companies; 11, in commercial airlines; and 9, in railroads. Ninety-eight congressmen were involved in numerous capital gains transactions; each of them netted a profit of over $5,000 (and some as high as $35,000).

In the executive branch, upper-income, business-oriented individuals have had a majority of all the important positions throughout U.S. history. This includes the members of the cabinet, their assistants and department heads, and heads of most regulatory agencies. They quite naturally, with no conspiracy, tend to consult big businessmen and business groups as experts (such as the Committee for Economic Development or the Council on Foreign Relations). Wealthy families have also contributed a majority of federal judges, top military men, and top leaders of intelligence agencies. Finally, it should be noted that there is much crossing over at the top: Ex-generals often become corporate executives, and corporate executives often get to be cabinet members.

Of course no serious radical would state the thesis of big-business control of government quite as strongly as President Wilson did in his anger at the moment he wrote. There are many qualifications. For example, although there are many men of means in Congress, the influence of wealth is much, much less than in the cabinet and other executive offices. Similarly, in state and local governments the influence of the wealthy is very strong, but certainly they do not have exclusive control. Moreover, even among the members of the capitalist class in high positions there are many differences of opinion, mistakes in perceiving their own interests, and conflicts of interest between different business groups. Thus the rule of the capitalist class is by no means monolithic; it rules through the forms of shifting coalitions and liberal or conservative styles, as reflected in the Democratic and Republican parties. Finally, the working class (including farm workers, industrial workers, intellectual and professional workers, the poor and unemployed, and workers from minority groups) can sometimes organize sufficiently to overcome the power of money by pure weight of numbers, may exert pressure, elect representatives, and sometimes even prevail on particular issues.

EFFECTS OF GOVERNMENT
ON ECONOMIC INEQUALITY

Although everyone knows that there is extreme inequality in the United States, liberals argue that the inequality is much reduced by higher tax rates on the rich, welfare payments to the poor worker, subsidies to the poor farmer, public education for the poor, and antitrust laws, which decrease the concentration of income and power. Thus Paul Samuelson asserts that the U.S. government has reduced income inequality, though he admits that it has not been much of a change: "The welfare state, through redistributive taxation and through educational opportunity . . . has moved the system a bit toward greater equality."[16] Radicals object to this conclusion on several grounds.

First, the facts on the history of income distribution show that (1) there was very, very little overall change in income distribution between 1910 and 1970; (2) the share of the poorest 20 percent of the population has actually declined; (3) the share of the richest 20 percent has fluctuated, going down very, very slightly by 1970. Therefore, in spite of many promises by several liberal U.S. government administrations (such as Wilson, Roosevelt, and Kennedy), there has been no reduction of inequality since 1910.

Second, the main function of the capitalist governmental system is the preservation of "law and order," which means that police and armies and courts and prisons all protect the private ownership of vast fortunes for the rich. Government thus preserves capitalist control of land and factories. With the help of government in breaking strikes, the rich can continue to pay low enough wages to farm and industrial workers to continue to make the high profits by which they grow richer.

Third, radicals have shown that the administration of every program from taxation to welfare has been such that the rich have benefited more and the poor less than the law would seem to indicate at first glance. Some of these programs are discussed in the following sections.

Taxation

It is certainly true that income tax rates rise as income rises, so that in theory individuals in the higher income brackets not only must pay more taxes but also must pay a higher percentage of their income in taxes. Indeed the theoretical tax rate today seems to take most of an individual's income, once that income exceeds $1 million.

In practice rich taxpayers find many loopholes that allow them to pay much lower tax rates. Thus in 1957, the highest tax rate had risen to an apparently confiscatory 91 percent, yet that category of taxpayers actually paid only 52 percent to the government.[17] In 1969, the tax rate paid by all taxpayers with incomes reported over $1 million had fallen to 34 percent.[18]

Loopholes, such as low taxes on capital gains from property and stock sales, mean that some of the rich income receivers pay little in taxes and some pay nothing. In 1959 (the last year for which full data are available), some 21,317 people earning more than $20,000 paid no federal taxes—and that included 56 people with incomes over $1 million in that single year. It has been estimated that the total loss of government revenue from all loopholes in the income tax laws is about $77 billion a year.[19]

Whereas the rich, with their income from property, can find many tax loopholes, there are no loopholes for the average worker with wage income. Consequently, there is in fact only the slightest redistribution of income as a result of the federal income tax. Even more important is the fact that the federal income tax amounts to only 40 percent of all taxes. The other 60 percent of taxes are mainly *regressive,* in that they fall more heavily on the lower income groups. "We might tentatively conclude that taxes other than individual income taxes do not reduce, and probably increase, income inequality."[20]

When all kinds of taxes—federal, state, and local—are added together, the proportionate burden on the poor seems to be actually larger than on the rich. Although the rich pay a larger total of taxes, the percentage of their income going to taxes is actually less than the percentage of poor families' income going to taxes. In 1967, the poorest families, those with less than $3,000 income, paid 34 percent of their income in taxes. In the same year, the richest families, those with incomes over $25,000, paid only 28 percent of their income in taxes. In fact, in 1967 the richest 5 percent of taxpayers had 15 percent of all income before taxes: but they had 17 percent of all income after all federal, state, and local taxes were paid.[21]

In the last 30 years, the tax burden has actually been shifting further away from rich capitalists and toward all workers and the poor. In 1944 corporate income taxes were 34 percent of all federal income taxes, but corporate taxes fell to only 15 percent of federal taxes by 1974.[22] At the same time, social security taxes (paid mostly by workers) rose from 4 percent of federal taxes in 1944 to 29 percent in 1974. Similarly, among the federal individual income taxpayers, the share paid by the lowest 20 percent of income recipients rose from 4 percent in 1950 to 11 percent in 1970—while the share of taxes paid by the top 4 percent of income recipients fell from 43 percent to just 27 percent.[23]

Welfare

The rich cry that the poor are getting vast amounts of welfare payments. Actually, the total of all federal, state, and local welfare expenditures are still fairly small. Moreover, it has been declining as a percentage of personal income. All welfare payments—including unemployment payments, workmen's compensation, health, education, medical, and housing programs—as a percentage of personal income were only 6.7 percent in 1938, 3.9 percent in 1950, 3.3 percent in 1960, and 3.8 percent in 1968.[24] Furthermore, there are many kinds of welfare payments to the rich, such as business subsidies and loan guarantees. It is no wonder, then, that our tax and welfare systems have not resulted in any significant redistribution of income.

Farm Subsidies

The rural poor have suffered the most pathetic poverty. For most of the twentieth century the incomes of small-farm owners and farm workers have lagged far behind other U.S. incomes. For that reason, liberals have persuaded Congress to pass various bills aiding farmers with subsidies. What has been the practical effect of these subsidies?

First, economic concentration among the business firms engaged in farming has increased. At present the richest 10 percent of all farms produce over 50 percent of total agricultural output. Second, the farm support programs benefit mainly the richest farmers and give very little support to the poorest farmers. From 1963 to 1965, the richest 20 percent of all farms (with the highest incomes before subsidies) received 83 percent of the farm subsidies given in sugar cane, 69 percent of those in cotton, 65 percent of those in rice, 62 percent of those in wheat, 56 percent of those in feed grains, 57 percent of those in peanuts, 53 percent of those in tobacco, and 51 percent of those in sugar beets.[25]

Third, it appears in fact that the net result of the farm program is to increase the percentage of total farm income going to the richest farmers and to decrease that going to the poorest farmers. Roughly, this can be seen from the fact that in 1963 the poorest 20 percent of all farmers and farm managers received 3 percent of farm income, whereas the richest 20 percent received 51 percent of farm income. Yet the data on subsidies show that many of the farm programs gave much less than 3 percent of the benefits to the poorest farmers and much more than 51 percent to the richest farmers. Clearly income inequality in farming is actually increased by the farm programs!

Education and Inequality

Government subsidized education is often thought to decrease the inequality of incomes. "The government gives free education to all," goes the argument, "so anyone can improve his station in life by going to school for a longer period."

It is a fact, however, that individuals from high-income families are able to get more schooling in the United States than individuals from lower-class families. This may be seen in the following data from a survey that classified students graduating from high school in 1966 according to their family's income in 1965. Of those in the under $3,000 income group, only 20 percent started college by February 1967. Other figures for the same period are 32 percent in the $3,000–4,000 group, 37 percent in the $4,000–6,000 group, 41 percent in the $6,000–7,000 group, 51 percent in the $7,000–10,000 group, and 61 percent in the $10,000–15,000 group. Fully 87 percent of those with family incomes over $15,000 started college.[26] Thus the higher one's family's income, the greater one's chance of going to college. Moreover, many students must drop out of college simply because they have no money on which to live while in school.

GOVERNMENT AND BUSINESS

In the United States the Industrial Revolution commenced after the Civil War. In more than a century of American industrial capitalism, the relationship between government and big business is seen by some observers as having been desultory and often contradictory. This is because many government programs and legislative acts were designed to promote big business, whereas some laws, particularly antitrust legislation, were ostensibly designed to curb the size and power of big business.

Thurman Arnold, former "trust-busting" head of the federal government's antitrust division, believes that these contradictory policies and laws have stemmed from "a continuous conflict between opposing ideals in American economic thinking."[27] The power of economic thinking, taken alone, however, explains very little. A more realistic explanation of these seeming contradictions would be based on the two broadest objectives of government in its dealings with big business.

First, the government has been committed to the maintenance of the capitalist system and the promotion of the interests of big business. This commitment has generally dominated the relationship between government and business. The interests of various capitalists and business firms, however, are not always mutually compatible. Many conflicts are so intense that, if left unresolved, they could eventually threaten the very existence of the capitalist system. Government's second objective, therefore, is to act as the arbiter in these rivalries and to resolve the difficulties before they become so extremely serious.

The antitrust laws have given the federal government a measure of power to enforce its function as arbiter. Interpreted in this way, the government's policy toward business has not been contradictory. Nor has this policy been designed, as many liberals believe, to curb the immense power of giant corporations. Rather, it has always attempted to promote the general interests of all capitalists and all businesses, as, for example, in the late nineteenth-century attempt to crush labor unions. But in instances of industrial or commercial rivalry between two giant corporate empires, the interests have been in conflict. In such cases the general interests of all capitalists would depend on at least partial restriction of one or both of the rivals.

The Sherman Anti-Trust Act of 1892 was passed under pressure of a broad labor and populist coalition. Yet it has not only been used to attack monopoly, but mostly to arbitrate business disputes over the rules of the game. Moreover, it was first used as an antilabor weapon. In the first four years after its passage, the government prosecuted five labor unions under the antitrust laws, and won four cases. In those same years, the government prosecuted five trusts, and won only one case.

American industrialization was aided significantly by the intimate association of government and business. Big business was supported by protective tariffs, which began with the Morrill Tariff of 1861 and were expanded significantly in 1890, 1894, and 1897. Thus large corporations were protected from foreign competition and could use fully their domestic monopoly powers to charge high prices.

The due process clause of the Fourteenth Amendment was passed on the argument that it would give equal rights to blacks. In the late nineteenth century, however, it was not used to help blacks at all. Rather, it was interpreted to prohibit state regulation of corporations (who were considered legal persons). The courts denied state governments the right to interfere in any way with even the most abusive, malicious, and socially deleterious corporate behavior.

The railroad magnates were among the most important entrepreneurs in the American Industrial Revolution. Through bribery, chicanery, and fraud, they amassed great personal fortunes. Building railroads was never more than the vehicle from which they launched their financial schemes. The federal government responded by generously giving federal lands to the railroads. Between 1850 and 1871, the railroads were handed 130 million acres of land, an area as large as all the New England states plus Pennsylvania and New York. During the same period, state governments gave the railroads another 49 million acres. All this, and yet some economic historians still refer to the second half of the nineteenth century as an age in which government stayed out of business affairs!

Toward the end of the nineteenth century, the relationship between the federal government and big business became a symbiosis in which the government governed in ways big business wanted it to govern and big business furnished the money, organization, and power structure through which politicians could come to power in the federal government. When progressive elements of the Democratic party saw that Democratic President Cleveland's relationship with big business was hardly distinguishable from the Republican big-business relationship, they captured control of the party and nominated William Jennings Bryan, a champion of the workers and farmers. William McKinley, the big-business Republican candidate, raised campaign funds estimated to total as much as $15 million, 50 times more than Bryan's $300,000. From that time on, the Democratic party has been more careful about picking a candidate of whom at least a large segment of big business approves.

REGULATORY AGENCIES

Since the late nineteenth century the U.S. government has established many regulatory agencies, such as the Interstate Commerce Commission, supposedly designed to protect consumer and environmental interests. Thus telephone and electric companies are given monopolies, but public agencies are placed above them to regulate their profits. These commissions are commonly thought to be the watchdogs of the public interests, but they often turn out to be merely a legal way to give monopoly powers to an oligopoly. The commissions are generally dominated by those they are supposed to regulate, and neglect the public interest. For example, when the public does not give them careful attention, the public utilities commissions normally grant most price increases desired by the regulated companies.

While public agencies have always been dominated by business interests, some of the most obvious cases have occurred during the Nixon administration. The Federal Power Commission is an important agency which is supposed to protect consumer and environmental interests concerning gas and electricity. All five of the members appointed by Nixon were either businessmen in the gas or electric businesses or lawyers for these firms. As is usual, the Senate went along with the appointments in the first four cases. In the fifth case, however, Robert Morris was rejected when, on June 13, 1973, the Senate finally asserted its power to turn down such openly biased appointments—mostly because the Watergate scandal had weakened the usual coercive influence of the president over Congress. Senator Magnuson said that in the case of Morris the Senate was "again asked to accept . . . one more nominee whose professional career has been dedicated to the furtherance of the private interests of that industry." He pointed out that Morris had represented Standard Oil of California for 15 years. In fact, from 1964 to 1971 he had spent most of his time lobbying for Standard Oil against public interests on natural gas matters before the Federal Power Commission!

FISCAL POLICY

The economic role of government that most directly influences the level of output, income, and employment is its taxing and spending of money, or *fiscal policy*. During most of American history the federal government has based its taxing and spending decisions on the political value of the project on which the money was to be spent. The effects of fiscal policy on output, income, and employment were ignored until the depression of the 1930s.

The prevailing economic philosophy was that taxes should be used only to finance necessary government expenditures. It was thought to be an unsound financial practice for governments to borrow money. If a balanced budget, in which expenditures equaled taxes, could not be achieved, it was thought to be preferable to have taxes exceed expenditures so that any debts incurred in the past could be retired. Only the Great Depression and the World War II experience forced a change in this policy. Since that time, government spending has often risen much more rapidly than taxes.

Federal government spending in the United States in 1921–1929 was only 1 percent of GNP. In 1930–1940, as the New Deal responded to the Depression, it had increased to 4 percent of GNP. With World War II, government spending rose to the incredible height of 41 percent of GNP in 1943 and 1944. After the war it fell somewhat, but it bounced up again in the Korean War, so federal spending averaged 11 percent of GNP in 1945–1959. In 1960–1970, partly owing to the Vietnam War, federal spending averaged 13 percent of GNP—about two-thirds or more being military.[28] Total government spending—including state and local as well as federal—rose to 31 percent of GNP in 1970.

Since World War II, the U.S. economy has entered a new stage of government-with-business. Since the 1890s, the economy has been dominated by the giant monopoly corporations; now the economy is dominated by these same corporations working intimately with a government that strongly affects the economy and is itself a major part of the economy.

How does the U.S. government affect the aggregate demand for goods? Leaving aside international relations, we may say:

$ consumption + $ investment + government spending
= $ demand

Aggregate demand is increased by more government spending and decreased by more taxes. If there is unemployment—because of deficient demand—then the government can add to demand in one of two ways. It can directly increase government spending, which is a component of demand. It can also lower taxes, which increases the income available to be spent for consumer or investor demand.

On the other hand, if there is inflation because demand is at too high a level (perhaps because of vast government military spending), then the government can reduce demand in one of two ways. First, it may lower the level of government spending. Second, it may raise taxes, which reduces the amount people have left over for consumer or investor spending. These are the simple mechanics of fiscal policy; we will now proceed to its problems.

AUTOMATIC STABILIZERS
Excessive or deficient demand can be combated in two ways: with *automatic* fiscal devices and with *discretionary* fiscal policies. Automatic fiscal policy is built into the present structure of governmental taxing and spending to react automatically to inflation or depression. Discretionary fiscal policies are changes in the fiscal structure made by current and conscious government decisions. Since World War II the government has placed more reliance on automatic than on discretionary fiscal measures. The fiscal structure is supposed automatically to expand net government demand in depressions and to decrease net government demand in inflations.

On the spending side of the ledger, the government makes many types of welfare payments that automatically increase in depression and automatically decrease in expansions. For example, as full employment is approached, there will be very little unemployment compensation; but in a depression, with growing unemployment, this may become a significant source of buying power.

On the taxation side, the total amounts of federal income tax collected had declined in most recessions faster than personal income, so it usually left people with more to spend. The federal income tax acted this way because the individual automatically pays a lower tax rate if his income declines. Therefore, the federal tax system was an important automatic stabilizer.

Unfortunately, the depression of 1973–1975 was in a continued price inflation. Therefore, personal incomes rose in the depression in money terms, though it fell in terms of purchasing power. Thus the percentage of taxes rose in the 1973–1975 depression. For middle-income taxpayers, with an intermediate income by government standards, in 1974 personal income taxes went up 27 percent and Social Security taxes went up 22 percent over 1973.[29] As a result of the inflation, this was the first depression in American history in which the burden of personal income taxes actually increased. Instead of being the most important automatic stabilizer, the federal income tax operated as a major automatic destabilizer!

DISCRETIONARY FISCAL
POLICIES AND SOCIAL PRIORITIES

Because the automatic devices have failed to stabilize the economy, liberal Keynesian economists maintain that discretionary fiscal measures are necessary to eliminate depression and inflation. They contend that the legislature merely needs to increase spending and lower taxes in depression, and lower spending and increase taxes in inflation. But these measures also are subject to political and economic complications.

There are three different policy views of what government discretionary fiscal policy ought to be. The most conservative economists, such as Adam Smith or the contemporary American Milton Friedman, argue that no discretionary fiscal measures are needed. The government should stay out of the economy. Friedman agrees with Adam Smith that the less government the better. He attributes many of our economic problems to too much government interference with private enterprise, which would otherwise automatically adjust to all situations in a near-perfect manner. To the extent that conservatives admit any need for government policy, they say that only monetary measures are necessary. Conservatives favor measures affecting the money supply (via interest rates, for example) rather than any fiscal measures of spending or taxation because they feel that monetary measures do not directly interfere with business. They view an adequate money supply merely as one of the prerequisites for a private enterprise economy. Other prerequisites which they believe government should provide include police and armies to maintain "law and order," primarily to protect private property from its domestic and foreign enemies.

The second, the liberal, view is that of such economists as John M. Keynes or the contemporary American Paul Samuelson. Liberals admit that capitalism has real problems, such as general unemployment and inflation. Liberal Keynesians argue that adequate government measures of increased or decreased spending and increased or decreased taxation are necessary to correct these problems. Finally, they used to maintain that such measures can always successfully bring about full employment with stable prices. Now, many of them, including Samuelson, simply admit that ending inflation and getting full employment at the same time is one little thing not yet solved by establishment economists: "Experts do not yet know . . . an incomes policy that will permit us to have *simultaneously* . . . full employment and price stability."[30]

The radical view is expressed by Karl Marx or the contemporary American Paul Sweezy. Radicals argue that problems like periodic unemployment are deeply rooted in the capitalist system and cannot be cured by any amount of monetary or fiscal measures. They contend that the U.S. economy has reached full employment only during major wars. In normal peacetime years, they believe unemployment and/or inflation is the usual state of capitalism. They argue that the necessary drastic fiscal measures cannot be taken by capitalist governments because powerful vested interests oppose each such step, aside from military spending.

All economists know and agree that government intervention can theoretically prevent large-scale unemployment or runaway inflation. The basic fiscal formula, to which may be added certain monetary measures, is to raise taxes and lower spending during inflations and lower taxes and raise spending during depressions. Moreover, corporate executives and congressmen alike are by now well aware of and receptive to these techniques. But that by no means settles the issue (even aside from the problem of simultaneous unemployment and inflation discussed below).

The problem remains one of finding suitable ways of spending the amounts of money necessary to maintain full employment. Many outlets that would be socially beneficial conflict with the vested interests of large corporations or wealthy individuals. Larger welfare payments tend to raise the wage level; government investment in industrial ventures or in public utilities tends to erode monopolistic privileges. The issue is the political constraints to economic policies.

In the years immediately after World War II, the goal of full employment required spending $15 to $20 billion annually. This might have been a very agonizing social and political issue except for the advent of the cold war.

Dollars for cold war armaments did not violate any vested interests. Military spending is considered an ideal antidepression policy by big business for three reasons. First, such expenditures have the same short-run effect on employment and profits as would expenditures on more socially useful projects. Second, military spending means big and stable profits, whereas welfare spending may shift income from rich taxpayers to poor recipients. Third, the long-run effect is even more favorable because no new productive equipment is created to compete with existing facilities. During the past 25 years, the main change has been that the necessary addition to the income stream—if full employment is to be maintained—has risen to at least $90–100 billion a year. If it were politically possible, the whole amount could be spent on public commodities, such as housing, health, or education, rather than on military waste. Such useful types of public spending are not politically feasible in such large amounts, however, as long as the U.S. government is dominated by big business.

One popular cure for depression is reduction of taxes to allow more money to flow into private spending. Given the composition of the U.S. government, however, tax cuts always end up benefiting mainly the rich and the corporations. Even in the liberal Kennedy administration, the taxes of the poor were reduced very little and those of the rich very much, resulting in a redistribution of income to the members of the wealthy class. Especially in a depression, however, the wealthy will not spend their increased income. The consumption of the wealthy remains at adequate levels even in a depression, and they have no desire to invest in the face of probable losses. Hence the political restriction as to *who* gets the tax cuts makes this policy economically ineffective.

Similarly, all economists (and even most businessmen) may see a need for more and more vast government spending under capitalism. The prime political question, however, is spending on what, for it is here that vested interests come into play. Thus even small vital expenditures on medical care have sometimes been defeated by the American Medical Association. Powerful vested interests oppose almost every item in the civilian budget as soon

as expansion proceeds beyond the necessary minimum. What
kind of interests must be defeated to have the necessary spending to fill a $90–100 billion deficiency in demand? Constructive
projects such as the Missouri Valley Authority could develop
dams, irrigation, and cheap power, but these have been fought
tooth and nail by the private power interests (and, indeed, might
lower private investment by direct competition). There could be
large-scale public housing, but private contractors have long kept
such programs to a minimum.

There might be other welfare spending—for example, on
hospitals and schools. The rich, however, see these as subsidies
to the poor for things that the rich can buy for themselves out of
their own pockets. Proposals to increase unemployment compensation or lower taxes paid by the poor encounter even greater
resistance because they would transfer income from the rich to
the poor. Likewise, billions could usefully be spent in aid and
loans to the less developed world, where poverty and human
suffering is so widespread. That, however, could be passed on a
massive scale only over the bodies of hundreds of congressmen,
who represent well the wishes of their self-interested con-
stituents and have no concept of the long-run gain to world trade
and world peace. If any of these measures are to some extent
allowed, it is only after a long political fight, certainly not
promptly enough to head off a developing depression.

In every area of possible constructive government spending,
powerful vested interests stand in opposition to the satisfaction of
some of the nation's most basic social needs. These interests will
not tolerate government competition with private enterprise,
measures that undermine the privileges of the wealthy, or
policies that significantly alter the relative distribution of income.
They therefore tend to oppose all government nonmilitary
spending—except direct business subsidies. The only major exception to this generalization is government spending on high-
ways, which is actively promoted by two large and lucrative industries: the automobile producers and the oil industry.

MILITARY SPENDING
VERSUS WELFARE SPENDING
From all of the facts just given, it must be concluded that
welfare or constructive spending on a large scale is opposed by
too many special interests to be politically feasible. My hypothesis is that only large-scale military spending brought the United
States out of the great depression of the 1930s, and only large-

scale military spending has kept the United States out of a major depression. The liberals like Samuelson are much more complacent; speaking about mass unemployment and galloping inflations, he says they are things of the past. He asserts that these are ancient problems that are solvable and have been solved: "For example, however true it might have been in the turn-of-the-century era of Lenin, . . . it is definitely no longer the case in the age after Keynes that prosperity of a mixed economy (i.e., capitalism plus government) depends on cold-war expenditures and imperialistic ventures."[31]

It is a fact, however, that our economy boomed by spending immense sums of money to kill the people of Vietnam, and continues to spend vast amounts on unnecessary military hardware. How would Samuelson replace that crutch to the economy? He says: "Does building missiles and warheads create jobs . . . ? Then so too will building new factories, better roads and schools, cleaning up our rivers, and providing minimum income-supplements for our aged and handicapped."[32] Certainly it is true that jobs could be created in all these constructive ways rather than the destructive ways of warfare. *But*—and it is a big *but*—we are talking about government spending, so we must remember that vested interests will obstruct programs that might harm them. Yet for the government to build new factories means direct competition with private industry. For the government to build schools means to take money from rich taxpayers and transfer it to the education of poorer citizens. To clean up the rivers means both more use of tax money and forcing private industry to spend money on purifying its wastes. Giving to the aged and handicapped means again adding taxes and shifting income to the poor.

The political reality is that vested interests oppose each of these programs with violent rhetoric and successful political pressure. Thus Congress does not even talk about building government factories for peaceful use; in fact, government atomic energy plants have been given away free to private capitalists. President Nixon, who was elected with big-business support, vetoed bills and impounded money intended to clean up the rivers. President Ford has vetoed hosts of bills for more health, education, or welfare benefits, including a bill for school lunches for poor children.

Samuelson says that radicals have asked: "Politically, will there be as much urgency to spend what is needed for useful, peacetime full-employment programs as there is urgency and willingness to spend for hot- and cold-war purposes?" And he answers: "It was proper to ask this question back in the 1950s. But . . . experience since then has shown that modern electorates have become very sensitive to levels of unemployment that would have been considered moderate back in the good old days. And they do put effective pressure at the polls on their government."[33] But in the first place, the pressure is only to get jobs, not necessarily to get welfare rather than warfare jobs. Thus the Nixons and Fords continue military spending to avoid unemployment, but do not do constructive spending to improve people's lives.

In the second place, Samuelson just assumes that the people make our governmental decisions, but we saw in the beginning of this chapter that the dominant power in governmental decision making in the United States is big business. The liberal Democratic administrations have been just as militaristic as the conservative Republican administrations. The Kennedy administration vastly increased military spending, invaded Cuba in the Bay of Pigs, and expanded the Vietnam War; while the Johnson administration invaded the Dominican Republic and further expanded the Vietnam War on a vast scale.

THE MILITARY ECONOMY
To measure the full extent of the military impact on the economy, we must recall that the U.S. Department of Defense is the largest planned economy in the world today outside the USSR. It spends more than the net income of all U.S. corporations. By 1969, it had 470 major and 6,000 lesser installations, owned 39 million acres of land, spent over $80 billion a year, used 200,000 primary contractors and 100,000 subcontractors—thus directly employing in the armed forces and military production about 10 percent of the U.S. labor force.[34] Some key areas of the economy are especially affected. As early as 1963, before U.S. entry into the Vietnam War, studies show that 36 percent of the output of producers' durable goods were purchased directly or indirectly by the federal government, mostly for military use.

How did the U.S. economy come to have such an enormous military sector?[35] Of course in World War II the United States had a huge amount of military production. It was assumed by every policy maker, including economists, businessmen, and political leaders, that the United States would mostly disarm after the war. It was also assumed that this would lead to a depression; therefore every possible solution was considered, with most analyses leading to the sole suggestion of renewed military spending. It was in this atmosphere that the cold war was born; it provided every possible increase in military spending. In fact, since the United States had a monopoly of atomic bombs, the USSR was very unlikely to be aggressive. Moreover, Soviet foreign policy was mostly very cautious and conservative, so much so that revolutionaries in other countries accused them of betrayal for not supplying arms. In reality, the USSR had its sphere of influence—Eastern Europe—which the United States has not invaded, while the United States has spheres of influence and imperial power in much of Latin America, Africa, and Asia, which the USSR has never invaded. Thus, despite the cold war rhetoric, the two major powers have never clashed militarily (except by indirectly supporting others).

Therefore the armaments spending justified by the cold war rhetoric was not militarily necessary. It was utilized, as in southeast Asia, to protect U.S. investments abroad but also in large part to support the U.S. economy at home. Thus we find in both world wars that the industrialists dictated to the government exactly how the procurement process should be run, completely dominated the Department of Defense, and made enormous rates of profit. This condition has continued ever since.

How big is U.S. military spending? It certainly includes all Department of Defense spending, but it goes considerably beyond that. How far is controversial, but the most careful study to date (by James Cypher) includes half of all international affairs spending, veterans' benefits, atomic energy and space appropriations (all military-related), and 75 percent of the interest on the public debt (since at least 75 percent of the debt was used to pay for wars). Other things that are too hard to get exact data on are: major parts of the budget for research and development, the CIA, and other intelligence agencies, and of course the deaths, wounds, and alienation of young Americans. For the five quantifiable items in military spending, Cypher adds up the grand total of $1.7 trillion from 1947 through 1971—enough to buy our entire gross national product for 1969 and 1970.

Yet this amount of direct military spending (even if it included the things we can't quantify) still underestimates the impact of military spending on the U.S. economy. There is a very large indirect or secondary effect on (1) additional consumer goods from the spending of those who receive dollars and (2) additional investment in plant, equipment, and business inventories by military industries. Economists measure the secondary effects of military spending by the government multiplier, which measures the ratio of the total increase in all spending to every dollar of increase in government spending. Estimates of the multiplier from military spending range from about $1.85 to $3.50 of total spending for every dollar of military spending.

The most important measure of military spending is as a percentage of our whole gross national product (GNP). From 1947 to 1971 it ranged from a low of 10.1 percent of GNP in 1948 to a high of 21.9 percent in the Korean War year of 1952. It was at 13.5 percent and 13.2 percent in 1967 and 1968, during the Vietnam War peak, and slowly fell to 12.6 percent in 1969, 11.6 percent in 1970, and 11.1 percent in 1971 (with another major rise in 1972). For the whole 1947–1971 period, direct military spending averaged 13.2 percent of GNP. Now if we are quite conservative and assume that the indirect effects are only as large as the direct effects, it is apparent that direct and indirect military spending accounted for the demand for 26.4 percent of GNP. This means that if military spending and its indirect effects had not been present in this whole period and all other things had been the same (which is very unlikely), we would have had a depression greater than that in the 1930s, when unemployment was 24.3 percent.

It is worth noting just how military spending has affected the U.S. economy at various times. As late as 1939, it had very little effect, being only 2.6 percent of GNP. In World War II, it rose to about 40 percent of GNP, which brought full employment (and even a shortage of labor). After World War II, there were several times when the drop in military spending seems to have been the main catalyst setting off a recession. Thus in 1948, it fell by 11 percent, followed by a recession in 1949. In 1953, it fell by 17 percent and in 1954 by 30 percent; and there was a recession in 1954. In 1957, military spending grew only 2.6 percent, followed by recession in 1961. In 1969, it grew by only 3 percent, and it fell by 2 percent in 1970, in which year there was a recession. All this suggests that military spending must keep rising at a considerable rate to prevent recessions and that when it falters it sets off a recession.

Obviously this is no simple case of cause and effect. In the first place, it holds true only when the economy does not have other sources of major demands, but that has not occurred since the first rush of consumer spending after World War II. And there is still an underlying private cyclical mechanism that makes the economy react as it does. Moreover, it can be offset by other policies on the required scale. Thus, in addition to the years mentioned, there is one other time when military spending faltered but did not set off a recession. In 1965 military spending did not change at all, but this lack was offset by the massive tax cut of 1964–1965, which did stimulate some private spending.

On the other side, it should also be noted that military spending does seem to have increased each time the U.S. economy needed to get out of a recession. Thus in the recession of 1949, military spending was immediately increased by 7.6 percent; in the recession of 1958, it was increased by 8.1 percent; and in the recession of 1961, it was increased by 6.6 percent. It was also increased by 7.6 percent in 1955, which may have helped us out of the 1954 recession. In 1971 wage-price controls were used in the new unemployment-inflation situation, but it appears that military spending did take another jump upward in 1972 to help with the continuing unemployment.

Thus our automatic and inherent pattern of business cycles has now been overlaid with a more politically motivated business cycle. When there is an all-out boom, business influence gets government to reduce military spending. This reduction is desired (1) to avoid inflation and (2) to avoid full employment, which means "uppity" workers and higher wages. Since, however, it is hard to time the military spending reductions exactly when desired and very hard to estimate exactly how much is needed, this always seems to do more than just limit the boom; it almost always seems to turn into a full-scale recession. Indeed, the capitalist economy never stands still but always has cumulative forces pushing it rapidly up or down once it gets going. Thus when vested interests reduce military spending a bit—in order to limit the boom—this action may help to set off a recession. As the recession gets worse and profits decline, the same political-economic power is used to start increasing military spending again, which may help to set off another boom. This, of course, is much too sketchy and rigid a schema to encompass all the many factors affecting current economic history, but it is an important framework for understanding.

Finally, we must note why big business is so happy with a normally high level of military spending. On the aggregate level, we saw that it is used to protect U.S. investments abroad, to get the economy out of recessions, and to prevent a major depression; but there is an additional incentive for the individual defense contractor. This incentive is based on the fact that the rate of profit is very high in military production and that most of these profits go to a few very large firms. Almost all military contracts go to some 205 of the top 500 corporations, and just 100 of them get 85 percent of all military contracts.

There are some government studies of military profits, but all of them understate the profit rates. In reporting to the government the military firms overstate their costs, and since they do not operate under competition but in a cosy relation with the Pentagon, they probably overstate costs more than most firms. Thus they allocate costs of other parts of their business to military contracts and add in all sorts of other unrelated costs—some have even tossed in the costs of call girls to influence government inspectors (called entertainment in their accounts). They also make many hidden profits through the use of complex subcontracting procedures to subsidiaries, unauthorized use of government-owned property, and getting patents on research done for the government.

Still, a study by the General Accounting Office (GAO) of the U.S. government has definitely spelled out their high profit rates. First the GAO asked 81 large military contractors by questionnaire what their profit rates were for 1966 through 1969. The replies, which were limited by self-interest, still admitted an average profit rate of 24.8 percent—much higher than nonmilitary profits in the same industries. But spot checks showed that these profit rates were still very much underreported. So the GAO did its own audit of the books of 146 main military contractors. The study found that the profit rate of these merchants of death was a fantastic 56.1 percent rate of return on invested capital!

GOVERNMENT POLICY IN STAGFLATION

Since World War II, the American economy has experienced a first in the nation's history: simultaneous unemployment and inflation. This situation appears impossible, according to elementary Keynesian analysis, because inflation implies an excess of demand over supply, while unemployment implies an excess of supply over demand. The answer to the riddle, as demonstrated in Chapter 8, lies in the monopoly power of American capitalism. In spite of a certain amount of unemployment, the largest corporations actually still have the power to continue to raise their prices, which might be called *profit-push* inflation.

No aggregate fiscal policy can remedy or prevent both inflation and unemployment in these circumstances. To end unemployment by increasing aggregate demand sufficiently to affect output in all sectors allows the monopoly sector to set off another inflation spiral. To end inflation by reducing aggregate demand sufficiently to affect monopoly prices causes catastrophic unemployment in the whole economy. The capitalist governments of America and Europe have generally chosen to combat inflation at the expense of more unemployment. Yet even high levels of unemployment have failed to end inflation; only truly catastrophic levels of unemployment would end inflation given the present monopoly structure of the economy.

Wage-Price Controls

Since neither monetary nor fiscal policy is much good against stagflation, even the conservative Nixon administration was forced to try the drastic solution of direct wage-price controls. On August 15, 1971, Nixon announced a new economic policy designed to save America and increase corporate profits.

Phase 1 ran for 90 days from August to November 1971. All wages, prices, and rents were frozen. Profits were not frozen. In actuality all wage increases were prevented, but some prices continued to creep upward. Nixon explained that the controls were necessary because we had combined inflation and unemployment, and all other monetary and fiscal policies had failed.

Phase 2 lasted from November 1971 until January 1973. The freeze was ended, but there were mandatory controls of wages, prices, and rents, though not of profits. Under this system inflation continued, though at a reduced rate of "only" about 4 percent per year. Unemployment fell from its highest level (in the official data) of about 6 percent in the 1971 recession down to about 5 percent. When one realizes that the official data leave out many people and do not even try to count part-time unemployment, this is still a very high level. Wages were successfully kept to a very, very slow increase in this period, but profits rose spectacularly (as we shall see in detail).

Phase 3 was supposed to "phase out the economic stabilization program back to the free market, since the price target was being achieved," according to administration spokesmen. It removed all controls over prices in all industries except food, health, and construction, and substituted voluntary controls. The voluntary controls were no controls at all because they had no enforcement procedure; therefore business paid no attention to them, so prices skyrocketed, rising at about 8 percent a year. In the end even the administration admitted failure in holding down prices and had to institute a new freeze. Phase 3 lasted only from January to June 1973. A striking feature of it was the pressure kept on the unions to abide by voluntary controls and the extent to which the unions did restrain workers from asking for wage raises, so that there was a very, very slight rise in money wages, and the earning power of workers declined. Again there were no controls on profits, which continued to soar.

Phase 3½ was a second freeze. All prices were frozen, but there were no controls on unprocessed food or on rents. Neither wages nor profits were frozen, but wages remained under Phase 3 controls. This phase lasted only 60 days, from June to August 1973.

Phase 4 began in August 1973 and ended in April 1974. It was again a mandatory system of controls over prices, wages, and rents, but not over profits. It was very effective in holding down wages, but prices continued to rise at about 10 percent per year. The lack of enforcement on the price side was apparent in the case of the oil industry. The Cost of Living Council allowed the price of "old oil" (from existing wells, averaging less than $1 to produce) to rise from $4.25 to $5.25 a barrel. The council allowed the price of "new oil" (which costs no more than $2 a barrel to produce) to rise to $10.50. Then during the (phony) shortage winter of 1974, the Federal Energy Office allowed the retailers' profit margin to rise from 7.25 cents a gallon to 11 cents—and this increase was not rescinded in the later period of surplus.[36]

In all of 1973, the actual buying power of workers declined by 4 percent, while profits rose rapidly. In the first half of 1974, unemployment rose to 6 percent, real gross national product declined, and the rate of inflation rose to 12 percent. According to the usual definitions, the U.S. economy was in a recession in the midst of an unprecedented inflation. Nixon, however, denied it was a recession, preferring to call it a slight readjustment. Much later, President Ford finally admitted it was a recession, but not a depression, even though unemployment was over 9 percent. Ford still resisted any attempts to cure unemployment until late 1974; even in October 1974, he was still talking about *raising* taxes.

Controls, Inefficiency, and Corruption

Economists of all ideological views criticized the controls, but for different reasons. The conservatives, such as Milton Friedman, were horrified at the violation of the First Commandment of laissez-faire economics: Thou shalt not interfere with the market process of setting wages and prices.[37] They have always argued that resources, including capital and labor, cannot be efficiently allocated if prices are not set by competition in the mar-

ket. If the government arbitrarily sets prices, how can a businessman calculate most efficiently what to produce or what
technology to use? If a businessman does follow the arbitrary
prices set by the government, then he will not produce what
consumers desire, nor will he produce it in the cheapest possible
way. It will not be produced as cheaply as possible because those
prices do not correctly reflect the true scarcities of resources, and
it will not be the combination of goods that consumers desire
because those prices do not correctly reflect true consumer pref-
erences. Thus wage-price controls doom a capitalist economy to
inefficiency.

Radicals agree with the truth of this insight. Radicals—and
some conservatives—go further along these lines to point out that
a huge bureaucracy would be needed to really enforce these
controls. Not only would that bureaucracy have enormous repressive power, but it would also be wide open to corruption.
After all, if a businessman cannot freely raise his prices when
opportunity arises, then he is better off spending his time and
money bribing a bureaucrat to raise his prices than worrying
about producing a better quality product. At the same time, the
controls do not end the money-grubbing aspect of capitalism. If
capitalists cannot freely raise prices, then they will either bribe
the bureaucrats as described or else evade the controls by selling
illegally (that is, on a black market, the way much gasoline was
sold during the crisis). In this sense, comprehensive wage-price
controls in a capitalist system combine the worst aspects of
capitalism and Soviet-style socialism: a huge and inefficient bureaucracy plus private greed.

Controls and Income Distribution

When the conservatives, such as Friedman, argued against
the controls, their own solution was an unregulated private capitalism. The liberals, such as Paul Samuelson, pointed out politely
that Nixon had already tried that solution, and that it was private
capitalism that had resulted in our present unpleasant mixture of
inflation and unemployment.[38] Moreover, they pointed out that
even the usual monetary and fiscal policies could not cope with
inflation and unemployment at the same time. In fact, it was the
liberals who first advocated the controls; they expected controls
to hold down prices, while welfare spending would increase demand to eliminate unemployment. At first the liberals applauded
Nixon's controls. Even in their naiveté, though, their initial reactions were a little doubtful on two points: Would Nixon actually

hold down prices or just wages? And would he actually spend
enough on welfare programs to end unemployment?

They were right to worry and wrong to applaud at all. Nixon
actually (1) held down wages, (2) allowed prices to continue to
rise, and (3) did nothing to cure unemployment, except some
military spending. The important thing to understand is that this
was not accidental, nor would Nixon be the only president to do
such a thing. It was shown above that all U.S. governments have
been strongly pro-business, for the very good reason that business
money elects them (and many other reasons). Any wage-price
controls under a business-dominated government can be expected to favor business.

The only difference with Nixon is that there was a great deal
of evidence in his case that he accepted business bribes (such as
those of ITT and the dairy industry) beyond the usual legal election campaign contributions, and he was much more blunt about
his pro-business biases than most presidents have been. For
example, in his speech announcing the wage-price controls,
Nixon said: "All Americans will benefit from more profits. More
profits fuel the expansion. . . . More profits means more investment. . . . And more profits mean there will be more tax revenues. . . . That's why higher profits in the American economy
would be good for every person in America."[39] Vice President
Agnew repeated the theory, saying: "Rising corporate profits are
needed more than ever by the poor."[40] Can you think of some
things the poor might need more than rising corporate profits?

Nixon and Agnew were really telling the truth this time.
They succeeded quite well in their objectives of limiting wages
and raising profits. Thus in all of Phase 1 and Phase 3½ wages
didn't rise at all. During all of the longer Phases 2 and 3, average
hourly earnings rose only 5.9 percent a year. At the same time the
cost of living rose by about 4 percent yearly in Phase 2, and 8
percent yearly in Phase 3, and about 10 percent yearly in Phase 4.
Since the cost of living rose faster than wages in 1973, for the first
time on record in a year of economic expansion, the buying power
of workers declined. In 1973, during Phases 3 and 4, wages rose
by about 5 percent and retail prices by about 9 percent, so real
wages (that is, what the worker can buy) declined by 4 percent.[41]

One way Nixon achieved these results was by appointing a
pro-business Pay Board to make wage decisions. The big unions
first joined it, hoping to salvage some crumbs, then withdrew
when they found they were to be allowed nothing. The AFL-CIO
said: "We joined the Pay Board in good faith, desiring—despite

our misgivings—to give it a fair chance. . . . The so-called public members are neither neutral nor independent. They are tools of the Administration, and inbued with its viewpoint that all of the nation's economic ills are caused by high wages. As a result, the Pay Board has been completely dominated and run, from the very start, by a coalition of the business and so-called public members. . . . The trade union movement's representatives on the board have been treated as outsiders—merely as a facade to maintain the pretense of a tripartite body."[42]

While real wages were declining in Phases 3 and 4, profit rates were actually climbing. Profit rates on investor's equity (before taxes) in all of manufacturing were "only" 16.5 percent in 1971, but rose to 18.4 percent in 1972; then—under Phase 3— rose to 21.6 percent in 1973; then—under Phase 4—rose to 23.4 percent in 1974 in the first year of the depression.[43] A strange depression!

Finally, in the first quarter of 1975, the profit rate fell to 15.0 percent (not seasonally adjusted). When this fall in the profit rate occurred, Congress and President Ford took immediate action to stimulate the economy by lower taxes, and the profit rate jumped back up to 19.2 percent in the second quarter of 1975.

One must conclude that the inevitable results of wage-price controls under a capitalist government are additional corruption and inefficiency, as well as a shift in income distribution away from wages and toward profits. The meaning of the political business cycle is also clarified. At the peak of expansion, when workers are pushing for higher wages, the U.S. government talks about inflation; and it uses restrictive monetary or fiscal or direct controls to lower wages and even promote a little unemployment. At the bottom of the depression, the U.S. government is moved by corporate pleas to stimulate the economy. The capitalist system would generate boom and bust cycles without government interference, but the government does reinforce them and may often serve as the catalyst setting off the downswing as well as the upswing (at such times as the economy was ripe for a change in direction anyway).

STAGFLATION POLICY AND
THE IDEOLOGY OF ECONOMISTS

It was noted earlier that most traditional economists see high wages as the cause of economic downturns. According to Leftwich and Sharp: "The general solution to involuntary unemployment is a reduction in real wage rates until the amount of labor demanded equals the amount supplied. In a competitive market, the reduction in real wage rates would take place automatically."[44] In their view, the problem is that unions use monopoly power to prevent workers' wages from falling, since competition among workers would force wages to drop when unemployment exists. So they imply that government should control wages. Of course, it is true that lower labor costs would induce capitalists to hire more workers if demand for products remains the same. But demand is the fly in the ointment. Wage income is the largest component of consumer demand, so lower wages mean less demand for products, which means less demand for workers.

When conservatives tire of discussing unions, they discuss government. Thus Milton Friedman and the monetarist school explain depressions in this way:

> *Most of the blame is assigned to misguided policies of the government. . . . For example, a considerable amount of government activity was generated in an effort to combat the [great] Depression, which is usually blamed on instability of the private sector. However, monetarists contend that the Depression was caused by improper monetary policies. . . . The government is seen as using intervention as a cure for problems which are actually caused by intervention. . . . The [private] economy can restore equilibrium through appropriate changes in prices with relatively little instability in output, employment, or other real factors.*[45]

Friedman's monetarist views involve a whole catalogue of errors, which can only be briefly listed here. First, as was proven in Chapters 3, 4, and 5, the Great Depression and most other depressions were created by the normal workings of the private capitalist system. Government policies may worsen, or sometimes set off, depressions but they are not the basic cause of capitalist systemic instability and its proclivity to cycles of boom and bust. Second, monetary policy played a very small role in the 1930s, and Roosevelt's fiscal policy did help somewhat in the mid-1930s (but it was too little and too late). Moreover, it was the conservative Republican Hoover who let the depression intensify; just as the recent depression was at first encouraged by the Nixon-Ford administration. How much more conservative and noninterventionist than Hoover could a president be? Earlier in this chapter, we saw that the U.S. government is not an independent factor above the battle, but the servant of private capitalism, so it can only do as private capitalism desires.

Third, the modern monetarists repeat the ancient advice of Say's law: that the private economy left to itself will automatically restore full employment. As a main mechanism, they rely on prices dropping under competitive pressures as demand drops; this would sell more goods and keep a high level of production and employment. Unfortunately, as demonstrated in Chapter 8, the competitive process now operates only in one small sector where prices and profits drop drastically. In the larger monopoly sector, prices do not fall and even rise in the recession, while production and employment fall rapidly. Moreover, as shown above, even if wages and prices moved downward with alacrity, this would more likely result (as it often did in earlier depressions) in a downward spiral of falling demand than in an immediate cure.

Faced with simultaneous inflation and unemployment, the liberal Paul Samuelson saw a dilemma with no obvious way out of it. Milton Friedman and his friends see it simply as a case requiring the sacrifice of heavy unemployment (by workers, not by Friedman) to keep stable prices. He claims that in any given situation there is a *natural rate* of unemployment, which is the level of unemployment that will prevent further inflation. This unemployment rate is thus consistent with any rate of inflation, and they argue that attempts to move the unemployment rate permanently below . . . this 'natural rate' by use of aggregate demand policies will result in an *acceleration* of the rate of inflation."[46] Since it is natural, nothing can be done about it, and any attempt to reduce the natural unemployment will only make things worse. Perhaps high unemployment with stable or rising monopoly prices *is* natural in the monopoly stage of capitalism; but then why stick with capitalism?

ANTITRUST POLICY

There are many liberal economists, and even more U.S. senators, who agree that monetary and fiscal policy are inadequate to stop an inflation generated by monopoly power. In fact, they perceive monopoly power as the prime cause of many U.S. political and economic problems. Their solution is to break up the monopolies through stronger antitrust laws. For several reasons, the trust-busting solution is not a good one, though any radical can sympathize with it.

The liberals see monopoly as an accident, a temporary aberration. Chapter 6 proved, however, that the monopolies are the

very heart of U.S. capitalism. Giant monopoly corporations produce and sell the majority of American goods. Therefore, to break
up all the monopolies is not a simple reform, but would constitute
a major revolution.

It must also be emphasized that breaking up a monopoly into
just four or five parts does little good. Most of our so-called
monopoly industries are right now technically oligopolies, with
four to eight major firms dominating them. They all play follow-
the-price-leader, however, so they all act exactly like a single
monopoly firm. To achieve something approaching pure competition requires many thousands of small firms in each industry, so
each monopoly must be broken into thousands of parts. Would it
make technological sense to break up the auto, oil, or steel industries into thousands of tiny firms?

Even if Americans were willing to sacrifice that much efficiency and extra effort in production, is it politically feasible? As
long as U.S. capitalism is to be preserved, how could there be the
political-economic power to cut up its very heart into thousands
of pieces. To make a major revolution without disturbing the
basic system is not feasible. At present, as we saw above, the
antitrust laws are much too mild to be any barrier to increasing
economic concentration. But even if stronger laws were passed,
that would not be enough because the antitrust laws are never
enforced. The antitrust division of the Justice Department always
operates on a shoestring, with a budget far less than the legal
department of any of the giant corporations. And if the laws are
totally rewritten, and the enforcement budget multiplied a
thousand times, the conservative Supreme Court always nar-
rowly restricts the antitrust laws (and might declare a sweeping
one unconstitutional). There is thus no feasible political hope
within the capitalist system for substituting millions of competitive firms for the present monopolies.

Suppose, however, such a political revolution within
capitalist boundaries were successful. A country of all small,
competitive firms would presumably resemble the present competitive sector. This sector is characterized by (1) sweat shops,
low wages, more exploitation of workers; (2) self-exploitation of
the small businessman and his family, with long hours and little
rewards; (3) little or no research and very little efficiency; and (4)
violent swings downward in depression, with big losses and
thousands of bankruptcies. Is this what one wants as an ideal
situation resulting from the vast effort of a political revolution?

NOTES

1. Woodrow Wilson, *The New Freedom* (Garden City, N.Y.: Doubleday, 1914), pp. 57–58.
2. This study is reported in Marian Irish and James Prothro, *The Politics of American Democracy* (Englewood Cliffs, N.J.: Prentice-Hall, 1965), p. 38. To avoid the imputation of a radical bias, the data in this section is taken from their widely used traditional textbook. In turn, all of their footnotes refer to well-known conventional political scientists.
3. Ibid., p. 165.
4. Ibid., p. 38.
5. Ibid., 193.
6. Ibid., p. 165.
7. Ibid., p. 183.
8. Ibid., p. 184.
9. Ibid., p. 245.
10. Ibid., p. 249.
11. Robert Dahl and Charles Lindblom, *Politics, Economics, and Welfare* (New York: Harper & Row, 1953), p. 313.
12. M. Cummings and D. Wise, *Democracy Under Pressure* (New York: Harcourt Brace Jovanovich, 1971), pp. 304–305.
13. Quoted in Mark Green, James Fallows, and David Zwick, *Who Runs Congress?* (New York: Bantam [The Ralph Nader Congress Project], 1972, pp. 7–8.
14. Cummings and Wise, op. cit., p. 39.
15. All these data were taken from statements filed with the House Committee on Standards of Official Conduct in April 1971; they were discussed in an article in the *Los Angeles Times* (May 24, 1971), pt. I, p. 12.
16. Paul Samuelson, *Economics*, 9th ed. (New York: McGraw-Hill, 1973), p. 804.
17. For this and much of the following information, see Gabriel Kolko, *Wealth and Power in America* (New York: Praeger, 1962), chap. 2.
18. John Gurley, "Federal Tax Policy," *National Tax Journal* (September 1967), pp. 12–27.
19. J. Lechman and B. Okner, "Individual Income Tax Erosion by Income Classes," in U.S. Congress, Joint Economic Committee, *Economics of Federal Subsidy Programs*, pt. I (Washington, D.C.: Government Printing Office, 1972), pp. 13–40.
20. F. Ackerman et al., "Income Distribution in the United States," *Review of Radical Political Economy* (Summer 1971), p. 24.
21. See Joseph Pechman, "The Rich, the Poor, and the Taxes They Pay," *The Public Interest*, Number 17 (Fall, 1969), pp. 113–137. The best discussion of all this tax and income distribution data is in Robert Lepachman, *National Income and the Public Welfare* (New York: Random House, 1972), p. 94 and ff.
22. Ralph Nader, *People and Taxes* (October 1974), discussed in Labor Research Association, *Economic Notes* (April 1975), pp. 3–4.
23. U.S. Department of Commerce, *Statistical Abstract of the*

United States (1960 and 1974), discussed in Labor Research Association, *Economic Notes* (April 1975), p. 4.

24. Richard Edwards, "Who Fares Well in the Welfare State?" in R. Edwards, M. Reich, and T. Weisskopf, eds., *The Capitalist System* (Englewood Cliffs, N.J.: Prentice-Hall, 1972), p. 244.

25. All data in this section from James Bonnen, "The Effect of Taxes and Government Spending on Inequality," in *The Capitalist System*, op. cit., pp. 235–243.

26. All data in this paragraph are from Ackerman et al., op. cit., pp. 25–26.

27. Thurman Arnold, "Economic Reform and the Sherman Antitrust Act," in J. A. Garraty, ed., *Historical Viewpoints: Volume Two, Since 1865* (New York: Harper & Row, 1969), p. 151.

28. James Cypher, *Military Expenditures* (Ph.D. dissertation, University of California, Riverside, 1973), chap. 6.

29. Survey by Joint Economic Committee of the U.S. Congress, reported in "Income Taxes Rise in Recession," *Riverside Press-Enterprise* (February 8, 1975), p. 1.

30. Paul Samuelson, op. cit., p. 823.

31. Ibid., p. 823.

32. Ibid., p. 824.

33. Ibid., pp. 824–825.

34. These data come from U.S. Defense Department documents that are reported in Seymour Melman, *Pentagon Capitalism* (New York: McGraw-Hill, 1970), pp. 83–94.

35. Most of the analysis and all of the facts in the rest of this section come from James Cypher, op. cit. This dissertation is a gold mine of information and the best discussion now available of military spending.

36. See Bennett Harrison, "Inflation by Oligopoly," *The Nation* (August 30, 1975), p. 147.

37. See Milton Friedman in *Newsweek* (August 30, 1971), p. 45.

38. See Paul Samuelson in *Newsweek* (August 30, 1971), p. 46.

39. President Nixon, in TV speech, August 15, 1971.

40. Vice President Agnew, at National Governors Conference, 1971.

41. Most of these data are from government sources, but they have been neatly compiled in a pamphlet by the AFL-CIO, *The National Economy, 1973.*

42. AFL-CIO Executive Committee, in ibid., p. 7.

43. Federal Trade Commission, *Quarterly Financial Report for Manufacturing Corporations* (1st quarter, 1974 and 1st quarter, 1975), pp. 12–16.

44. Richard Leftwich and Ansel Sharp, *Economics of Social Issues* (Homewood, Ill.: Irwin, 1974), p. 249.

45. William Mitchell, John Hand, and Ingo Walter, *Readings in Macroeconomics* (New York: McGraw-Hill, 1975), pp. 271–272.

46. David Ott, Attiat Ott, and Jang Yoo, *Macroeconomic Theory* (New York: McGraw-Hill, 1975), p. 260.

10
STAGFLATION IN INTERNATIONAL CAPITALISM

Stagflation has engulfed all the advanced capitalist countries. In western Europe and Japan, depressions in the United States did not cause major downturns in the 1950s and 1960s. In the 1973–1975 depression, however, these countries joined the U.S. economic contraction. From peak to trough of this depression, industrial production fell 14 percent in the United States, 9 percent in the United Kingdom, 10 percent in West Germany, 15 percent in France, 17 percent in Japan, and 19 percent in Italy.[1] Unemployment reached 5 percent in West Germany, 4 percent in France, 5 percent in Italy, and 7 percent in Belgium. At the same time, in July 1975 inflation was still running at 6 percent in West Germany, 11 percent in France, 17 percent in Italy, and 11 percent in Belgium.[2] So we see the familiar phenomenon of continued inflation in the midst of unemployment and industrial stagnation. As in the United States, the rates of inflation remained very high throughout the entire depression, contrary to many predictions.

MONOPOLY POWER IN OTHER CAPITALIST COUNTRIES
By the 1950s all the leading capitalist countries showed high levels of concentration of output and sales by a few firms in each

industry. In Great Britain in the 1950s, for example, the top four firms had the following percentages of total sales in various industries: 91 in explosives, 56 in electric lamps, 73 in distilled liquors, 47 in aircraft, 93 in petroleum refining, and 90 in cement. In Japan the top four firms had the following percentages of total sales in various industries: 65 in electric lamps, 52 in steel ingots, 49 in cement, 98 in beer and ale, 42 in petroleum refining, and 56 in pharmaceutical products. In France, the top four firms had the following percentages of total sales in various industries: 57 in aircraft, 76 in shipbuilding, 72 in petroleum refining, and 53 in cement.[3]

Since the 1950s, concentration has increased in each of the leading capitalist countries. The share of the one hundred largest manufacturing firms in all manufacturing output in the United Kingdom rose from 21 percent in 1948 to 38 percent in 1963 to 51 percent in 1970![4] Similarly, in France by 1962 in 56 industrial groups, just four firms had over 50 percent of the sales in 21 of these groups. "French industry, since 1962, appears to have a market structure more concentrated than American industry itself."[5] Finally, in the entire European economic community (excluding the United Kingdom) the share of total output produced by the 50 largest firms was 35 percent in 1960, 35 percent in 1965, and 46 percent in 1970.[6] During the process of integrating several economies in the early 1960s, concentration held steady. When integration was completed in the mid-1960s, however, there were a large number of mergers and the share of the largest 50 rose rapidly.

Similar industrial structures lead to similar economic behavior and performance. For example, an important study in Japan finds that monopoly prices fluctuate much less than competitive prices, so that in recessions monopoly prices in Japan have fallen less (or risen more) than competitive prices.[7] It is, therefore, no surprise that increasing monopoly power in Europe and Japan has helped produce—as in the U.S. economy—the strange phenomenon of inflation in the midst of depression. Of course, this is not the only reason for the new phenomenon, but it is an important one.

There are also plenty of defenders of big business who put the whole blame for Japanese and European stagflation on the workers. One economist makes his class viewpoint very clear: "To put the case bluntly, the British labor movement has been independent, parochial, generally oblivious to modern economic thinking, and, moreover, apparently unaware of what policies will serve its own long-run interest, much less that of the general economy."[8] Isn't it surprising that British labor, like American labor, is oblivious to that "modern economic thinking" which tells it to lower its own wages in its own interest? And since workers are 80 percent to 90 percent of the population, what is the interest of "the general economy" that is different from labor's interest? Yet some economists seem to think that the interest of the "general economy" means the interest of big business.

There is no evidence that high wages in Britain—rather than low wages and low demand—have led to Britain's current unemployment and inflation. Moreover, one serious research study shows that a long-run falling profit share in England is a myth, that the profit share (after taxes) in national income has been constant from 1950 to 1973.[9] On the contrary, there is plenty of evidence that business monopoly power *has* increased in England.

The increase of business monopoly power in western Europe is the first factor explaining stagflation there. The second factor is the policy pursued by European governments. In England it is called the *stop and go policy*. At the peak of the cycle, the government tries to stop the rise of wages by direct controls or even by general restrictive policies. In the trough of the depression, the government tries to stimulate the economy, to make profits go upward by various means. These policies, which constitute a political business cycle of capitalism, are likewise pursued by all the other western European governments.[10]

The third factor explaining stagflation is the international situation. In the following sections, we examine (1) the degree of international concentration by the multinational corporations, (2) the profits extracted by the multinational corporations from developed and less developed capitalist countries, (3) the changing power of the U.S. economy vis-à-vis western Europe and Japan, (4) the problems of trade balances and supposed shortages caused by these changes, and (5) how international problems worsen stagflation in each country.

CONCENTRATION BY
MULTINATIONAL (OR GLOBAL) FIRMS

The new degree of economic concentration of assets in the whole capitalist world by a few enormous multinational or global corporations constitutes a new structural stage for international capitalism. The term *multinational* suggests management from many countries, whereas the truth is that each firm is governed mostly by the nationals of one developed capitalist country. The term *global corporation* may be less misleading. The one proposition uniting all these corporations is the notion that the whole globe is their oyster, that vast profits may be made by control of markets in several countries.

In pursuit of profit, U.S. based global corporations have been rapidly expanding abroad. In terms of total assets of U.S. industries, by 1974 about 40 percent of all consumer goods industries, about 75 percent of the electrical industry, about 33 percent of the chemical industry, about 33 percent of the pharmaceutical industry, and over half of the $100 billion petroleum industry was located outside the United States![11] Moreover, this expansion trend has increased and perhaps accelerated in recent years. In 1957, investment in plant and equipment by U.S. firms abroad was already 9 percent of total U.S. domestic investment in plant and equipment; but by 1970 that investment abroad rose to 25 percent of domestic investment. In 1961 sales of U.S. manufacturing abroad were only 7 percent of total sales by all U.S. manufacturing corporations, but that figure rose to 13 percent by 1970. In 1960, the foreign dollar deposits of the largest U.S. banks were only 8.5 percent of domestic deposits, but by 1970 foreign deposits rose to 65 percent of domestic deposits.[12]

The pattern of ownership by foreign-owned global corporations is most striking in the less developed countries. In Chile, before Allende's socialist government, global corporations controlled at least 51 percent of the 160 largest firms. In Argentina, global corporations control more than 50 percent of the total sales of the 50 largest firms. In Mexico, global corporations control 100 percent of rubber, electrical machinery, and transportation industries. Moreover, in Mexico foreign ownership in the metal industry rose from 42 percent in 1962 to 68 percent in 1970, while foreign ownership in tobacco rose from 17 percent in 1962 to 100 percent in 1970. In Brazil, global corporations own 100 percent of automobile and tire production, while their share of machinery rose from 59 percent in 1961 to 67 percent in 1971, and their share of electrical equipment rose from 50 percent in 1961 to 68 percent in 1971.[13]

A more complex case is Canada, which invests much money in less developed countries, but is itself largely foreign owned. Thus, in 1968 in Canada 54 percent of all manufacturing industry was directly owned by foreigners, including 97 percent of automobile production, 97 percent of rubber, 78 percent of chemi-

cals, and 77 percent of electrical apparatus. In addition, foreigners owned 62 percent of mining and smelting and 64 percent of
the petroleum and natural gas industry. About 80 percent of the
foreign   ownership   was   lodged   in   U.S.   based   global
corporations.[14]

It is also important to note that many transactions within and
between capitalist countries are conducted solely between subsidiaries of the same parent corporation. A large-scale sample
found over 50 percent of total foreign trade transactions in the
capitalist world are of this nonmarket intracorporate variety between subsidiaries of the same company.[15] This means that taxes
can be shifted to those countries where the rates are lowest. It
also means that fiscal policies may not operate—or may operate
mainly to the benefit of the global giants. Several studies show
that the largest corporations in the United States absorb a disproportionate part of all government spending and tax reductions
designed to stimulate the economy.[16]

The global manufacturing corporations are serviced by
global banks with tenacles almost everywhere. At their urging,
additional credit has been created as a new currency, the $110
billion dollar pool of Euro-dollars (and the Special Drawing
Rights, which acts as currency). Since there are no reserve deposit requirements on the Euro-dollars, they are particularly unstable and contribute a strong impetus, by further credit creation,
to inflationary pressures. This international credit expansion, plus
rapid monetary flows between corporate subsidiaries across bor-
ders, makes it less possible than ever for any capitalist nation to
control its money supply by any conceivable monetary policies.

It should also be noted that union bargaining power has been
further weakened by the power of the global corporations to shift
production rapidly from areas of high wages to low wage areas.
For example, if the United States has high wages, they shift to
Mexico, and if even Mexican wages are considered too high, they
shift to Hong Kong.[17]

Finally, the international concentration of investment
decision-making in a relatively small number of corporations,
plus the very intimate ties of international trade and investment
among all the capitalist countries, bind these economies closely
together. Therefore, a contraction begun in one country, or in just
a few global corporations, spreads at lightning speed to the
others. If investor demand declines in several countries at once,
then their import trade in raw materials declines, lowering demand for exports in several other countries. If unemployment

rises in several countries at once, then their demand for consumer goods from abroad also declines. Thus the entire capitalist world tends to move in the same direction in its investment decisions as well as its demands from trading partners. This encourages either explosive expansion amidst spiraling optimistic speculations, or universal contraction amidst a downward spiral of lower profits and pessimism.

IMPERIALISM

To fully understand the present global scene, a brief historical sketch will prove very useful. Only then can one comprehend how a small number of giant corporations have come to dominate the international economy and what their impact has been.

From the fifteenth century onward, the developing capitalist economies of Europe grew economically and militarily at a rate then unparalleled in human history. From the fifteenth to the nineteenth centuries, they slowly came to dominate much of the rest of the world. They plundered, enslaved, and ruled so as to extract the maximum from their subjects.

Such havoc was created that ancient and culturally advanced civilizations disappeared, as in Peru and West Africa, and progress was set back hundreds of years by the destruction of native industries, as in India. On the other side, the plunder was so great that it constituted the main element in the formation of European capital and provided the foundation for prosperous trade and eventual industrialization.

By the end of the nineteenth century, almost all the present less developed countries were under the colonial rule of the more advanced countries. The imperialist countries invested in the colonial countries at astoundingly high profit rates, primarily because of a cheap labor supply and enforced lack of competition. The capital was invested mainly in extractive industries, which exported raw materials to the imperial country. In the imperial country, the cheap raw materials were profitably turned into manufactured goods, part of which were exported back (tariff free) to the colonial country.

The tariff-free imports of manufactured goods generally completed through competition the destruction (often begun by plunder) of the colonial country's manufacturing industries. An example of this may be seen in colonial India, especially in its textile industry:

> *India, still an exporter of manufactured products at the end of the eighteenth century, becomes an importer. From 1815 to 1832, In-*

dia's cotton exports dropped by 92 per cent. In 1850, India was buying one quarter of Britain's cotton exports. All industrial products shared this fate. The ruin of the traditional trades and crafts was the result of British commercial policy.[18]

The development of the colonial areas was thus held back by the imperialist countries, while the development of the imperialist countries was greatly speeded by the flow of plunder and profits from the colonies. The exception that proves the rule is Japan. Japan escaped colonialism as a result of several more or less accidental factors. Thus it was able independently to industrialize and develop its own advanced capitalist economy. Japan achieved this alone among the countries of Asia, Africa, and Latin America because the others had all been reduced to colonies and had their further development prevented.

The half century from 1890 to World War II was the peak period of colonialism, when all the world was divided among the western European and North American powers. In the late 1940s and 1950s, a new era began, with formal independence achieved by hundreds of millions of people throughout Asia and Africa as a result of struggles fomented by the impact of two world wars, the Russian and Chinese revolutions, and long pent-up pressures for liberation. The day of open colonialism is over, but the pattern still holds by which the ex-colonial countries export food or raw materials. In fact, the less developed countries are often dependent mainly on exports of just one product, and they still import most of their manufactured goods. Foreign investment still dominates their industries. Because of the continuance of the underlying colonial economic pattern, we are justified in describing this situation as *neocolonialism,* in spite of formal political independence.

In fact, formal independence has changed the essential economic relationships very little. On the one side are all the less developed, newly independent countries, still under foreign economic domination, still facing all the old obstacles to development. On the other side are the advanced capitalist countries, still extracting large profits from the dependent Third World. The imperialist group includes all the countries that extract profits by trade and investment. Thus it includes most of western Europe, Japan, and the United States. Neocolonial profits from the less developed countries flow even to countries like Switzerland that never held colonial power over any less developed country.

Although military power is occasionally used (as in Vietnam), most neocolonial control comes through economic and monetary penetration. This ranges from blatant forms such as subsidies and military supplies to highly complex monetary agreements. It also seems to be characteristic to grant independence to small territories, tiny divisions of former colonial domains. Thus they have no political or economic power with which to resist continued domination.

It should also be noted that the economic control often is not direct but built up in a complex pyramid. For example, some American companies directly invest in northeast Brazil. More control of that area, however, is achieved through American domination of major southern Brazilian companies, which in turn buy controlling interests in companies in the northeast. Still more control is achieved through American domination of some western European companies, which in turn own some major Brazilian firms or directly own some of the local firms in the northeast.

PROFITS AND IMPERIALISM

The multinational or global firms are the present instrument whereby enormous profits are extracted from the neocolonial countries and sent back to the imperialist countries. U.S. firms' profits from abroad were only 7 percent of total U.S. corporate profits in 1960, but rose to 30 percent by 1974.[19] The top 298 U.S. based global corporations earn 40 percent of their entire net profits overseas, and their rate of profit from abroad is much higher than their domestic profit rate. In office equipment, for example, the overseas rate was 26 percent and domestic only 9 percent. There is dramatic evidence for specific companies: In 1972, the overseas profit rate was 72 percent for United Brands, 51 percent for Parker Pen, and 53 percent for Exxon.[20]

In the neocolonial countries, the global corporations skim off a very large percentage of all profits for themselves. For example, in 1971 in Brazil the global corporations grabbed 70 percent of the total net profits of the five important sectors of rubber, motor vehicles, machinery, household appliances, and mining.[21] Moreover, much of these corporate investments are not U.S. funds at all, but are provided by local capitalists. In all of the Latin American manufacturing operations of U.S. based global corporations from 1960 to 1970, about 78 percent of the investments were financed by local funds. Yet the same corporations, between 1965 and 1968, sent 52 percent of all their profits back to the United States.[22]

As a result of the use of local funds for investment, plus high profit rates and the sending of most profits to the United States, the neocolonial or Third World countries actually have a net outflow of capital to the United States. This surprising fact has been documented by the U.S. Department of Commerce for the period 1950–1965, in which there were striking differences in the flow pattern to and from the advanced capitalist countries and to and from the less developed Third World.[23]

U.S. corporations made direct investments of $8.1 billion in Europe and transferred $5.5 billion of profit from their European investments to the United States, for a net flow of 2.6 billion U.S. dollars into this advanced capitalist area. Similarly, U.S. corporations invested $6.8 billion in Canada and extracted $5.9 billion of profit, for a net flow of 900 million U.S. dollars into that advanced capitalist area.[24]

In the less developed Third World, the situation was different. In Latin America, U.S. corporations invested $3.8 billion but extracted $11.3 billion, for a net flow of 7.5 billion U.S. dollars from that area to the United States. Yet profit rates were so great that at the same time the value of U.S. direct investments in Latin America rose from $4.5 billion to $10.3 billion. In fact in the period 1957–1964, only 12 percent of direct U.S. investment in Latin America came from the United States; 74 percent was reinvestment of profits or depreciation funds from Latin American operations. Similarly, in Africa and Asia in the period 1950–1965, American corporations invested only $5 billion but transferred to the United States $14 billion of profits, for a net flow of $9 billion to the United States. Yet enough profit remained for reinvestment so that U.S. direct investments in Africa and Asia rose from $1.3 to $4.7 billion.[25]

Two facts are blatantly obvious from these data: (1) The rate of profit in U.S. investments abroad is several times higher in the less developed than in the advanced capitalist countries, and (2) the less developed neocolonial countries generously make a good-sized contribution to U.S. capital accumulation.

STAGFLATION AND IMPERIALISM
What is the impact on the U.S. economy of the extraordinarily high profits that flow in from the neocolonial countries? When each U.S. based global firm finds and grabs a new market, its excess investment funds can now be invested abroad. Moreover, the new investment can be expected to yield high profits year after year. The problem is that for the economy as a whole, these new profits pour in from overseas faster than new investment

areas can be found for the mounting funds. This capital accumulation is in excess of the investment opportunities domestically or abroad. Therefore, in a depression the situation is worsened by adding to savings when there is already a surplus of saving beyond what can be invested profitably.

For the less developed Third World countries, the outflow of immense amounts of capital (in the form of profits) is disastrous for their growth and feeds their own peculiar type of stagflation. These neocolonial countries have long suffered the odious combination of inflation and unemployment. In September 1974 inflation rates in the advanced capitalist world averaged a high 12.6 percent, but inflation rates in the less developed capitalist countries averaged 19.1 percent.[26] The rates of unemployment in the less developed capitalist countries have been scandalous for many years, often over 30 or 40 percent of the urban labor force.

To understand their type of stagflation, it must be stressed that the less developed neocolonial countries suffer from a tremendous lack of capital. This is quite unlike the advanced capitalist countries, who usually suffer from a surplus of capital far beyond the profitable investment opportunities. Lack of capital means not only a small amount of new factory construction, but also little new equipment, very little in research funds and very slow technological improvement. Lack of capital also means few funds for the education and training of human beings, the most important lack in the long run.

The Third World countries lack capital because of the institutional-structural arrangements within most of them and vis-à-vis the capitalist world. First, most have an internal ruling class that spends much of its income on luxuries, spends government revenues on unnecessary public monuments or on vast military establishments, and banks much of its wealth in Switzerland or the United States. Second, most of them have very poor terms of trade for large parts of each business cycle, because prices of raw materials from the Third World fall much faster in depressions than prices of finished goods from the advanced capitalist world. Thus in the 1973–1975 depression prices of most raw materials rose very slowly (with the partial exception of oil prices), while prices of finished goods went sky high.

Finally, as shown above, the outflow of profits and interest from the Third World countries is much, much larger than the flow of foreign investment into them. For all these reasons there is a horrendous lack of plant and equipment, a lack of technological progress, and a lack of highly trained workers.

The lack of plant and equipment means that millions and millions of workers have little or nothing with which to work. Therefore, these millions cannot be profitably employed. Since the rate of profit would be insufficient, these millions of human beings are left unemployed. Because it is due to lack of capital, this unemployment continues even in the face of demand for products and severe shortages leading to inflation.

The stagflation in the less developed capitalist world is thus characterized by lack of capital, while stagflation in the advanced capitalist world is characterized by surplus capital. This difference is reflected in the fact that mass unemployment of workers in the advanced capitalist countries is accompanied by high rates of nonutilization of capital (idle machines and factories).[27] Mass unemployment of workers in the less developed capitalist countries, on the contrary, often coexists with full utilization of their tiny supply of capital plant and equipment.

Of course, stagflation in the neocolonial countries is worsened by their dependent position. The global corporations generally have little competition and exercise their monopoly power to keep prices of goods within these countries high even during global depressions. Moreover, the global corporations often reduce all their investments during a depression (though not as much as competitive firms must do), but they continue to extract and return to their home countries as much profit as possible throughout the depression, thus intensifying the lack of capital. Finally, it is worth repeating that the raw material products of the Third World suffer the greatest price declines or the smallest price rises in depression periods, so they bear a considerable part of the international burden of the slump.

RISE AND DECLINE
OF THE U.S. EMPIRE

Until the Civil War, American capitalism was far behind European capitalism. It had the advantage, however, of having no feudal or semi-feudal encumbrances. After the Civil War, it also abolished slavery and opened the whole country to capitalism. Moreover, the U.S. economy was relatively short of labor, so it was forced to use the most advanced technology. As a result, U.S. industrialization proceeded very rapidly after 1870, and it eventually overtook and passed British and other European industry. Finally, the two world wars devastated much of Europe, but stimulated the U.S. economy. By 1945 the United States emerged completely dominant in the capitalist world.

Between 1945 and 1950 the U.S. Gross Domestic Product (GDP) was equal to that of the whole rest of the world combined. Thus in 1950 the French GDP was only 10 percent of the American, West Germany's only 8 percent, Italy's only 5 percent, Japan's only 4 percent, the United Kingdom's only 13 percent—and all five only 39 percent of the American GDP. In 1950, the United States produced 82 percent of all the world's passenger vehicles, produced 55 percent of the world's steel production, and consumed 50 percent of the world's energy consumption.[28]

Throughout this period U.S. firms also extended their control over much of European industry. By 1965 American firms or their subsidiaries owned 80 percent of computer production, 24 percent of the motor industry, 15 percent of the synthetic rubber industry, and 10 percent of the production of petrochemicals *within* the entire European Common Market. Furthermore, it is well to remember how concentrated this ownership is. About 40 percent of all U.S. direct investment in Britain, France, and Germany is owned by Ford, General Motors, and Standard Oil of New Jersey.[29]

American firms have maintained a relative superiority over western European firms because of (1) greater size of capital assets and (2) greater technological advances. The size advantage of U.S. corporations is indicated by the fact that, of the hundred largest global corporations, 65 are based in the United States, 11 in the United Kingdom, 18 in other Common Market nations, and 5 in Japan. Because they have greater size and financial power, U.S. firms are able to do more technological research. Furthermore, the continued enormous U.S. military spending has subsidized much technological research for U.S. firms. U.S. spending on research per capita is still three to four times European research spending. Finally, the United States has drained away many of the best brains in Europe (after they were trained in Europe). Between 1949 and 1967, about 100,000 of the best doctors, scientists and technicians left western Europe for the United States.[30]

In spite of all these initial and continuing advantages, the absolute superiority of the U.S. economy in world production has slowly faded away. It was restricted and then reduced by three main factors. First, the Soviet Union broke away from the capitalist world in 1917 and has steadily gained on the U.S. economy since the late 1920s. Despite the one awful hiatus of the Second World War, Soviet production now rivals the U.S. total.

Second, the old colonial empires were overthrown at the end

of World War II. At first, the new "independent" neocolonial countries turned to the U.S. economy for aid and investment, so U.S. power expanded further. Later, however, wars of liberation (as in Vietnam) spread and were focused against the United States as the main policeman of imperialism.

Lastly, as a counterweight to the Communist countries and the increasing resistance of the Third World, the United States was forced to give strong support to the rebuilding of the capitalist economies of Japan and western Europe. These economies began in 1945 with a skilled labor force but devastated factories. As their industry was rebuilt from scratch, they used the latest technology and began the long march to catch up with the U.S. economy. Whereas the data show that the United States ruled supreme in the early 1950s, it was being challenged by the growing power and competition of Japan and western Europe in every market by the early 1970s.

The United States was still the largest, but it no longer was far larger than the combination of all the rest. Thus, by 1972 the French gross domestic product (GDP) had risen to 17 percent of American GDP, West Germany's rose to 22 percent, Italy's rose to 10 percent, Japan's rose incredibly to 24 percent, the United Kingdom's to 14 percent—all five of these together now had a GDP equal to 86 percent of American GDP. In specific areas of basic production, the U.S. share of the world total fell between 1950 and 1972 from 82 to 29 percent of passenger vehicles, from 55 to 20 percent of steel production, and from 50 to 33 percent of world energy production. The competitive position of Japan and western Europe was also strengthened by the fact that their productivity per labor-hour, especially Japanese productivity, rose much faster than U.S. productivity. On the other hand, Japanese and west European wage levels also rose faster than U.S. wage levels, which hurt their competitive position a little, but they are still somewhat lower than U.S. wage levels.[31]

BALANCE OF PAYMENTS PROBLEM
Problems with the U.S. balance of payments have arisen largely because of the resistance of the Third World and the increasing competition of Japanese and west European capitalists. To demonstrate this, we must understand what the balance of payments is and how it works.

Suppose a U.S. firm exports $1000 worth of Coca Cola to Germany. Then the German importer sells the Coca Cola for deutschemarks (DMs), say for DM 4000. If the exchange rate is

$1 = 4 DM, then the importer buys $1000 U.S. dollars with the 4000 DMs, and pays the U.S. exporter $1000 dollars. Suppose at the same time a U.S. importer imports beer worth 4000 DM from Germany. The U.S. importer sells the beer for $1000 U.S. dollars (or more). Then the U.S. importer buys 4000 DM for $1000 U.S. dollars, and pays 4000 DM to the German beer firm. In this case, both sides are satisfied, the trade between the two countries is in balance, and the monetary exchanges balance.

There are two reasons why this example worked out so neatly. First, the demand for *foreign exchange* (which is generally what foreign currencies are called) was exactly equal to the supply of foreign exchange. The demand for foreign exchange, it should be noted, arose from the import of foreign goods, while the supply of foreign exchange arose from the export of domestic goods. Second, the supply of and demand for foreign exchange were equal because the *exchange rate* at which dollars could be converted was $1 = 4 DM. There are, then, two important considerations in the financing of foreign transactions: (1) the number and magnitude of transactions giving rise to a demand for and supply of foreign exchange and (2) the rate at which dollars can be converted to foreign exchange, or the exchange rate between American dollars and the various foreign currencies. Each of these must be considered.

We begin by taking the exchange rate as given and examining the international transactions that give rise to a demand for and supply of foreign exchange. The *balance of payments* is a systematic accounting of all such transactions for one country for a given period, usually one year. Transactions are aggregated into different categories. The *current account* records all sales and purchases of goods and services between Americans and foreigners.

Table 10.1 summarizes the U.S. current account for 1970. All items on the left side of the table are transactions that created a supply of foreign exchange. The transactions listed on the right side created a demand for foreign exchange. From the current account transactions in 1970, the United States earned $6.9 billion more foreign exchange than it spent. How did the U.S. economy achieve this favorable balance in its current account? We must examine three paired items: (1) imports and exports, (2) U.S. and foreign transport costs, and (3) U.S. and foreign investments.

In 1970 the United States exported more than it imported, a favorable situation (for money flowing in) which has existed in

TABLE 10.1 CURRENT ACCOUNT OF U.S. BALANCE OF PAYMENTS FOR 1970 (IN BILLIONS OF DOLLARS)

Transactions that Created a Supply of Foreign Exchange		Transactions that Created a Demand for Foreign Exchange	
U.S. exports of merchandise	$42.0	U.S. imports of merchandise	$39.9
Foreign purchases of U.S. transportation, insurance, and other private services	9.8	U.S. purchases of foreign transportation, insurance, and other private services	9.5
U.S. income from private foreign investments	9.6	Foreign income from private investments in the U.S.	5.1
Total	$61.4		$54.5
Net balance	$ 6.9		

SOURCE: *Federal Reserve Bulletin*, April 1971, p. 270.

almost every year of the twentieth century. The gap, however, was much smaller in the early 1970s than it had been in the 1950s. In the 1950s the U.S. economy had done most of the exporting and little importing; and all other countries complained of dollar shortages needed to pay for their imports. By 1970 the flows of merchandise were more equal. Thus Japanese exports were only 2 percent of U.S. exports in 1948, but rose to 58 percent in 1972. Exports of the European economic community rose from 53 percent of U.S. exports in 1948 to 254 percent in 1972. Even exports of the Communist countries rose from 30 percent of U.S. exports in 1948 to 79 percent in 1969.[32]

Secondly, U.S. firms supplied slightly more transport and other services to foreigners than vice versa. The gap here has also narrowed, but it is a smaller item. Finally, U.S. income from private investments abroad—profits and interest—is far higher than the income of foreigners from investments in the U.S. economy.

Unfortunately, as Table 10.2 shows, there are other transactions influencing the balance of payments. For one thing, the outflow of money into U.S. investments abroad is a little higher than the inflow of foreign investments to the United States (but remember the offsetting profit flows). Most important are the military items. U.S. firms bring in some money by selling military

TABLE 10.2 REMAINDER OF U.S. BALANCE OF PAYMENTS FOR 1970 (IN BILLIONS OF DOLLARS)

Transactions that Created a Supply of Foreign Exchange		Transactions that Created a Demand for Foreign Exchange	
Net balance carried forward from current account	$ 6.9	Remittances and pensions (net)	$ 1.4
Military sales	1.5	Military purchases abroad	4.8
Foreign investment in U.S.	4.4	U.S. government grants and investments abroad	3.5
		U.S. private investments abroad	6.4
		Change in U.S. liabilities to commercial banks abroad	6.5
		Errors and omissions	.9
Total	$12.8		$23.5
Net balance		($23.5 − $12.8 =)	$10.7

SOURCE: *Federal Reserve Bulletin*, April 1971, p. 270.

supplies to other countries. Far larger, however, is the outflow of U.S. government money for military purchases abroad and military and economic aid to an assortment of dictators abroad. These are the two largest items causing the deficit, since they are only slightly offset by military sales. On the other hand, private investments abroad are offset by foreigners' investments here and by the large inflow of private profits.

This outflow of money for military purposes is obviously linked to U.S. opposition to the liberation movements of the Third World. The United States has spent $1.4 trillion on militarism since 1945 at home and abroad.[33] This staggering burden has been a major factor in causing both inflation at home and balance of payments difficulties abroad.

THE INTERNATIONAL MONETARY CRISIS
Because the United States spends more abroad each year than it takes in, this payment deficit must somehow be balanced in the foreign arena. The deficit was actually made up in two ways. The United States paid out gold, and foreigners were forced to extend low-cost loans to Americans.

The first way, the drain of U.S. gold stock to foreign countries, is easy to understand. When U.S. corporations and the U.S. government spend more abroad than they earn from trade and investments, then some of the difference is paid in gold. In 1945, the United States had 75 percent of the world's gold reserves. But two-thirds of that gold stock has now fled abroad. By 1968 American reserves had fallen to only $15 billion, or less than the $24 billion of the European economic community alone.[34]

The second source for financing excess foreign investments has been cheap foreign loans. To understand why foreigners must make these loans, consider the role of the American dollar in the financing of international transactions. Since every country has a different currency and some of the currencies have unstable values, it is necessary to have a currency with which to conduct international business. The American dollar is used far more extensively than any other currency for this purpose. The American dollar is, then, the currency of which other countries must keep a balance in order to facilitate their foreign financial transactions, just as the individual must keep a small balance of currency to finance his day-to-day transactions.

But the worldwide volume of international transactions has grown rapidly and continuously since World War II. This means other countries have been forced continuously to build up their American dollar bank balances. If U.S. currency were not the international medium of exchange, foreigners would immediately demand that the dollars be taken back in exchange for more U.S. exports or for gold. These commodity exports or gold exports would represent the *real* payment for the foreign resources U.S. corporations have taken over. But because foreign countries must continuously build up American dollar balances if they are to continue to engage in international transactions, they are forced to keep them. This means they get no real payment for the resources they hand over to U.S. corporations. They are in effect extending low-cost loans that need never be repaid as long as the American dollar is the international medium of exchange.

By 1972, foreigners in the rest of the world held 82 billion U.S. dollars.[35] They were accepted because the dollar is used in international trade and was allegedly as good as gold. But the strength of the dollar was declining, both because of the gold and dollar drain outward and because of U.S. inflation. Fewer U.S. goods could be bought with a dollar, so there was pressure for a lower exchange rate of dollars to other currency.

Although U.S. businessmen and the U.S. government had

spent too many dollars abroad, the United States tried to maintain a fixed rate of exchange and to force foreigners to hold on to large reserves of dollars. In 1968 and again in early 1971, attempts by foreigners to convert their dollar holdings into gold or into other currencies created minor crises. Throughout the 1960s and early 1970s, it had been obvious that the size of the recurring American balance-of-payments deficit was too large. This meant U.S. currency was *overvalued*—that is, in order to make the deficit manageable, the value of the U.S. dollar should be decreased. Otherwise, the value of undervalued currencies such as the German DM or the Japanese yen should be increased.

The problem with removing the fixed exchange rate for dollars was that in 1970 foreigners held $43.3 billion in American dollars.[36] If the value of the American dollar were decreased by 10 percent, these foreigners would suddenly lose the equivalent of about $4.33 billion. This large amount of wealth would simply evaporate. Consequently, if foreigners received the slightest hint that the American dollar was about to be devalued, they immediately sought to exchange their dollars for gold or other currencies before the devaluation could take place.

In the 1968 and early 1971 crises, the governments of the United States and the western European countries succeeded in convincing dollar holders that the exchange value of the dollar would be maintained. This averted a major crisis, but the problem remained. If the United States continued to spend lavishly on a worldwide military empire and continued to attempt to extend its worldwide economic hegemony, then the pressure of foreigners attempting to convert unwanted dollar balances into gold or other currencies would constantly present the threat of a worldwide run on the dollar any time the fear of devaluation became widespread. Most economists agreed that if such a run on American dollars were to develop, the international monetary structure would collapse. If this were to occur, foreign trade would undoubtedly be drastically reduced, as it was after the international financial crisis of the early 1930s.

In the face of these dangers President Nixon took drastic action on August 15, 1971. The fact that America's exports were substantially less than its imports for the first time in many years precipitated extreme policy measures. In order to end America's persistent balance-of-payments deficit, the president did three things. First, he imposed a 10 percent tariff surcharge. In order to reduce demand for imports, Americans were forced to pay 10 percent more for all imported foreign goods. Second, the president announced a 90-day wage-price freeze (with wages frozen but leaving profits free to increase). This was designed mainly for domestic effects, but its foreign effect was to make American exports more competitive in foreign markets.

The third and most extreme measure taken by the president was to sever the direct link between the American dollar and gold. The American dollar had maintained a fixed exchange rate with other currencies by maintaining a fixed price of gold. Since the value of gold in terms of other currencies was also fixed, this fixed the exchange rates between any two currencies. For example, if gold costs 35 American dollars per ounce and also 15 British pounds per ounce, then the price (in American dollars) of one British pound would be fixed at $2.33.

When the president cut the tie between gold and the American dollar, the United States no longer had a fixed exchange rate. The value of the dollar in relation to other currencies was allowed to fluctuate according to supply and demand.

It soon became apparent, however, that other countries were unwilling to allow their currencies to appreciate substantially in relation to the American dollar. The entire capitalist world was experiencing a recession during this period, and a decline in the value of the American dollar would stimulate demand for American exports because they would now cost foreigners less of their own currency. This increased export demand would add to aggregate demand in the United States and help us pull out of our recession. But by the same reasoning, an upward revaluation of foreign currencies in relation to the American dollar would decrease the exports of these countries to the United States because they would cost Americans more dollars than before. The decreased demand for their exports would decrease aggregate demand in these countries, worsening the problems of recession and unemployment.

By December 18, 1971, the American dollar had depreciated by over 10 percent. That meant, of course, that holders of American dollars had lost nearly $4 billion because of the dollar's depreciated value. Resistance to further depreciation had stiffened appreciably, so the United States returned to a fixed exchange rate on that date.

Over the next year and a half, it required extensive intervention in the foreign exchange market by various governments and central banks to maintain that fixed exchange rate. It became increasingly obvious that some fundamental realignment of currency values was needed. By early 1973, the economic situation in the capitalist world had changed from one in which recession and unemployment were the principal problems to one in which rapid inflation was the main concern. The United States took advantage of this economic change and in March 1973 announced that once again the dollar was to be allowed to fluctuate according to supply and demand.

Since that time the dollar has dropped in value in a number of periods. Yet the U.S. government and other governments have also worked to stabilize it. Moreover, when the European economies themselves weakened in the stagflation of 1974–1975, their currencies did not remain stronger than the dollar.

It is important to understand the domestic impact of these international payments and monetary problems. When different capitalist countries wish to help their firms compete for the export market, they traditionally do this by lowering wage costs. Wages may be held down by direct controls a la Nixon, or by increasing unemployment through restrictive monetary and fiscal controls. Real wages may also be reduced by lowering the exchange value of the dollar or by higher tariffs, in either case causing higher prices for imported goods. The idea of the Nixon-Ford administration has been to end the international U.S. payments deficit by selling U.S. goods more cheaply on the basis of lower wages, or by forcing U.S. consumers to buy fewer imports (German beer or small foreign cars) through higher prices for these goods. Thus the international problems are seen as constraints or excuses for greater burdens on American workers in the shape of lower wages and unemployment as well as more inflation. The inflationary policy is particularly evident in President Ford's efforts to increase oil prices.

SHORTAGES

International shortages—that is, supply less than demand at present prices—certainly played a part in the inflationary spiral. These shortages, however, were not natural accidents (except in a few minor cases) nor were they acts of God; they were clearly contrived by human actors. In the case of food and fuels, the two most important categories, conservatives have blamed Soviet wheat buyers and Arab oil sheiks.

The evidence, however, indicates that the blame for the oil "shortage" must be placed much closer to home than Arabia. One careful investigator writes indignantly that it is hypocritical to blame the raw material producing countries for inflation. He stresses the fact that:

> the major imperialist powers control the marketing of raw materials—so that even when nationalizations are undertaken, profits are not seriously threatened. But most of the world's raw materials continue to be owned by the major imperialist monopolies, above all by U.S. firms.[37]

For many decades, U.S. and western European based global corporations controlled all the oil production, and made astonishingly high rates of profit. In the late 1960s and early 1970s, it was those global corporations that decided to restrict the expansion of supply—by reducing oil exploration or the building of new refineries, as discussed in Chapter 8—and thereby created an artificial shortage designed to raise prices. The Arab oil embargo was used as an excuse to make rapid price increases.

It is true that in recent years some of the oil-producing countries have taken larger shares of revenue by taxes or even by nationalization. They were able to do this by the increased power of the whole Third World and the Communist countries, so this does represent a shift of power that accounts for some small part of the U.S. and western European inflation. It has meant the rise of a new ruling class in the Arab countries, Iran, and Venezuela that is a peculiar combination of semi-feudal attitudes, capitalist production, and some financial capitalist power—though they still act closely in coordination with the global corporations to the benefit of both parties.

Nor have the global corporations lost much, if anything; they are simply getting some new stockholders and new forms. Most of the production and financing companies in the oil-producing countries are not publicly owned even today (and most other raw materials are purely private). For example, in Kuwait one investment company is 25 percent privately owned and the other is 50 percent privately owned, with about half the private stock being foreign owned.[38] But even if production is all nationalized, the fact—as pointed out in the quotation above—is that the global corporations continue to control all the distribution and marketing of oil. Therefore, it is the global corporations who set the market prices, determine their profit margins, and continue to make enormous profits.

There are several facts indicating that the Arab oil boycott was nothing more than an excuse for the monopolies to raise prices. First, 60 percent of U.S. oil is produced at home and is unaffected by Arab production costs, yet the price of U.S. crude oil rose from $3.50 to $7.00 a barrel. Second, from March 1973 to March 1974 Arab oil producers raised their taxes by 17 cents a barrel, but U.S. gasoline prices rose almost 30 cents a gallon for all gas, regardless of origin. Third, the U.S. government allows the oil companies to deduct all payments to foreign governments from their U.S. taxes, so this cost was passed on to all other U.S. taxpayers (in addition to passing it on to consumers at the pump). Finally, the minute the embargo was over, the companies suddenly found large reserves of oil on hand, so they didn't need to buy any more, but did not lower the prices.[39]

The high price of U.S. food was blamed on a shortage created by sales to the Soviet Union. Yet the main blame seems to fall on agribusiness and the U.S. government. First of all, for many years the U.S. government paid large farm subsidies to get farmers *not* to plant food over large areas of the best farmland. "As late as 1973, after the shortages of 1972, the government was still paying over $3 billion to keep roughly 50 million productive acres out of farming use."[40] Then, when deficits in the balance of payments became a problem, the U.S. government reversed itself and tried to stimulate production, not for domestic consumption, but for exports. The government encouraged the export of food as fast and as fully as possible in order to get foreign currency to pay for U.S. investment and military spending abroad. Thus, exports of U.S. food on the world market tripled between 1969 and 1973 as a result of careful planning by agribusiness and the government.[41] Of this enormous planned outflow of food for profit, the Soviet wheat deal formed a very minor part even of the sales of wheat.

In conclusion, the inflation and the so-called shortages have several not surprising bases. The inflation was not caused by accidental natural calamities because these tend to even out over a few years time. The inflation, however, has not evened out, but has picked up over some years. A small part was caused by a shift in power toward the Arab ruling classes away from the oil companies. But this was fairly minor and cannot account for the long inflation. Most of the inflation and "shortages" were caused by the global monopolies in collusion with the U.S. government, begun by the Vietnam War spending and always made worse by the continued excessive outflow of money for military purchases and military aid abroad.

NOTES

1. "Organization for Economic Cooperation and Development," reported in *Newsweek* (Sept. 15, 1975), p. 57.
2. "Worldwide Depression Policies," *Riverside Press-Enterprise* (Sept. 14, 1975), pp. A2, A4.
3. Joe Bain, *International Differences in Industrial Structure* (New Haven: Yale University Press, 1966), p. 130.
4. P. Sargent Florence, "Stagflation in Great Britain," in John Blair, ed., *Roots of Inflation* (New York: Franklin, 1975), p. 88.
5. Data and quote from French National Institute of Statistical and Economic Studies, reported in Joel Dirlam, "The Process of Inflation in France," in Blair, op. cit., p. 114.
6. See H. W. de Jong, "Experience Within the European Economic Community," in Blair, op. cit., p. 187.
7. Yoshihiro Kobayashi, "Movements of Price and Profit in the Periods of Rapid Growth in the Japanese Economy," *Economic Studies Quarterly* (August 1971), in Japanese.
8. Florence, op. cit., p. 76.
9. M. A. King, "The United Kingdom Profits Crisis: Myth or Reality," *The Economic Journal*, vol. 85 (March 1975), pp. 33–54.
10. See the description of the most recent depression policies country by country in "World-wide Depression Policies," *Riverside Press-Enterprise* (Sept. 14, 1975), pp. A2, A4.
11. See Richard Barnet and Ronald Muller, *Global Reach* (New York: Simon & Schuster, 1974), p. 17.
12. Ronald Muller, "Global Corporations and National Stabilization Policy," *Journal of Economic Issues*, vol. 9 (June 1975), pp. 183–184.
13. Barnet and Muller, op. cit., p. 147.
14. Canadian Privy Council Report, *Task Force on the Structure of Canadian Industry* (Ottawa: Queens Printer, January 1968).
15. See Muller, op. cit., p. 194.
16. See ibid., p. 188 and his footnote 6.
17. See Barnet and Muller, op. cit., Chapters 10 and 11.
18. Charles Bettleheim, *India Independent* (New York: Monthly Review Press, 1968), p. 47. Also see Romesh Dutt, *The Economic History of England*, 7th ed., (Boston: Routledge & Kegan Paul, 1950), pp. viii–x.
19. Muller, op. cit., p. 183.
20. Barnet and Muller, op. cit., pp. 16–17.
21. Ibid., p. 147.
22. Ibid., p. 153.
23. U.S. Department of Commerce, *United States Business Investments in Foreign Countries* (Washington, D.C.: Government Printing Office, 1970), p. 85.

24. Ibid., p. 86.

25. Ibid., p. 87.

26. First National City Bank of New York, *Monthly Economic Letter* (September 1974).

27. There is a detailed description of the underutilization of capacity in the United States and western Europe in Ernest Mandel, *Europe vs. America: Contradictions of Imperialism* (New York: Monthly Review Press, 1970), p. 145.

28. Albert Syzmanski, "The Decline and Fall of the U.S. Eagle," in David Mermelstein, *The Economic Crisis Reader* (New York: Random House (Vintage Books), 1975), pp. 65–70.

29. Mandel, op. cit., pp. 22–23.

30. Data and most of the ideas for this section on "Rise and Decline of the American Empire" come from Ibid., pp. 30–43.

31. Syzmanski, op. cit., pp. 66–69.

32. Ibid., p. 70.

33. Sidney Lens, "The Shortage Economy," in Mermelstein, op. cit., p. 107.

34. Mandel, op. cit., p. 95; also Lens, op. cit., p. 107.

35. Lens, op. cit., p. 107.

36. *Federal Reserve Bulletin* (Washington, D.C.: Government Printing Office, April 1971), p. 270.

37. Dick Roberts, "Ripening Conditions for Worldwide Depression," in Mermelstein, op. cit., p. 97.

38. Ernest Mandel, "The Emergence of Arab and Iranian Finance Capital," in Mermelstein, op. cit., p. 316.

39. Dave Pugh and Mitch Zimmerman, "The 'Energy Crisis' And the Real Crisis Behind It," in Mermelstein, op. cit., pp. 278–279.

40. Union for Radical Political Economics, National Food Collective, "The Capitalist Food System," in Mermelstein, op. cit., p. 357.

41. Ibid., p. 359.

11
WHAT IS TO BE DONE? THE NEED FOR SOCIALISM AND DEMOCRACY

Previous chapters have demonstrated the need for a drastic change away from the present capitalist system: Chapter 1 illustrated the vast extent of unemployment under the present capitalist system in the United States, and later chapters indicated the same high unemployment rates throughout the capitalist world. Chapter 1 also illustrated the enormous amount of price inflation under capitalism, and Chapter 8 proved that most of this inflation is traceable to the existence of monopoly power.

Chapter 7 found that monopoly power rises inevitably from capitalist competition in which the big fish eat the little fish. Chapters 2 and 3 discussed the very unequal income distribution in the United States, ranging from a few very wealthy individuals to a very large number of families living under the official poverty level. Chapters 3, 4, and 5 proved that the phenomenon of cyclical large-scale unemployment is inherent in the capitalist system, and so cannot be completely eliminated without eliminating that system. Chapter 1 showed the much higher rates of unemployment among women, blacks, and other minority groups. Other radical studies have shown that the high unemployment and low

wages for working members of these groups is caused by discrimination and that the discrimination and prejudice is supported by the capitalist class, which increases its profits from
these sources.[1]

Chapter 9 demonstrated that the U.S. government, like the
governments of western Europe and Japan, is dominated by the
capitalist class and its representatives. As a consequence, this
government takes economic measures in the interest of big business and contrary to the interests of small business, farmers,
white collar workers, blue collar workers, and all other workers.
Specifically, the U.S. government will stimulate demand in a
deep depression, but will actually work to produce a little unemployment when full employment threatens higher wages and less
control over workers. Specifically, the regulatory agencies regulate in the interests of big business, not the consumers or the
workers; antitrust laws are seldom enforced, except against up-
start businesses which do not follow the rules of the game; and
wage-price controls must always mean strict controls over wages,
with little control over business prices.

The same giant monopoly corporations that control the U.S.
government, charge high prices, and cause drastically lower employment, have now extended their operations worldwide. In the
underdeveloped capitalist countries, from Vietnam to Angola,
they have extracted enormous profits. These high profits transmit-
ted back to the United States or other capitalist countries resulted
in very low rates of growth and misery in the underdeveloped
countries, eventually involving U.S. forces in armed attempts to
hold back movements of national liberation.

For all these reasons and others, such as the pollution of the
environment caused by capitalist greed for profits,[2] we must get
rid of this economic system.

EXISTING SO-CALLED SOCIALIST SYSTEMS

All radicals agree on the need for socialism, but there are
many conflicting versions of what socialism means. In my view,
and that of most U.S. radicals, none of the existing countries that
calls itself socialist has the kind of system we want for the United
States. On one extreme is the Swedish system, which has as
much or more of the forms of democracy than the United States,
but has very little public ownership of the economy. At the other
extreme, the Soviet Union has almost complete government
ownership of the economy, but little or no democratic control of

the government. Notice that public ownership and government ownership may be two very different things: Socialist public ownership, then, by definition, means government ownership, but it also means that *the people own the government* through the democratic political process. In this definition, the Soviet Union is not democratic, so neither is it socialist.

The Soviet Union has:

1. government ownership
2. national economic planning
3. wages according to work done (while private profit, rent, or interest are illegal)
4. a dictatorship running the government through a single party and a small self-perpetuating group at the top of the party.

Because the Soviet Union has government ownership and national planning, it has no general unemployment, no cycles of boom and bust, and a steady growth.[3] In fact, it has a shortage of labor because the planners are always too optimistic about the number of projects that can be accomplished. It suffered extreme inflation in its early industrialization and in the Second World War; since that time, however, it has had *no* inflation. At times, when consumer goods fell short of the planned amount, there have been some inflationary pressures expressed in long lines of customers, but the Soviet Union has succeeded in having constant or actually lower prices in most years.

Soviet income distribution is far more equal than U.S. income distribution because of the lack of private profits, interest, or rental income; but the spread of their wage and salary income is still very considerable, being about the same as that in the United States. In addition, there is always the question as to what the wages of the top leadership really are and whether they are paid strictly for their labor. The wages of the top leadership are decided by the top leadership themselves and are kept secret. Therefore, we properly suspect that the Soviet leadership practice some exploitation of Soviet workers for their own benefit, but the top leadership group is so small (ten or fifteen at most) that this exploitation must be on a much smaller scale than the billions of dollars that U.S. corporations take away from U.S. workers.

It is also to the credit of the Soviet Union that there are lower levels of racist and sexist discrimination than in the United States, lower levels of environmental pollution, and no private profits flowing in from investments in the neocolonial world. These strengths are due to the lack of private economic profit from any of these sources. The fact that some prejudice and discrimination still exists is due to the fact that some political leaders have found it advantageous to play up the racist prejudices, such as Stalin's anti-Jewish propaganda, and the fact that the dictatorship allows no independent movements such as an autonomous women's movement. The fact that some pollution exists is related to the drive of the political leadership at every level for production successes to bolster their prestige. It is easy to put environmental protection on a low level when no independent movements of consumers are allowed.

The Soviet Union has engaged in imperialist attempts to dominate other countries, as in eastern Europe. This has not been done for direct economic gain in most cases, since no individual can receive foreign profits and the country as a whole has as many expenses in keeping an empire as it is able to extract from it. The domination of other countries results rather from the drive of the top political-military leadership to bolster its own power and prestige. They are able to do this in a situation where there can be no democratic control or anti-militarist movements against the government.

If the Soviet Union allowed more democratic participation in decision-making, it would have less discrimination, less pollution, and fewer attempts to dominate other countries (such as Czechoslovakia). If the Soviet Union were more democratic, it would have wider discussion of economic shortcomings and correction of bureaucratic mistakes. If the Soviet Union were more democratic, Stalin could not have jailed hundreds of thousands of people for political opposition nor could he have "legally" murdered thousands of people.

WHAT IS TO BE DONE IMMEDIATELY?

The lessons to be drawn from this book—in depth on the United States and briefly on the Soviet Union—indicate the need in the long run for a socialist democracy. What can radicals reasonably fight for in the short run in the United States?

In spite of the propaganda saturation in favor of capitalism, a remarkable number of Americans dislike capitalism. A 1975 opinion poll by Hart Research Associates found that 32 percent believe the capitalist system is beyond its peak and is declining, while only 22 percent think it is still improving. Moreover, the poll found 41 percent in favor of a drastic change in the economic system, 37 percent in favor of minor reforms, and only 17 percent for the status quo. Furthermore, 49 percent think big business is the source of most of our economic problems, while a majority believe that both major parties put the interests of big business above those of the average voter.[4]

There are also a number of reforms that Democratic liberals are willing to support under pressure from the working class. First, there is a real chance to pass a law guaranteeing full employment and jobs to everyone, with the government as an employer of last resort. This is an impossible bill to fully enforce under capitalism, but the struggle to enforce it would lead many people to see the need for socialism. Secondly, 45 senators voted for a bill in 1975 to break up the oil companies into somewhat smaller pieces. While such a bill would accomplish little even if it passed and were enforced, it does show the depth of sentiment against the oil companies.

There have also been some recent struggles and victories for municipal ownership of public utilities. Again, this doesn't accomplish too much under capitalism because the private energy corporations still control most of the supplies of power to the municipal utilities. Yet even under an overall capitalist system a 1974 study did find a benefit in municipal ownership. The study found that the average cost of 1000 kwh of electric power to the consumer was $13.48 by privately owned utilities and only $11.02 by municipally owned utilities. Moreover, the municipally owned utilities included $1.26 of retained earnings in that cost, but such retained earnings are public funds, so the actual municipal cost could be said to be only $9.76 per 1000 kwh.[5]

Finally, going beyond limited reforms, a poll of participants at a liberal Democratic party forum to meet the presidential candidates in Los Angeles in November 1975 found that 90 percent of the participants (*not* the candidates) supported public ownership of the whole energy industry.[6] Radicals, therefore, will find wide support for the proposition: *the people* (through Congress) *should take over the oil companies*. This is now a viable political slogan with wide support; even George Meany supported it in one speech.

Of course, public ownership of one industry can have only a limited effect so long as most of the economy is under capitalist domination. For example, the Tennessee Valley Authority was a great radical achievement which brought cheaper power to that region. Yet today corporate interests appear to control TVA in the same way they control most government agencies:

> *TVA . . . has become the world's largest user of strip-mined coal, and it has resisted citizen efforts to make it use coal scrubbers. Also TVA's agricultural aid programs have disproportionately helped the wealthy farmers, and its low rates have been especially important to industry.*[7]

Thus, TVA has encouraged environmental destruction and has subsidized big business in the surrounding area.

There is also a tendency for capitalist governments to willingly nationalize industry only in the most backward and bankrupt sectors. For example, the U.S. government is giving enormous subsidies to the railroads, while Amtrak has taken over the least profitable operations. If the government takes over all the bankrupt railroads, this will be done to give another subsidy to the corporations that use rail transport. It will not be a good test of the performance of public ownership.

Even more suspicious are the current moves—supported by Rockefeller—to set up an apparatus for national planning. All such planning in capitalist countries, from Hitler Germany in the 1930s to present-day Labor England, has been planning in the interest of big business, not labor or consumers.

WHAT IS TO BE
DONE IN THE LONG RUN?

The long-run goal of radicals is a democratic socialist system. Socialism in the United States could be achieved for the most part by the national expropriation and ownership of the 1000 largest corporations. These corporate giants control about two-thirds of all corporate assets, sales, and profits. There is no need to nationalize the corner grocery store if it is family-run.

If a corporation is nationalized, exactly who should control it? Surely a large measure of control should be given to our duly elected democratic government. This would extend democracy into the economic sphere. If a corporation is purely on a local scale, then local government would have most control. On a state scale, state government would have a major role. For most corporations that are on a national scale, the national government must play the largest role. For those corporations that operate on an international scale, we may hope that someday a democratic socialist world government would run them.

To return to the near future, it would be sensible for the 1000 largest U.S. corporations to have 50 or 51 percent of their boards of directors appointed by local, state, or federal government. The other 49 or 50 percent of the boards of directors could be elected by the workers in each enterprise. The demand for workers' control of corporate enterprises strikes a sympathetic chord in many American workers. It is already a central demand of the European labor movement.

Workers' control is another important aspect of economic democracy. Why should local workers not elect *all* the board of directors? The fact is that the interests of workers in a specific plant are not identical to the interests of the whole working class. To take one example, if General Motors' workers ran all of GM to their own benefit, would they pay enough attention to the reduction of automobile pollution? Moreover, some of the surplus or profits of each enterprise must be used for collective consumption, such as free local or national health care and education.

Once the economic power of the 1000 largest corporations is totally eliminated from the political scene—by giving their assets to the workers and the whole public—our government would be very much changed. Big business would no longer dominate Congress and the president because big business would no longer exist. If our government process then becomes far more democratic in content than today, it makes sense to include such a government as a partner with the workers in each enterprise.

After this revolutionary change, radicals must continue to work just as hard as ever to deepen and extend democratic processes. This means continuing the formal democratic processes through elections, competing political parties, and freedom of discussion. When the Soviet Union abolished all competing parties and freedom of discussion, the ultimate result was Stalin's tragic dictatorship. Socialist democracy means continuing and extending all formal democratic rights and procedures. But it also means the content of those procedures will change. When the present concentration of economic power is ended, every citizen will have far more equal access to the governmental process. The government will be dominated by working people of all types—blue collar, white collar, and intellectual workers—and not big business. There is no magical way to determine the representatives of the whole working class (which will then be the whole public) without free discussion and an open election process.

THE LONG, LONG RUN

In the very long run, when there is abundance for all and a broad humanist education for all, we may be able to fashion a still better society. The good society would presumably be one in which all goods would be free, there would be no wages, and everyone would work for the job of contributing to the social good. Any such proposal for the immediate future is utopian and not very feasible.

We can, however, slowly make progress in that direction. Even under capitalism, it should be possible to fight for and obtain a minimum guaranteed family income (or negative income tax) to provide some income to the poorest groups. Under any real socialist system, a large portion of private profit and interest income will be eliminated immediately. That alone will drastically reduce income inequality. Further moves to reduce income differences can be made slowly.

A different approach, which could be pursued at the same time, is the expansion of the free public goods sector. Even under capitalism, it should be possible to fight for and obtain free public education at all levels and free public health care. Many countries already have free health care and it is barbaric that the wealthy United States does not have it.

With a socialist democracy, we can slowly increase the free goods sector to cover the basic necessities of life, public transportation, some food staples, and a certain amount of housing space. The demand for these goods is not elastic and would not increase much when they become free. Surely most workers would not have less incentive to work if the program is done slowly and is accompanied by a thorough reeducation of all of us to improve our social attitudes.

But this is science fiction speculation for the future. For now, we must concentrate on full employment legislation, nationalizing the oil industry, and free health care—as well as the continuing fight against discrimination. This can be expanded—as a socialist movement expands—to the control by all the workers and consumers over *all* the monopoly corporations. Only by that means can we eliminate unemployment and inflation, ending the disease of stagflation forever.

NOTES

1. The profitability of sexist discrimination is shown in Barbara Deckard, *The Women's Movement* (New York: Harper & Row, 1975).

The profitability of racist discrimination is shown in Victor Perlo, *Economics of Racism* (New York: International Publishers, 1975); also see Raymond Franklin and Solomon Resnick, *The Political Economy of Racism* (New York: Holt, Rinehart and Winston, 1973).

2. The political-economic bases of continued environmental pollution are revealed in Mathew Edel, *Economics and the Environment* (Englewood Cliffs, N.J.: Prentice-Hall, 1974).

3. For a detailed discussion of Soviet economic performance, see Howard Sherman, *The Soviet Economy* (Boston: Little, Brown, 1968).

4. "Poll Uncovers Hostility to U.S. Business," in *Riverside Press-Enterprise* (August 31, 1975), p. A–4.

5. Brom and Kirschner, "Buying Power," *Working Papers* (Summer, 1974), pp. 1–15.

6. *ADA News*, newsletter of Americans for Democratic Action, Southern California Chapter, vol. 6, no. 6 (November–December 1975), p. 4.

7. "Public Ownership of Industy," *Dollars and Sense*, no. 9 (Sept. 1975), p. 13.

FOR FURTHER READING

1. A more comprehensive discussion of all of economics is in E. K. Hunt and Howard Sherman, *Economics: An Introduction to Traditional and Radical Views* (New York: Harper & Row, 3d ed., 1975).

2. The fullest data on monopoly power are in John Blair, *Economic Concentration* (New York: Harcourt Brace Jovanovich, 1972).

3. Almost every issue of the journal *Review of Radical Political Economics* has further discussion of the points discussed in this book. The address of the journal is: Union for Radical Political Economics, 41 Union Square West, Room 201, New York, N.Y. 10003.

4. Several models of the business cycle are presented in Howard Sherman, *Radical Political Economy* (New York: Basic Books, 1972).

5. The best recent article on stagflation theory and data is Howard Wachtel and Peter Adelsheim, "The Inflationary Impact of Unemployment," U.S. Congress, Joint Economic Committee, *Hearings* (Washington, D.C.: Government Printing Office, forthcoming).

6. An outstanding discussion of recent monetary developments is in Paul Sweezy, "Capital Shortage: Fact or Fancy," *Monthly Review* (April 1975). This radical journal, *Monthly Review*, edited by Paul Sweezy and Harry Magdoff, consistently has the clearest analyses available of contemporary economic events. The address of this journal is *Monthly Review*, 62 West 14th Street, New York, N.Y. 10011.

INDEX

76 77 78 7 6 5 4 3 2 1